JOHNNY DEPP DIAGNOSED

Unauthorized PSYCHOLOGICAL DIAGNOSIS

Of His Secret Life

Dr. Paul Dawson

VISTAR PICTURES, LTD.

Published by Vistar Pictures Ltd.

JOHNNY DEPP DIAGNOSED

UNAUTHORIZED PSYCHOLOGICAL DIAGNOSIS of HIS SECRET LIFE

Copyright © 2013 by Dr. Paul Dawson

All rights reserved. No part of this book may be reproduced in whole or in part without written permission from the publisher and author, except by reviewers who may quote brief excerpts in connection with a review in a newspaper, magazine, or electronic publication; nor may any part of this book be reproduced, stored in a retrieval system, or transmitted in any form or by any means electronic, mechanical, photocopying, recording, or other, without written permission from the publisher and author. Printed in the United States of America.

Other Books by Dr. Paul Dawson

ANGELINA JOLIE PSYCHOANALYZED

BORDERLINE PERSONALITY DISORDER

DEMON OF HADES

DEMON OF LUISON

DEMON OF XIBALBA

GET A LIFE! BORDERLINE PERSONALITY DISORDER RECOVERY

MASKS of PREDATORS

MARILYN MONROE DIAGNOSED

NARCOTERRORIST PSYCHOPATHS

PRINCESS DIANA DIAGNOSED

PSYCHOLOGY OF MEN WHO ABUSE WOMEN

ROCK STARS DIAGNOSED

SEX CRIMES

SEX, LOVE & SMART DATING

SPYING WITH THE ENEMY

CONTENTS

Chapter 1: "My self-image, it still isn't that alright. No matter how famous I am..." 9

Chapter 2: "We're all a mishmash of extremes. I know that I have demons..." 37

Chapter 3: "I've also gotten weird letters, suicide letters, girls threatening to jump if I don't get in touch with them..." 55

Chapter 4: "I see kids who are complete cynics. They're not dreaming. They're out there with high-powered weapons, smoking crack..." 79

Chapter 5: "This is a rumor-filled society and if people want to sit around and talk about whom I've dated..." 89

Chapter 6: "Novelty boy, franchise boy. Fucked and plucked with no escape from this nightmare..." 100

Chapter 7: "I guess I still feel a little bit outside it all...ish. I mean, not so much outside as just not inside..." 130

Chapter 8: "I despise those prick actors who say, 'I was in character'...It's just masturbation at the highest level." 140

Chapter 9: "I'm not a Blockbuster boy..." 156

Chapter 10: "America is dumb. It's like a dumb puppy that has big teeth that can bite..." 189

Chapter 11: "I smoked with Jesus Christ! Jesus is a Marlboro man!"   214

Chapter 12: "The only gossip I'm interested in is... 'Woman's bra bursts, 11 injured...'"   219

Chapter 13: "Tim Burton can ask me...to have sex with an aardvark..."   233

Chapter 14: "I sat there snarling at him in that deeply expressive way that only teens possess, decompressing too fast back into reality..."   246

Chapter 15: "I watched *Rebel Without a Cause*...James Dean was the catalyst..."   254

Chapter 16: "Kids write to me and say they are having these problems...It's scary...If you need help..."   262

Chapter 17: "I'd been in high school...I was bored out of my mind and I hated it..."   272

Chapter 18: "On fame...They say, 'It's you!' But you don't know them. That's bad for an actor..."   278

Chapter 19: "If you love two people at the same time, choose the second. Because..."   286

Chapter 20: "You can never, ever understand fully what a woman's life might be like until you step into her shoes. The same thing goes for transvestites..."   291

Chapter 21: "I am doing things that are true to me. The only thing I have a problem with is being labeled."   296

Chapter 22: "With every part you act, there must be a little of yourself in it. If there isn't, it's not acting. It's lying."   302

Chapter 23: "You can close your eyes to the things you don't want to see but how can you close your heart to the things you don't want to feel?"   308

Chapter 24: "I don't care. I'm just gonna smoke…I'll go get a brand new pack, smoke the shit out of that one…"   314

Chapter 25: "The beauty, the poetry of the fear in their eyes. I didn't mind going to jail for, what, five, six hours? It was absolutely worth it."   321

Chapter 26: "Me, I'm dishonest, and you can always trust a dishonest man to be dishonest. Honestly, it's the honest ones you have to watch out for."   329

Chapter 27: "As a teenager I was so insecure. I was the type of guy that never fitted in…I was convinced I had absolutely no talent at all…"   336

Chapter 28: "People say I make strange choices, but they're not strange for me. My sickness is…"   341

Chapter 29: "I was always fascinated by people who are considered completely normal, because I find them the weirdest of all"   345

Chapter 30: "On buying a private island… Money doesn't buy you happiness, but it buys you a big enough yacht to sail right up to it."   349

Chapter 31: "Throughout my lifetime I've left pieces of my heart here and there..."   354

Chapter 32: "I don't think of myself as being a celebrity, it's too mortifying..."   358

Chapter 33: "It's all kinds of these profound things crashing on you when..."   363

Chapter 34: "France...has a great culture...I'm afraid that the American culture is a disaster."   369

Chapter 35: "Better to not know which moment may be your last..."   373

Chapter 36: "Just keep moving forward and don't give a shit about what anybody thinks..."   380

Chapter 37: "There's a drive in me that won't allow me to do certain things that are easy."   385

Chapter 38: "If there's any message to my work, it is ultimately that it's OK to be different..."   392

Chapter 39: "I pretty much try to stay in a constant state of confusion just because of..."   400

Chapter 40: "When kids hit one year old, it's like hanging out with a miniature drunk..."   406

Chapter 41: "I like the challenge of trying different things and wondering..."   411

Chapter 42: "I am doing things that are true to me. The only thing I have a problem with is being labeled."   417

Chapter 43: "For a long time I tried to manage an honesty and openness about my personal life because..."   423

Chapter 44: "Everything here is edible; even I'm edible. But that, dear children, is cannibalism, and is..."   434

Chapter 45: "I think everybody's nuts."   440

Chapter 46: "One of the greatest pieces of advice I've ever gotten in my life was from my mom..."   448

Chapter 47: "They stick you with those names, those labels -- 'rebel' or whatever..."   454

Chapter 48: "If someone were to harm my family or a friend or somebody I love, I would eat them..."   469

Chapter 49: "We're all damaged in our own way. Nobody's perfect. I think we're all somewhat screwy..."   473

Chapter 50: "I think everybody's weird. We should all celebrate our individuality and not be embarrassed or ashamed of it."   488

Appendix – Photos   493

Selected References   553

Chapter 1

"My self-image, it still isn't that alright. No matter how famous I am. No matter how many people go to see my movies…"

Johnny Depp seems to be very mysterious, complex and inscrutable. He's one of the top-ranked, highest paid movie stars in the world. But he's had an incredible-dark side that's been haunting him for years.

In doing research on Depp's background I was able to shine some light on his dark side. I found bits and pieces that seemed to hint at some elusive mental disorder. Johnny did not have a strong sense of self. He had an unstable or volatile identity or self-concept, took on many different personas throughout his life and thus was better able to play roles as an actor.

Some of the fragments of Depp's personality – little puzzle parts – were reported on separately. He was quoted as having some phobias such as a fear of clowns which is called clourophobia. At times Johnny was reported to also have a panic disorder.

He admitted to substance abuse of drugs and alcohol – particularly in his teenage-bad-boy and twenty-something-party-monster days; self-mutilation, cutting himself; was a rebel – antagonistic with cops, arrested on various charges including fighting, assault or trashing hotel rooms.

Johnny's love life was a never-ending, perpetual series of romantic relationships punctuated by extremes: intense, passionate, quixotic, starry-eyed honeymoon stages, dreamy-romanticized-clingy engagements followed by frenzied, chaotic fights, tumultuous break-ups, muddled make-ups and messy endings. His lovers were put on a pedestal at first, viewed through rose-tinted glasses and then the "angel" would become demonized and dumped.

Depp would then move on to the next tender, adoring "love of his life." If asked, Johnny always discounted, diminished and minimized the negatives of his past relationships. His comments were always vague – the relationship "got a little bumpy." He always claims to be friends and have kept a platonic connection with his ex-lovers.

Tabloid media even breathlessly report Johnny hanging-out or having a rare dinner with Winona Ryder or Kate Moss. When interviewed, Depp visualizes his former girlfriends in glamorized, sentimentalized clichés, puts his rose-tinted glasses back on and rhapsodizes about the upside of his past loves which "naturally" ended or the split was after they "grew apart" or he was "gone too much on film shoots."

I don't get the latter "career-travel" excuse which Depp has said caused him to not "give her the attention she wanted." All of Johnny's lovers knew he was an actor who went to film locations – his excuses imply it was a secret that he is an actor who travels. What about when Johnny hangs-out with his romantic partner and it's later reported they were fighting, bickering; he was boring, smothering and clingy?

Or what about when Depp has said a woman (e.g., Vanessa Paradis) "bored him senseless"? Too much attention then? I found that it was impossible to apply logic to Depp's life including his romances. The key was to read the subtext of reports or evidence and excavate deeper into his life.

I'm a big fan of Depp's film acting work. I admire his entertainer talent. But if you're looking for a book that over-idealizes him, presents a star-struck, sugar-coated portrayal – an idolization of Depp, this is not my aim. My approach is to fit the puzzle parts of his personality together and arrive at an overall psychological diagnosis.

I've researched and analyzed Johnny with the objective of arriving at a valid psychological diagnosis in my opinion – hopefully it will help Johnny and others. Johnny is a very elusive, obscure, and tenuous research subject. He often minimizes, denies and avoids deeper personal conflicts and sensitive issues. Depp is hard to get hold of and pin down.

In interviews he tends to shrug off, dismiss or discount the significance of his past impulsive, self-destructive behavior and romantic relationships However, I've dug down and researched relevant evidence of his mental disorder symptoms – which he's been hiding or keeping secret.

Johnny has remarked:

"**My self-image, it still isn't that alright**. No matter how famous I am. No matter how many people go to see my movie, I still have the idea that I'm that pale no-hoper that I used to be. A pale no-hoper that happens to be a little lucky now. Tomorrow it'll be all over, then I'll have to go back to selling pens again…"

If we shine light on Depp's shadowy foundation, his skeletons in the closet include signs and symptoms of a serious mental disorder – red-flag symptoms which can be grouped into these categories:

Impulsive behavior: non-suicidal self-injurious behavior (cutting himself); substance abuse (abusing alcohol and mood-altering drugs); petty theft, shoplifting, burglary, vandalism and trashing hotel rooms.

Unbalanced emotions: mood swings and depression; intense experience of anger, difficulties controlling anger.

Erratic relationships: sex-love affairs with a series of women including well-known women such as Winona Ryder, Kate Moss, Sherilyn Fenn and Vanessa Paradis – intense and volatile personal relationships.

Insecure self-identity: persistent uncertainty about self-image, long-term goals, friendships and values; chronic feelings of emptiness and boredom.

Depp revealed, "As a teenager I was so insecure. I was the type of guy that never fitted in because he never dared to choose. I was convinced I had absolutely no talent at all. For nothing. And that thought took away all my ambition too…"

Johnny Depp came to Los Angeles in the mid-1980s to be a rock-and-roll musician, not an actor. His wife introduced him to Nicholas Cage. He went to his first audition on a whim, at the urging of Cage, and was cast in a featured role in Wes Craven's breakthrough horror film, *A Nightmare on Elm Street* (1984). Depp then found success as an actor.

Now 50 in 2013, he was born John Christopher Depp in Owensboro, Kentucky on June 9th, 1963. Johnny Depp was raised in Florida. He's the youngest of four children of Betty Sue Palmer, a waitress, and John Christopher Depp, a civil engineer.

In a 2002 interview, Depp stated that he believed he has Native American ancestry – although a Cherokee Indian Nation representative said he's not a member of the tribe; in 2011, he claimed:

"I guess I have some Native American in me somewhere down the line. My great-grandmother was quite a bit of Native American, she grew up Cherokee or maybe Creek Indian. Makes sense in terms of coming from Kentucky, which is rife with Cherokee and Creek."

But controversy arose over Depp's portrayal of a Native American character (Tonto in *The Lone Ranger*), as Depp was not raised in, nor has confirmable ancestry from, a Native American community, though he has said he "guesses" he may have some distant Cherokee or Creek ancestry.

He dropped out of high school in his mid-teens in the hopes of becoming a rock musician. He fronted a series of garage bands including The Kids, which once opened for Iggy Pop.

Depp got into acting after a visit to Los Angeles, California, with his former wife, Lori Anne Allison (Lori A. Depp), who introduced him to film industry contacts. He made his film debut in *A Nightmare on Elm Street* (1984).

In 1987 he shot to stardom when he replaced Jeff Yagher in the role of undercover cop Tommy Hanson in the popular TV series *21 Jump Street* (1987). However, he complained about being under contract in the *21 Jump Street* role – Depp wrote in 1995:

"On *21 Jump Street* I was bound by a contract doing assembly-line stuff that, to me, was borderline Fascist (cops in school...Christ!)...Dumbfounded, lost, shoved down the gullets of America as a young Republican. TV boy, heart-throb, teen idol, teen hunk..."

"Plastered, postered, patented, painted, and plastic!!! Stapled to a box of cereal with wheels, doing 200 mph on a one-way collision course bound for Thermos and lunch-box antiquity. Novelty boy, franchise boy. Fucked and plucked with no escape from this nightmare..."

While Depp's rebel-side quotes appeal to his young fans, he lacked gratitude because, as a young, mid-20s actor starting his career, he was making $45,000 per episode of *21 Jump Street* (1987-1990) which was good money then and still is.

In 2007, it was reported by Forbes Magazine that his earnings for the year 2006 were estimated to be $92 million. He was reported to be the highest paid actor in 2012 – Depp was paid $75 million that year alone. His estimated net worth as of 2012 was over $350 million.

Breaking-out his salary from some of his films shows Depp earned from *The Rum Diary* (2011) $15,000,000; *Pirates of the Caribbean: On Stranger Tides* (2011) $35,000,000; *Rango* (2011) $7,500,000; *The Tourist* (2010) $20,000,000; *Alice in Wonderland* (2010) $50,000,000; *Pirates of the Caribbean: Dead Man's Chest* (2006) $20,000,000; *Charlie and the Chocolate Factory* (2005) $18,000,000; *Pirates of the Caribbean: The Curse of the Black Pearl* (2003) $10,000,000; *Donnie Brasco* (1997) $5,000,000; and *Nick of Time* (1995) $5,000,000 (*IMDb*).

Johnny was quoted commenting on the money he makes:

"You use your money to buy privacy because during most of your life you aren't allowed to be normal."

Depp remarked on buying a private island: "Money doesn't buy you happiness, but it buys you a big enough yacht to sail right up to it."

Johnny commented on his **childhood and teen years**:

"We moved like gypsies. From the time I was five until my teens we lived in 30 or 40 different houses. That probably has a lot to do with my transient life now. But it's how I was raised so I thought there was nothing abnormal about it..."

"Wherever the family is, that's home. We lived in apartments, on a farm, in a motel. Then we rented a house, and one night we moved from there to the house next door. I remember carrying my clothes across the yard and thinking, '*This* is weird, but it's an easy move'."

"Like Edward D. Wood Jr. I also grew up feeling like an obtuse piece of machinery. It was the same feeling I had about Edward Scissorhands."

"Years and years I watched my Mother, Betty Sue, wait tables. I'd count her change at the end of the night. She cursed like a sailor, played cards and smoked cigarettes."

"I was a weird kid. I wanted to be Bruce Lee. I wanted to be on a SWAT team. When I was five, I think I wanted to be Daniel Boone."

"My cousins had a gospel group and they came down and played gospel songs, and that was the first time I ever saw an electric guitar. I got obsessed with the electric guitar, so my Mom bought me one from them for $25. I was about twelve years old."

"Then I locked myself in a room for a year and taught myself how to play, learned off records, and then I started playing in little garage bands. The first group I was ever in was called Flame. Then I was in The Kids. They were the ones who moved to Hollywood."

"Miramar (the small town where Depp lived) was like Endora, the town in *What's Eating Gilbert Grape* (1993). It had two identical grocery stores opposite each other and nothing much ever happened there."

"At first we'd wear T-shirts that said 'Flame' on them. At 13 I was wearing plain T-shirts. Then I used to steal my mom's clothing. She had all these crushed velvet shirts with French-cut sleeves. And, like, seersucker bell bottoms. I dreamed of having platforms, but couldn't find any."

"I'd been in high school three years, and I may have just walked in yesterday. I had, like, eight credits. I was in my third year of high school and I didn't want to be there. **I was bored out of my mind** and I hated it."

"I hung around with bad crowds. We used to break and enter places. We'd break into the school and destroy

a room or something. I used to steal things from stores."

"One of my old teachers asked for my autograph. I mean, what was I supposed to say? He'd failed me. I remember one time this teacher yelled at me so heavily in front of the entire class. He didn't have any time for me then, and now, all of a sudden, he wants my autograph? They all thought I was going to end up a drug addict, in jail."

"I started smoking at 12, lost my virginity at 13 and **did every kind of drug there was by 14. Pretty much any drug you can name, I've done it. I wouldn't say I was bad or malicious, I was just curious. I certainly had my little experiences with drugs.** Eventually, you see where that's headed and you get out."

"I played rock 'n' roll clubs in Florida. I was underage, but they would let me come in the back door to play, and then I'd have to leave after the first set. That's how I made a living, at about $25 a night. At times we could make $2,100 - we used to make that for the entire group and the road crew, which is a lot."

Depp revealed some **abandonment fears** from his childhood dysfunctional family:

"My father left and my mother was deeply hurt and sick physically and emotionally. That's a very traumatic thing for a family to go through, so we all pulled together and did the best we could."

"I can remember my parents fighting and us kids wondering who was going to go with whom if they got divorced."

Johnny seems to have bottled-up a lot of **inappropriate anger and resentment** as the next quote indicates:

"These are the most important people in my life. You know, I would die for these people. If someone were to harm my family or a friend or somebody I love - I would eat them. I might end up in jail for 500 years - but I would eat them."

"I remember carving my initials on my arm and I've scarred myself from time to time since then. In a way your body is a journal and the scars are sort of entries in it."**

Depp discounts his self-injury, cutting, as a sort of journal or diary entry. **However, non-suicidal self-injurious behavior, such as cutting himself is a serious symptom of a mental disorder.** Johnny has observed insouciantly:

"I remember carving my initials on my arm and I've scarred myself from time to time since then. In a way your body is a journal and the scars are sort of entries in it."

The irony is that now that Depp is famous, he gets letters from young people threatening suicide – Johnny discussed it:

"Kids write to me and say they are having these problems or they want to commit suicide or something. It's scary. I have to say, Listen, I'm just an actor, not a professional psychologist. **If you need help, you should go and get it.**"

"I've gotten weird letters, suicide letters, and girls threatening to jump if I don't get in touch with them. So you think, 'This is bullshit, but then you think, What if it's not?

Who wants to take that chance?' I write them back, tell them to hang in there - if things are that bad they have to get better. **But I'm not altogether stable myself, so who am I to give advice?"**

Recently, Depp remarked that he isn't an addict-alcoholic and claimed he was giving up alcohol in an interview – from his comments **I'd say he's in denial. The quotes and subtext of what he's saying sound like the behavior pattern of an alcoholic-addict**:

In the News: Johnny Depp Opens Up about Alcohol Use; Denies Being an Alcoholic (J. Hunt; July 3, 2013):

In the new issue of *Rolling Stone*, Johnny Depp opens up about his past alcohol use, but unlike his infamous on-screen character, Captain Jack Sparrow, he says he is not an alcoholic. Depp denies ever having to depend on alcohol, though he made a conscious decision over a year ago to give up drinking.

"No, I don't have the physical need for the drug alcohol," he tells *Rolling Stone*. ***"No, it's more my medication, my self-medication over the years just to calm the circus. Once the circus kicks in, the festivities in the brain, it can be ruthless..."***

Depp, who turned 50 in 2013, adds that his decision to give up alcohol stemmed from his own realization that though he was able to function just fine with alcohol on a day-to-day basis, he could manage almost just as well without it.

"I just decided that I pretty much got everything I could out of it," he says about his drinking. ***"I investigated wine and spirits thoroughly, and they certainly investigated me as well, and we found out that we got along beautifully, but maybe too well…"***

The actor, who created rules for himself like drinking wine but no hard liquor, found a partner in crime in the writer Hunter S. Thompson, who he would binge drink with for weeks.

"Maybe that's why Hunter and I got along so well. I'm able to continue for great periods of time, weirdly. For weeks. There's no great point to it, ultimately. You realize that you wouldn't treat your car that way…"

Depp is so dedicated to his new pledge of sobriety, he says, that even after he split with longtime girlfriend Vanessa Paradis last year, he hasn't been turning to alcohol the way that he might've for previous breakups.

"In terms of the breakup, I definitely wasn't going to rely on the drink to ease things or cushion the blow or cushion the situation," he explains. ***"Cause that could***

have been fatal. I felt it was my duty to be real clear throughout that..."

The couple were together for 14 years and had two children together — Lily-Rose, 14, and Jack, 11.

While I'll review Johnny Depp's life in this book, he seems to have a number of symptoms of Borderline Personality Disorder (BPD). However, I'm not reaching a diagnostic conclusion at this early point in the book.

What is BPD? The *Mail Online* recently summarized it:

"People with borderline personality disorder (BPD) suffer from a disorder of emotion regulation. While less well known than schizophrenia or bipolar disorder, BPD is more common, affecting two per cent of adults, mostly young women. Patients account for 20 per cent of psychiatric hospitalizations."

"While a person with depression typically endures the same mood for weeks, a person with BPD may experience intense bouts of anxiety that may last only hours. Sometimes people with BPD view themselves as fundamentally bad, or unworthy."

"People with BPD often have highly unstable patterns of social relationships. While they can develop intense but stormy attachments, their attitudes towards family, friends, and loved ones may suddenly shift from love to intense anger and dislike.

People with BPD exhibit other impulsive behaviors, such as excessive spending, binge eating and risky sex."

The above summary is somewhat misleading. Consider the current BPD diagnostic requirements – you'll see that I've already mentioned a number of these BPD signs or symptoms which Johnny Depp has shown. I'll indicate Depp's suspected symptoms in **bold**:

Current Diagnostic Criteria - Borderline Personality Symptoms or Signs:

Individuals with BPD usually have several of the following symptoms, many of which are detailed in the *DSM-IV-TR (Diagnostic manual of the American Psychiatric Association). For a diagnosis, five of the nine following criteria must apply*. Most of them can be reduced down to instability in five critical areas: emotions, relationships, behavior, identity, and temporary psychotic.

Volatile, on-the-edge emotions: **1) Marked mood swings with periods of intense depressed mood**, irritability and/or anxiety lasting a few hours to a few days (but not in the context of a full-blown episode of major depressive disorder or bipolar disorder). 2) **Inappropriate, intense or uncontrollable anger** (frequent displays of temper, constant anger, recurrent physical fights).

Insecure, unstable relationships: 3) **Unstable, intense personal relationships**, sometimes alternating between "all good," *idealizations,* and "all bad," *devaluation*. 4) Frantic efforts to avoid abandonment. (Not including suicidal or self-mutilating behavior). **Abandonment fears.**

Impulsive, self-destructive, erratic behavior: 5) **Impulsive behaviors that result in adverse outcomes and psychological distress**, such as excessive spending, sexual encounters, **substance use (abusing mood-altering drugs & alcohol), shoplifting**, reckless driving or binge eating. 6) Recurring suicidal threats or **non-suicidal self-injurious behavior, such as cutting** or burning one's self.

Variable, unhinged, unsteady identity: 7) **Persistent uncertainty about self-image, long-term goals, friendships and values. 8) Chronic boredom or feelings of emptiness.**

Temporary psychotic: 9) Transient, stress-related paranoid ideation or severe dissociative symptoms.

    I've tentatively identified 8 out of the 9 symptom total as applying to Depp which qualifies him as a possible BPD sufferer. But let's finish the book and see if there is some cross-validity to my initial assessment. Since I have not met Johnny Depp, I want to review his whole life and make a fair diagnostic evaluation based on research.

    In researching Depp's symptoms such as non-suicidal self-injury – cutting himself – one theory is that he got into self-harm as a result of his family problems as a teenager. The assumption is that because his mother and father were in conflict and broke-up, he then proceeded to cut himself at times. I don't buy this.

Millions of dysfunctional families break-up or fight and have conflicts. Very few young people then take a knife and cut their arms up. It is more likely the self-injury was part of a BPD mental disorder. Johnny discussed his self-injury scars on his arm:

"My body is a journal in a way. It's like what sailors used to do, where every tattoo meant something, a specific time in your life when you make a mark on yourself, whether you do it yourself with a knife or with a professional tattoo artist".

Depp has had run-ins with the police and legal problems related to his **inappropriate, intense or uncontrollable anger (frequent displays of temper, constant anger, recurrent physical fights) – which is a symptom of BPD**. For example:

Johnny was accused of selling drugs out of his Hollywood club, the Viper Room, at the time River Phoenix died of a drug overdose in front of The Viper Room in 1993. Depp closed down the Viper Room for two weeks after River Phoenix died there and he also closed it on every October 31st which was the date of Phoenix's death. Johnny then sold his share in the club in 2004.

He received further bad publicity when he was arrested for trashing and smashing a New York hotel suite in 1994. Depp rationalized the incident with a nutty excuse: an armadillo did it, saying that he had found the animal hidden in a closet and it had gone crazy, wrecking the hotel room before leaping out the window.

Depp was arrested for fighting in 1999 – he was brawling, punching paparazzi outside a restaurant in London while he was with his girlfriend Paradis.

An example of a legal case involves a U.C. Irvine medical professor (Robin Eckert) who was roughed-up by Depp's bodyguards at a concert in Los Angeles in 2011. Apparently Eckert was injured after being dragged 40 feet across the floor while hand-cuffed by Depp's bodyguards.

She argued in court that Johnny Depp did not intervene - since he supervised the security men – and was responsible for the battery, her dislocated shoulder and other injuries. A trial date was set for August 12, 2013 when she'll seek compensation and punitive damages against Depp.

Johnny has also gotten into trouble by being critical of Americans and America. He moved to France saying it was a better country. Here are some of his anti-American quotes:

"One of the greatest things I've ever seen happen was the morning I opened the newspaper and it said that some very powerful government officials had decided to change the name of 'French fries' to 'freedom fries' and 'French toast' to 'freedom toast'. It was impressive. I wanted to write a letter to them just to thank them, just for proving globally that they were absolute imbeciles."

"America is dumb. It's like a dumb puppy that has big teeth that can bite and hurt you, aggressive. My daughter is four, my boy is one. I'd like them to see America as a toy, a broken toy. Investigate it a little, check it out, get this feeling and then get out."

After Depp got into trouble for his anti-America remarks, he tried to alibi his way out of it by saying:

"It is a shame that the metaphor I used was taken so radically out of context and slung about irresponsibly by the news media. There was no anti-American sentiment. In fact, it was just the opposite…"

"I am an American. I love my country and have great hopes for it. It is for this reason that I speak candidly and sometimes critically about it. I have benefited greatly from the freedom that exists in my country and for this I am eternally grateful."

"France and the whole of Europe have a great culture and an amazing history. Most important thing, though, is that people there know how to live! In America they've forgotten all about it. I'm afraid that the American culture is a disaster."

Johnny has been quoted idealizing France, his girlfriend Vanessa Paradis and his kids he had with her:

"I pretty much fell in love with Vanessa the moment I set eyes on her. As a person, I was pretty much a lost cause at that time in my life. She turned all that around for me with her incredible tenderness and understanding…"

"I love our house in the country (in France). I can walk to the nearby village and have a coffee and no one pays any notice. I'm just another dad with my daughter on my knee…"

"The time I've spent in France with my girlfriend Vanessa Paradis has solidified my belief that I can keep a major distance from Hollywood and still keep in the game. Acting is my living, but I don't want to live it. Living in France is the first time I can honestly say I feel at home."

To illustrate Depp's **unstable relationships**, I should point out that he has broken-up with his girlfriend Paradis and moved out of France because he doesn't want to pay taxes in France and the United States. So what happened to the paradise of France and his girlfriend Paradis – he claimed he loved them both?

Johnny doesn't like people to talk about his romantic life – here's a quote:

"This is a rumor-filled society and if people want to sit around and talk about whom I've dated, then I'd say they have a lot of spare time and should consider other topics... or masturbation."

Depp tried to be objective in evaluating his failed relationships and marriages. He attributed the problem that he was too young (or the wrong timing) and not in "true love" – like he was with Vanessa Paradis who he loved. He claims he could not be in love before he was 30. Oops! Johnny split with Paradis also. Anyway, here's what he said about his first marriage:

"I guess I have very traditional kinds of sensibilities about that kind of stuff - you know, a man and a woman sharing their life together and having a baby, whatever - and I think for a while I was trying to right the wrongs of my parents because they split up when I was a kid, so I thought I could do it differently - make things work. I had the right intentions, but the wrong timing - and the wrong person. But I don't regret it; I had fun and I learned a lot."

"You know, I was married, when I was 20. It was a strong bond with someone, but I can't necessarily say I was in love. That's something that comes around once, man, maybe twice if you're lucky. And I don't know that I experienced that, let's say, before I turned 30."

A quote Depp has given in 1995 maybe applies to his unstable relationships – he was discussing a role in Ed Wood (1994):

"You can never, ever understand fully what a woman's life might be like until you step into her shoes. The same thing goes for transvestites."

And yet after an endless series of unstable relationships with women, Depp has claimed he's just an old fashioned guy who wants a long, stable marriage and kids. In Johnny's own words:

"I like to think that I'm very considerate of other people's feelings, and I was trained as a small child to always try my best at everything. I think I'm a mixture of romantic and realist..."

"I'm a realist about some stuff, but I also wholeheartedly believe that in a society where people get divorced every five minutes you can still stay married for 50 or 75 years. It's been done and it's beautiful. When I see a couple celebrating their 75th wedding anniversary, I just think that it's totally incredible."

Depp remarked on his early relationships or the string of sex-love affairs he dashed through:

"I don't regret any of them. I had a good time. Most of what's been written about me has been completely false. People have created an image that has absolutely nothing to do with me, and they have the power to sell it, to shove it down the throats of people. I'm an old-fashioned guy who wants marriage and kids."

This seems to be a common BPD syndrome. The BPD casualty fantasizes about a perfect, long-term marriage with kids just like Johnny does. Yet Depp, who has tremendous resources (over $350 million net worth) can't seem to find a woman to settle down with, marry and have the kids. He managed to have kids with French girlfriend Vanessa Paradis but didn't marry her and dumped her – despite claiming to love her eternally.

The usual merry-go-round BPD victims follow in unstable, intense personal relationships is alternating between "all good," *idealizations,* and "all bad," *devaluation* of their romantic partner. Johnny initially over-idealized Vanessa Paradis as the "love of his life." Okay, then why did he break-up with her? He got a tattoo "WINONA FOREVER" when he was with Winona Ryder – what happened to the "forever" love with Winona?

Reviewing Depp's track record with women, we have many sex-love affairs with some high-profile, celebrity girlfriends and a former wife. Lori Anne Allison was his wife from 1983 to 1985. He was engaged to Jennifer Grey and Sherilyn Fenn in the late 1980s. Winona Ryder was his fiancée in the early 1990s – and rated the "WINONA FOREVER" tattoo on his right arm.

Then it was Kate Moss – the British supermodel – who was Depp's next love and relationship until 1998. Vanessa Paradis, a French actor and singer, lasted in a relationship with Johnny from 1998 until 2012 when they separated. He had two kids with Paradis: Lily-Rose Melody Depp (born in 1999) and John "Jack" Christopher Depp III (born in 2002).

Depp is single and on the prowl for the next "Miss Right" to love and marry forever – since he's an "old-fashioned guy" as Johnny claims. He commented on his "deep love" and fatherhood – and now he's ready for the next "ride" that's part of his "destiny":

"Having children has given me a real foundation, a real strong place to stand in life, in work, in everything...You can't plan the kind of deep love that results in children. Fatherhood was not a conscious decision. It was part of the wonderful ride I was on. It was destiny. All the math finally worked."

Who knows? If you're a beautiful woman on the inside and outside, you might bump into Johnny Depp in Hollywood. You could be his next "ride" as part of his "destiny". The "ride" with Depp seems to be that the woman starts out as Depp's "love forever" because she's idealized as "all good" – romanticized, viewed through rose tinted glasses and put on a pedestal.

Then the loving relationship changes as the lady transforms to being "all bad," when Johnny coolly devaluates his romantic partner after a period of time. Then I'm afraid it'll be over for you because Johnny will unflappably move on to his next "eternal love" in his destiny ride. Unfortunately, Depp will take off his rose-tinted glasses, pull you off your pedestal and the romance ends.

While openly bisexual, lipstick-lesbian Amber Heard has been Johnny's romantic interest in 2013, how long can the triangle of Johnny, Amber and her lesbian lovers last? Depp has broken-up with exotic Amber once at least and has been in a second-round, open relationship with her – allowing her to romance her lesbian girlfriends – as long as Johnny is still number one.

Chapter 2

"We're all a mishmash of extremes. I know that I have demons. I don't know if I want to get rid of them altogether, but I would like to experience them in a different way. Maybe go face to face with them. I've never really had the time to go to therapy. Well, here and there. But not enough to help me."

–Johnny Depp

Depp's first feature film credit was *A Nightmare on Elm Street* (1984) – storyline synopsis:

Teenagers in a small town are dropping like flies, apparently in the grip of mass hysteria causing their suicides. A cop's daughter (Heather Langenkamp) traces the cause to child molester Fred Krueger (Robert Englund), who was burned alive by angry parents many years before.

Krueger has now come back in the dreams of his killers' children, claiming their lives as his revenge. With a supporting cast that includes horror veterans like John Saxon and Ronee Blakley, director Wes Craven creates moments of real dread by examining the line between nightmares and reality, as well as the "sins of the parents" theme (*rottentomatoes*).

JOHNNY DEPP'S LIFE BEHIND THE SCENES:

I'm going to jump around and not stick to a chronological order as I seek some underlying diagnostic clues to Depp's possible mental disorders.

In the early 1990s Johnny Depp had a breakthrough from a sexy TV-screen star, as Officer Tom Hanson on *21 Jump Street*, to enthralling film actor — which was a sort of charismatic coup.

Johnny went from TV pretty boy to leading roles in two 1990 films. As Wade Walker in John Waters' musical satire *Cry-Baby*, Johnny lampooned celebrity-mania (and his own recent past), yet brought unique film-star magnetism to the role.

What's Depp's relationship status today?

In June, 2012, it was reported that Depp and Paradis had split. Johnny has had a series of stormy relationships including his affair with Kate Moss and Winona Ryder which were conflicted. As I've said, a BPD symptom is **<u>unstable, intense personal relationships</u>**, sometimes alternating between **"all good,"** *idealizations,* and **"all bad,"** *devaluation*. Here's an article on one of his latest breakups:

Johnny Depp, Vanessa Paradis End 14-Year Relationship:

After Months of Denials, Publicist Confirms That Two Have Separated (*Celebrity Health & Fitness*, June 19th, 2012):

Johnny Depp and **Vanessa Paradis** have officially called it quits, after their 14-year relationship began to grow stormy last year. The breakup has been rumored for months, but it's official now.

Depp, 49, one of Hollywood's most bankable stars and Paradis, 39, a French actress, model and singer, "have amicably separated," his publicist confirmed today (June 19).

"Please respect their privacy and, more importantly, the privacy of their children," the publicist told *USAToday*.

Depp began dating the French actress in 1998. He'd previously dated actress **Winona Ryder** and had a stormy relationship with **Kate Moss**. The couple, Depp and Paradis, never married, but have two children, **Lily-Rose**, 13, and **Jack,** 10.

Their relationship seemed solid, although there were **occasional, public flare-ups**. The latest reports surfaced in January. The couple were reported to be constantly involved in **bitter arguing**, despite the idyllic relationship Depp portrayed in an interview around the same time.

Before that, Paradis was reported to have flown into a **jealous rage** when Depp film a steamy shower love scene with **Angelina Jolie** in their movie, *The Tourist*. The scene was allegedly dropped as a result, although the reports were later strongly denied.

The French singer was so distressed over the script's racy theme, she begged Depp to pull out of the project. But he'd already signed on for the role.

Depp and Paradis have homes in Meudon in the Paris suburbs, Los Angeles, Le Plan-de-la-Tour in the south of France and own an island in the Bahamas.

Split rumors have dogged the couple for months now, but they've remained relatively silent about their personal life. Depp has been busy recently promoting his movies *The Rum Diary* and *Dark Shadows*. He hasn't appeared with Paradis on a red carpet in a year, a source noted to *People*.

In contrast, Depp and **Amber Heard**, the **openly bisexual** actress he starred with in *The Rum Diary*, have been spotted together, and are said to be an **item after growing close** while filming the movie. By 2013 Amber and Johnny had already broken-up at least once, made-up and have been into a second-cycle of their relationship.

Another symptom of BPD is inappropriate, intense or uncontrollable anger (frequent displays of temper, constant anger, and recurrent physical fights). While it is understandable for Depp to be irritated when photographers take pictures of him and his family, it is not appropriate to threaten physical violence or assault photographers.

After all, Johnny picked the film acting profession and along with the $350 million or more he's earned, comes the celebrity of being a movie star. Photographers are naturally going to want shots of him and his family. But here's how Depp reacted after a photographer took some pictures:

"I had an incident with a really dumb magazine called *Voici* where they printed a photograph of Lily-Rose, a long-lens shot from very far away, and **I just went ballistic**. You can sue them — I've sued a couple of times, Vanessa's sued and we win every time — but this time I was beyond suing. I just wanted to **beat whoever was responsible into the earth — I just wanted to rip him apart**..."

"**So I tracked him down and gave him a few suggestions about how to live life and stay healthy** and he took my advice. Because that's just unacceptable. They can do anything they want to me — and most tabloids have — but not my kid, not my pure, innocent little baby. She didn't ask to be in this circus..."

Depp made the above comments in 2000. **He's pushed his self-righteous anger to the point where he's been arrested by the police in the past several times.**

Typical BPD Characteristics & Johnny Depp:

Disturbance in Self-Image or Self-Concept:

Depp has been quoted as indicating he has had a variable self-image or self-concept which in turn can cause wide mood swings. For instance:

"My self-image, it still isn't that alright. No matter how famous I am. No matter how many people go to see my movie, I still have the idea that I'm that pale no-hoper that I used to be. A pale no-hoper that happens to be a little lucky now. Tomorrow it'll be all over, then I'll have to go back to selling pens again..."

"The character I've played, that I've responded to, there has been a lost-soul quality to them..."

"We're all a mishmash of extremes. I know that I have demons. I don't know if I want to get rid of them altogether, but I would like to experience them in a different way. Maybe go face to face with them. **I've never really had the time to go to therapy. Well, here and there. But not enough to help me."**

"As a teenager I was so insecure. I was the type of guy that never fitted in because he never dared to choose. **I was convinced I had absolutely no talent at all. For nothing. And that thought took away all my ambition, too."**

With Depp's **variable self-concept**, he can experience painful emotions as a function of interpreting experiences personally and negatively.

Unstable Interpersonal Relationships:

There seems to be a **push-and-pull activity in Johnny's romantic relationships**, for example. He's very dependent and overly sensitive to others' emotions. Depp **over-idealizes and unrealistically devaluates** those close to him which leads to very **intense beginnings and endings to his relationships.**

I can trace some of his **unstable interpersonal relationship issues back to his parents' break-up** and his reaction including a **sense of abandonment** – Depp remarked:

"My father left and my mother was deeply hurt and sick physically and emotionally. That's a very traumatic thing for a family to go through, so we all pulled together and did the best we could."

His apparent BPD pattern has resulted in a string or series of love-sex affairs and unstable relationships. Details of his stormy relationships with Winona Ryder and Kate Moss, to illustrate, have reached the level of the tabloid press. Johnny remarked on Vanessa Paradis:

"**I pretty much fell in love with Vanessa the moment I set eyes on her**. As a person, I was pretty much a lost cause at that time in my life. She turned all that around for me with her incredible tenderness and understanding."

By Hollywood standards Johnny and Vanessa have stayed together for a respectable amount of time – 1998 until 2012. Although I've read reports about their stormy relationship. It still sounds like the **BPD pattern of excessive idealization** at the start of the relationship and then **unrealistic devaluation and discounting** of the romantic partner at the end.

Depp has idealized his girlfriend Vanessa Paradis, praised his kids and home in France as a paradise where he finally found his foundation and happiness. So why did he escape from that setting, break-up with Paradis and see his kids less? It seemed like the BPD push-pull mechanism was at work in him. Depp said:

"Having kids was a huge change for me. Becoming a father. But I think more than changing, I feel like I've been revealed to myself, I kind of found out who I was. When you meet your child for the first time and you're looking at this angel, you start realizing what an idiot you've been for so many years and how much time you've wasted."

"As far as being feet-on-the-ground, once again my kids and my girlfriend Vanessa Paradis have given me a proper foundation. A sense of home that I never had in my life, a real sense of a place to be."

Johnny **rationalizes his unstable relationships**, jumping from one woman to the next – one of his slogans is:

"If you love two people at the same time, choose the second. Because if you really loved the first one, you wouldn't have fallen for the second..."

Johnny has been connecting parts of his past family experiences to his later relationships with women to try to explain his crumbling, unstable, wobbly romantic relationships. He's commented:

"I can remember my parents fighting and us kids wondering who was going to go with whom if they got divorced."

"As far as my first marriage, I guess I have very traditional kinds of sensibilities about that kind of stuff - you know, a man and a woman sharing their life together and having a baby, whatever - and I think for a while I was trying to right the wrongs of my parents because they split up when I was a kid…"

"…So I thought I could do it differently - make things work. I had the right intentions, but the wrong timing - and the wrong person. But I don't regret it; I had fun and I learned a lot."

"You know, I was married, when I was 20. It was a strong bond with someone, but I can't necessarily say I was in love. That's something that comes around once, man, maybe twice if you're lucky. And I don't know that I experienced that, let's say, before I turned 30."

Depp is very glib and seemingly insightful concerning his rickety, volatile, unhinged romantic hookups or relationships. But if one understands the **BPD syndrome which consists of processes such as idealizing and demonizing ("splitting" – a person is "all good" or "all bad") or anxious attachment versus avoidant attachment**, Johnny's stormy love life comes into focus. I'll discuss this more in the next chapter.

Johnny often talks it one way and walks it in another direction. For example, he remarked on his prior relationship strife:

"I don't regret any of them. I had a good time. Most of what's been written about me has been completely false. People have created an image that has absolutely nothing to do with me, and they have the power to sell it, to shove it down the throats of people. **I'm an old-fashioned guy who wants marriage and kids.**"

His stated goal is to live like an "old-fashioned guy who wants marriage and kids." He's got over $350 million and has no excuses that he can't afford it financially – he could get a prenuptial agreement signed before marriage to protect his assets.

Why doesn't he do what he says he most wants? I understand finding "Miss Right" can be difficult for the average guy. But Johnny has his pick of an endless number of beautiful women. **Why can't he find one to marry, settle down and have kids?**

And when he does pick a woman, she always seems to be the wrong one – now it's openly bisexual Amber Heard who simultaneously has a lesbian lover. They've already fought bitterly, broken-up, made-up and now he's struggling to hang onto Amber by buying her expensive gifts and promising to help with her career by, for example, introducing her to his contacts.

However, Amber has complained Johnny has not helped her career and she's bored with him. Reportedly Depp's hurting her career by interfering with her choice of roles – he was against her taking a role in *Fifty Shades of Grey* because it was "smutty."

My theory is that his Borderline Personality Disorder will block him and interfere with his stated relationship goals. Even if he finds a woman to marry and have kids, it won't last. **If Depp got the right kind of effective psychotherapy combined with a Twelve-Step program like A.A. to handle his aim to quit drinking alcohol or using drugs, he'd have a chance at a more stable life.**

Cognitive Disturbances:

BPD people often suffer from temporary psychotic symptoms including:

1) **Dissociation** (An abnormal psychological state in which one's perception of oneself and/or one's environment is altered significantly).

2) **Derealization** (A sense one has lost contact with external reality).

3) **Depersonalization** (A sense one has lost contact with one's own personal reality – "My body feels strange like it's not my own...").

4) **Paranoia** (Having suspicions and beliefs that one is being followed, plotted against, persecuted, etc.).

Depp has commented: "I'm shy, **paranoid**, whatever word you want to use. I hate fame. I've done everything I can to avoid it."

If Depp "hates fame" and has "done everything I can to avoid it," then why did he sign-up to be a rock star or superstar movie actor? It is obvious he was going to lose some privacy and have photographers taking his photo and reporters writing up interviews to promote his films. **He seems to say socially acceptable things and his behavior often shows the opposite.**

Of course if you consider Depp's impulsive substance abuse (abusing alcohol and mood-altering drugs) tendencies combined with his inappropriate, intense or uncontrollable anger (frequent displays of temper, constant anger, recurrent physical fights) – then one can see flashes of temporary paranoia, dissociation, depersonalization and derealization. But in fairness to Depp, his cognitive distortions including paranoia (extreme mistrust) seem the least of his BPD symptoms.

Impulsive Behaviors:

Depp has admitted some of his impulsive behaviors:

"I started smoking at 12, lost my virginity at 13 and did **every kind of drug there was by 14. Pretty much any drug you** can name, I've done it. I wouldn't say I was bad or malicious, I was just curious. I certainly had my little experiences with drugs."

Labile Affect:

"Labile affect" refers to one having sudden and frequent changes in affect – wide mood swings. When Johnny expresses rage, bitterness or despondency, he may also have underlying anger, emptiness, boredom and abandonment fears.

Depp has revealed a **feeling of emptiness and boredom** as early has his high school years:

"I'd been in high school three years, and I may have just walked in yesterday. I had, like, eight credits. I was in my third year of high school and I didn't want to be there. **I was bored out of my mind and I hated it**."

At these stressful times Depp may demand more attention and support from others. BPD people have a problem in regulating their emotions. They may express negative emotions more deeply and have more fluctuations in pleasant emotions.

Functional Failures:

Many BPD individuals can't reach their potential and apply their abilities because their emotional instability and cognitive turmoil interferes. However, some BPD sufferers including Johnny Depp, Marilyn Monroe, Princess Diana and Angelina Jolie have functioned at a high level while experiencing the pain of BPD mental disorders.

For further information on them you can read my books: *Marilyn Monroe Diagnosed*; *Princess Diana Diagnosed*; and *Angelina Jolie Psychoanalyzed*. **With famous BPD victims, their sense of entitlement and over-inflated ego can lead them into denial of any mental disorders.**

Self-Destructive Activity:

Depp has shown self-destructive behavior in the form of <u>non-suicidal mutilation or cutting himself</u> and overlapped impulsive behavior such as substance abuse of various illegal street drugs and mood-altering drugs.

He's admitted to vandalizing property, petty theft, breaking and entering, burglary, trashing hotel rooms, and fighting or brawling with photographers and others. His anger in relationships has driven women away. Johnny said:

"I hung around with bad crowds. We used to break and enter places. We'd break into the school and destroy a room or something. I used to steal things from stores."

The initial assessment of Depp I've just made in this and the prior chapter have revealed a number of BPD signs and symptoms.

According to the current diagnostic criteria to establish Borderline Personality Disorder (BPD) individuals with BPD usually have several of the following symptoms, many of which are detailed in the *DSM-IV-TR (Diagnostic manual of the American Psychiatric Association)* – for a diagnosis, five of the nine following criteria must apply (I've put symptoms in bold which apply to Johnny Depp according to my research.):

1) **Marked mood swings with periods of intense depressed mood**, irritability and/or anxiety lasting a few hours to a few days (but not in the context of a full-blown episode of major depressive disorder or bipolar disorder).

2) **Inappropriate, intense or uncontrollable anger** (frequent displays of temper, constant anger, recurrent physical fights).

3) **Impulsive behaviors that result in adverse outcomes and psychological distress**, such as excessive spending, sexual encounters, **substance use (abusing mood-altering drugs & alcohol), shoplifting**, reckless driving or binge eating.

4) Recurring suicidal threats or **non-suicidal self-injurious behavior, such as cutting** or burning one's self.

5) **Unstable, intense personal relationships**, sometimes alternating between "all good," *idealizations,* and "all bad," *devaluation*.

6) **Persistent uncertainty about self-image, long-term goals, friendships and values.**

7) **Chronic boredom or feelings of emptiness.**

8) Frantic efforts to avoid abandonment. (Not including suicidal or self-mutilating behavior). **Abandonment fears.**

9) Transient, stress-related paranoid ideation or severe dissociative symptoms. **Some intense mistrust or paranoia at times.**

Chapter 3

"I've also gotten weird letters, suicide letters, and girls threatening to jump if I don't get in touch with them. So you think, "This is bullshit," but then you think, "What if it's not? Who wants to take that chance?" I write them back, tell them to hang in there, if things are that bad, they have to get better. But I'm not altogether stable myself, so who am I to give advice?"

--Johnny Depp

***Private Resort* (1985) was Depp's** second film – storyline:

A wacky teenage sex comedy of the sort that proliferated in the mid-1980s, this farce is notable for featuring two lead actors who would go on to bigger and better things.

Rob Morrow and Johnny Depp star as Ben and Jack, respectively, teen buddies who are on the sexual prowl for beautiful, wealthy girls at a posh Miami resort where they are weekend guests.

Also on the prowl is The Maestro (Hector Elizondo), a skilled jewel thief who evades detection by cross-dressing as a woman while he pursues the diamond necklace of society woman Amanda Rawlings (Dody Goodman).

When they accidentally run afoul of the Maestro, Ben and Jack suddenly have their hands full. *Private Resort* was the third in a series of comic teen sex romps from producer R. Ben Efraim, each of which had the word Private in the title (*rottentomatoes*).

JOHNNY DEPP'S LIFE BEHIND THE SCENES:

In order to get the pattern of Depp's unstable relationships, I'm including the following material on Johnny & Kate's stormy relationship. I've edited out irrelevant material.

You can see **Johnny's relationships with women follow the yo-yo BPD pattern of what's known as "splitting" – black or white thinking; either the woman is idealized unrealistically or unrealistically devalued as all bad.**

Johnny does not see any gray areas or nuances in his relationships with women. It's always "love at first sight" and "love forever" or "love eternally" which is followed by stormy relations, fights, conflicts and a split.

THE ROOM OF KATE AND JOHNNY (*THE TEMPLE OF KATE MOSS & JohnnyDeppfan*):

September 13, 1994, the event that will always be associated with their relationship occurred. **Johnny trashed his hotel room at the Mark Hotel in New York with Kate present in the room**. This incident set off a frenzy of speculation, rumor and innuendo in the tabloid press as well as the legitimate (?) press. It was reported Johnny and Kate were fighting.

Surely, Kate and Johnny were through. NAW! On September 24, they appeared together and were quite affectionate at the premiere of Johnny's movie, *Ed Wood* at the New York film festival.

On 11/17/95, Johnny participated in a chat for America Online. This question was posed to him, "Johnny, are you still talking to Kate Moss?" Johnny's answer, "As of about 3 minutes ago, yes". Also, on 11/20/95, Johnny escorted his mother to the premiere of his new movie and was quick to tell the press that Kate was in Japan working.

The above contradicted tabloid rumors that they were separated. However, there continued to be periodic reports in the press that Johnny and Kate had split.

As to the rampant rumors in August and September, 1995, regarding an impending wedding for Kate and Johnny, Kate said in a 10/95 interview with *Entertainment Tonight* when the marriage question was posed, **"He's just my boyfriend. That's all. We're not getting married"**.

In an interview with Playboy (1/96), Johnny said about the marriage rumors:

"It's fiction. I can guarantee you that if I woke up one day with a wild hair up my ass to get hitched, there wouldn't be invitations. We'd run out and do it."

Again in early February, 1996, there were tabloid reports that the duo had parted. This time the reports said that **Kate was tired of Johnny not paying enough attention to her** and she wanted to date other men.

Johnny reportedly went to his mother's farm to plan how to win Kate back. But the pair was together during fashion week in New York City in March, 1996. Johnny was in New York filming *Donnie Brasco* during the fashion shows.

According to an interview in *Select* magazine with Noel Gallagher of Oasis, Johnny and Kate were in Mustique with Noel and his girlfriend, Meg. Meg and Kate are long time-friends and Kate often stays with them when she is in Great Britain.

During their vacation together, Noel was writing songs for his new album and Johnny was writing the script for his directorial debut, *The Brave*. The ladies were evidently just hanging out and **disgusted with the lack of attention** they were receiving from their gentlemen friends. Johnny and Kate were together on November 11, 1996, in New York at a party for author Hunter S. Thompson.

It was been reported from several sources that Johnny moved in with Kate in December, 1996 at her apartment in New York. Johnny and Kate attended the premiere of *Donnie Brasco* together in Los Angeles on February 24th, 1997.

Kate also attended with Johnny the premiere of his film *The Brave* in Cannes on May 10th, 1997, during the 50th anniversary of the Festival.

Tabloid news the week of June 16, 1997, suggests that Kate and Johnny had again split. There was no confirmation about this from Kate or Johnny.

Here are the tabloid reports so you can judge for yourself:

The rumor began in the London *Sun* newspaper on 6/16 when they reported:

"Supermodel Kate Moss has finally split from Hollywood **hell-raiser Johnny Depp**. The couple are going their separate ways after a **stormy four-year relationship**. A source said they planned to remain friends and Kate will go to Depp's film premiers. Kate, 23 from Croydon, South London, had once talked about marrying the *Edward Scissorhands* star."

"Earlier this year, Depp 33, moved into Kate's New York flat. But instead of cementing the relationship, the **couple found they got on each other's nerves.**"

The June 23 *New York Magazine* added this to the *Sun* rumor:

..."According to fashion-world insiders, Kate has told friends that she called it **quits with the hot-tempered heartthrob last week because they were having too many fights**. Says the source, "**They've had small separations before, but this was a major breakup**...Depp's spokesperson didn't return calls; Moss's publicist declined to comment on his client's personal life..."

On 6/25 the *New York Post* had this to add to the rumors:

"...Sources say **things were already rocky for the couple** back in May at the Cannes Film Festival. They rented separate villas. Kate shared one with her pals from Oasis...and they never visited each other's pad. Friends say **Kate wants to keep the relationship alive, but Johnny won't change** to suit her...When Depp was in town recently, the pair didn't even see each other once. Depp's publicist Nancy Seltzer still maintains, "to our knowledge the breakup is untrue."

On June 26th Mitchell Fink of *People* magazine had this to say:

"...According to friends, **Moss wants to continue to date Depp occasionally, but Depp isn't into open relationships.** For the record, a Depp spokeswoman says, "To our knowledge news of the breakup is untrue."

Janet Charlton of *Star* magazine said on the *E! Gossip* show that Kate and Johnny had taken a vacation from one another while Johnny continues working on improving *The Brave* and will resume their relationship when he is through. And that **Winona Ryder has been calling Johnny since she still cares for him and that Kate should watch out**. (That definitely sounds like gossip.)

And last, *The New York Post* reported on June 27th that:

"...Moss has taken up with 32-year-old Tarka Cordell...and that **he and Kate were making a chump out of Johnny long before he gave the waif her walking papers**. Sources say that for the past year Cordell has stayed at Moss' apartment in New York whenever he's in town...'To my knowledge they've been friends for a while,' says Paul Rowland, owner of Moss' agency, 'but I don't think there's any romance involved.'"

Also the *Star* magazine had an article about a wild night Johnny supposedly had with Demi Moore but that one isn't worth my typing efforts. So there you have the gossip.

Johnny and Kate were together for a Rolling Stone Concert in New York on January 16, 1998. The *Daily News* had this to say about the event:

"**Johnny Depp and Kate Moss appear to be back together**. The fun couple joined Uma Thurman and Ethan Hawke at the Rolling Stones Concert on Friday. Exiting Madison Square Garden, Depp was in high spirits. When paparazzo John Barrett dropped his house keys, Depp picked them up, then asked Barrett to "prove" they belonged to him. Barrett did, prompting Depp to toss them back on the sidewalk"

This mention appeared in the *New York Magazine* dated February 2 1998:

"Stones Fan Gathers No Moss At least one supermodel makes it to her appointments on time. Kate Moss had promised record mogul and friend Chris Blackwell that she would attend the opening of the Aveda spa at his Strawberry Hill resort in Jamaica. What the prototypical waif didn't bargain for was how long her 24th-birthday celebration with ex-beau Johnny Depp would last."

"The pair began the evening at the Madison Square Garden Rolling Stones show and then headed back to guitarist Ron Wood's Palace Hotel suite for an all-night bender with Helena Christensen and Keith Richards's son Marlon."

"The crew was spotted roaming the halls till sunrise. But that morning, like a trouper, Moss raced to the airport, hopped a commercial jet to Kingston, and helicoptered into Strawberry Hill. She spent just four hours there before heading back to New York. Blackwell said affectionately, "**She looked like she had been through hell,** but I was impressed that she kept her word and decided to show."

Kate and Johnny appeared together in public for the last time at the 1998 Cannes Film Festival for the premiere of Johnny's film, *Fear and Loathing in Las Vegas*. They admittedly attended as friends.

Following is a quote from Johnny from the *New York Daily News* 5/17/98:

"**Kate is somebody I care about deeply. We were together for four years, and she's a great, lovely, sweet, pure girl, really a great kid, and I care about her. I love**

her on a very deep, profound level. Distance is very difficult when you're trying to maintain a relationship, when you're thousands of miles apart for a lot of time. We still see each other, hang out and talk on the phone. We're close, but I'm not with anybody at all."

Finally, here is a quote from CYBERSLEAZE 5/22/98:

"DEPP TAKES THE BLAME FOR SPLIT FROM MOSS: Heartthrob actor JOHNNY DEPP has revealed he was to blame for the break-up of his romance with top British model KATE MOSS. Talking at the CANNES FILM FESTIVAL, where he is promoting his latest movie *FEAR AND LOATHING IN LAS VEGAS*, **Depp admits that he didn't give Moss the attention she deserved - and says that he cried for a week after they split up."

"He says, '<u>**I was a horrific pain in the butt to live with. I can be a total moron at times.**</u> **I let my work get in the way which made me difficult to get along with.'** Depp, 34, was accompanied by Moss, 24, for the premiere for his movie last week - but simply as an old friend."

"**He admits he's been unable to find a replacement for Moss and is scared he will never find another girlfriend who can properly replace her**. The *EDWARD SCISSORHANDS* star says, "I want to have children, I'd really like to become a parent now, but finding the right woman to share that with is proving difficult."

Postscript: Johnny is expecting a child in May, 1999, with French Singer/Actress, Vanessa Paradis.

Why did Depp break-up with Kate Moss? Johnny has reported in interviews some socially-acceptable reasons such as his work demands and distance between them which led to his lack of attention to Kate.

But let's consider some possible BPD related causes which are at a deeper level. First, woven into stories about Depp's stormy relationships is his **inappropriate, intense or uncontrollable anger (frequent displays of temper, constant anger, recurrent physical fights) – a symptom of BPD.**

On moment the excuse is that Johnny did not have time to pay Kate the attention she required. After all, Depp claimed, he was busy with film projects, traveling to film shoots or too involved with his career. But Johnny's girlfriends have always known he's an actor who travels to film locations and promotes his movies. Why is this "lack of attention" suddenly an issue?

Then simultaneously there were reports that when Kate and Johnny were living together they **"got on each other's nerves" and were fighting when they were together**. Why wasn't Depp able to give her enough "attention" – it seems they gave each other too much attention then.

So I don't understand – first it is that Depp can't provide Moss with the attention she needs. **Then when he lives with her and she has access to Johnny's "attention," then fireworks seem to explode between them.**

How could Depp's Borderline Personality Disorder (BPD) have resulted in their split when it seemed like "eternal love" and "love at first sight" when Johnny and Kate first met?

One BPD theory is that BPD sufferers form "relationship schemas" or have developed other BPD "schemas" which they use to navigate their relationships – often unintentionally destroying the relationship or stressing-out their romantic partner.

BPD & Relationship "Schemas" and Johnny Depp:

"Schema" Definition:

According to "schema" theory, BPD and relationship "schemas" or powerful beliefs and attitudes are frequently held by Borderline people and result in unstable relationships. Complicating the Depp-Moss relationship is the fact that they were both celebrities who may have **conflicts arising out of a sense of special entitlement, narcissism and perhaps an ego-maniac mentality.**

"Schema" Development:

Schemas, if you accept the theory, are developed in BPD individuals in a process beginning in childhood and continuing into adulthood. Parents, teachers, peer groups and other factors can influence the development of schemas or BPD belief systems and attitudes held by BPD victims.

For example, **Depp's "schemas" developed** as a function of his peer group and teachers in high school. He ran with a "bad crowd," got into drug abuse, vandalism, breaking and entering, burglary, trashing other's property, petty theft and was failing in high school out of boredom and a lack of effort.

Johnny's belief and attitude – his BPD "schema" - in high school was that he was a failure which was reinforced by some of his teachers. His lowlife-peer group further conditioned him to expect he was headed down to the gutter as a misfit – that he'd end up in jail or dead like other drug-addict criminals. He assumed he had no talent for anything. Here's how Johnny saw it from his comments:

"I hung around with bad crowds. We used to break and enter places. We'd break into the school and destroy a room or something. I used to steal things from stores."

After he was famous as a movie star, one of his old high school teachers asked for his autograph. "I mean, what was I supposed to say? He'd failed me. I remember one time this teacher yelled at me so heavily in front of the entire class. He didn't have any time for me then, and now, all of a sudden, he wants my autograph? They all thought I was going to end up a drug addict, in jail."

"I started smoking at 12, lost my virginity at 13 and **did every kind of drug there was by 14. Pretty much any drug you can name, I've done it.** I wouldn't say I was bad or malicious, I was just curious. I certainly had my little experiences with drugs. Eventually, you see where that's headed and you get out."

Types of BPD "Schemas" or Beliefs and Attitudes:

According to some BPD theorists, Depp could have several **types of schemas** he has used to guide himself including:

1) **Self-concept schemas** (Who am I? What am I worth? Am I competent, capable, and talented?)

2) **Relationship schemas** (How do I deserve to be treated? How should I treat others? Can I trust others or should I avoid them?)

3) **World schemas** (Is the world predictable or unpredictable? Is the world safe or dangerous?)

Usually these schemas – self-concept, relationship or world schemas – develop out of experiences with the opposite extremes. So for instance, when Depp as a teenager in high school is failing in a class and his teacher yells at him in front of the class harshly, **he developed a self-concept or self-image schema that he was incompetent** to do school work or lacked talent for anything.

When Johnny was given a school assignment he felt overwhelmed and incompetent because his self-concept schema told him he was not capable and had no talent. In addition he hated and was bored by high school.

At the opposite extreme, another student in Depp's class could have an **omnipotent schema** indicating he/she could do anything without help – say a student who had an A-average and was highly praised by the teacher. This student might need help at times and yet impulsively take on any task.

The mid-point between the two extremes is a **competent schema** – a person with a sense of capability and competence will evaluate a problem they tackle and get help when needed.

Why were Johnny Depp's schemas or attitudes/beliefs about himself, relationships and the world hard to change?

There are four major reasons a person including Depp does not easily change developed schemas:

1) **Schemas act as filters** (For instance, a person with an **inferiority schema** such as Depp had about his competence doing high school work, will filter out contradictory evidence such as a good grade and focus on the negative.)

2) **Schemas encourage misinterpretation and misunderstandings** (An example of misinterpretation could be based on an "**anxious attachment schema**" – fearing a romantic partner will leave one. Johnny's parents split and perhaps set an example of abandonment up for him. So when his romantic partner does something such as leaving them alone for a time, he jumps to conclusions that he's being abandoned and panics.)

3) **Schemas lead to fear** (One could over-idealize a romantic partner and be afraid of finding out some contrary information. Or Depp could fear trying to do his high school work because he fears he'll fail again.)

4) **Schemas are invisible** (People can't change something they don't see. So when they are not aware of negative schemas, they can't make an effort to change them.)

If we take a look at Depp's self-concept schema in terms of his looks, he's said he's ugly. He prefers a shaggy-dog look, hair messy, uneven beard or facial hair, etc. *Starpulse* reported:

Johnny Depp Thinks He's Ugly (Jan. 13, 2011):

Johnny Depp recently talked about taking partner Vanessa Paradis on double dates with his *The Tourist* co-star Angelina Jolie and Brad Pitt.

He explained, "Angie is a stunner, so is Vanessa. And Brad, of course. When we all sat together, I was the only ugly one. I'm not the spick-and-span kind of guy. To be honest, I don't like cutting my hair or trimming my beard."

Of course Depp could be just making modest, socially-acceptable comments to explain his "trademark" look. But if a person seriously had an "**ugly schema**" about themselves, they could block out contrary evidence and misinterpret in line with their belief that they're unattractive.

No Midpoint or Middle-Ground Schemas:

The mind of the BPD creates and develops **extreme "schemas"** or beliefs/attitudes. If a man has an **undeserving schema**, he expects bad things to happen and not get what he wants in general.

Yet there can be a flip-flop from an undeserving to a **sense-of-entitlement schema**. If this guy's girlfriend slights him, he can flip into a rage because she does not pay attention to him or do something for him. Maybe she wants to spend a weekend with her girlfriends – he can get into a rage over her being "inconsiderate" of him.

Contrast another guy with a **middle-ground schema** of deserving and he can adapt to his girlfriend not spending time with him at times.

For example, Depp fights photographers or trashes hotel rooms because he has a fight with his girlfriend or whatever and he can't see the shades of gray in a situation. His **black-and-white thinking** views a conflict in an all-or-none context.

He doesn't get the room service in a hotel to his liking or his girlfriend doesn't behave the way he demands, so he destroys the hotel room. Johnny doesn't see that his girlfriends have rights and the photographer is trying to earn a living and as a celebrity actor, public exposure is part of his gig. Depp wanted to be a rock star or a movie star and this is what comes with it.

Self-concept Schemas:

Personal or self-concept schemas develop as a child and teen interacts with caregivers and peers. They influence a BPD sufferer feels, what he does and expects.

1) **Entitled versus undeserving schemas**: Sometimes parents who spoil or neglect their children set these schemas in motion. Rock stars or movie stars often have a **sense-of-entitlement schema**. Depp has often gotten into fights with women when the relationship doesn't go his way. This has led to a series of unstable relationships. A "normal" or non-BPD person might have a **balanced self-worth schema** – they expect to have their needs met but not at the expense of others. If one has an **undeserving schema**, he sets himself up for failure.

2) **Inferiority versus superiority schemas**: Apparently Depp struggled with an **inferiority schema** as a teenager – he said: "As a teenager I was so insecure. I

was the type of guy that never fitted in because he never dared to choose. I was convinced I had absolutely no talent at all. For nothing. And that thought took away all my ambition too." People with inferiority schemas feel inadequate, lack confidence in their abilities, give up easily and then feel more incompetent. The reverse is the **superiority schema** when the BPD feels he's better than others, may be narcissistic and self-centered while abusing others. The more adaptive schema is the **middle-ground schema** of self-acceptance.

I think ironically, Depp's **"inferiority schemas"** coming from the dark side have perhaps helped him make some interesting and varied choices in acting. For example, Depp remarked:

"People say I make strange choices, but they're not strange for me. My sickness is that I'm fascinated by human behavior, by what's underneath the surface, by the worlds inside people."

Relationship Schemas:

Relationship schemas impact interpersonal relationships for better or worse. People with BPD put up roadblocks in forming relationships by having such schemas as "anxious attachment" vs. "avoidant attachment" or "idealizing" vs. "demonizing."

1) **Anxious attachment versus avoidant attachment schemas**: Some BPDs with an **"anxious-attachment schema"** fear abandonment – that someone close to them will leave them. Depp appears to be vulnerable to that because of his parents' break-up and its impact on him and his family. At the other extreme is the **"avoidant-attachment schema"** which leads the BPD to stay away from people, seem aloof – often because they fear people will hurt them. BPD victims may switch from one extreme to the other. The **middle-ground schema** is the **"secure attachment schema"** which leads the person to have friends based on mutual caring and respect.

Johnny claimed that he was finally in the right place when he had kids and was in love with Vanessa Paradis. Yet he left Vanessa in 2012 and has been involved with another woman. Why does he keep splitting from these "ideal" women? Why did he run away from the perfect home?

Maybe it is because of his underlying **"anxious-attachment schema"** which, at times, flips over to an **"avoidant-attachment schema"** – stimulating him to split. Here's his idealized version of kids and Vanessa in his own words:

"Having kids was a huge change for me. Becoming a father. But I think more than changing, I feel like I've been revealed to myself, I kind of found out who I was."

"When you meet your child for the first time and you're looking at this angel, you start realizing what an idiot you've been for so many years and how much time you've wasted."

"As far as being feet-on-the-ground, once again my kids and my girlfriend Vanessa Paradis have given me a proper foundation. A sense of home that I never had in my life, a real sense of a place to be."

2) **Idealizing versus demonizing schemas**: BPDs often have **"idealizing schemas"** which they lay on new romantic partners – BPDs over-inflate their expectations and expect their new lovers to be perfect. Sooner or later they will be disappointed. Later in the relationship the BPD may then flip to a **"demonizing schema"** when they unrealistically discount, degrade and devalue their partner – interpret their behavior as hostile and malicious. The middle-ground, adaptive schema is the **"realistic view schema"** when a "normal" person tolerates the ups and downs in a relationship and sees gray areas in social relationships. Everything isn't all black or all white – good or bad which is known as "splitting." **"Splitting"** is jumping from one extreme to another.

Depp commented on interfacing, talking to others which implies a **"demonizing schema"** in operation: "You gotta be careful: don't say a word to nobody about nothing anytime ever."

World Schemas:

1) **Dangerous versus totally safe schemas**: If one develops a **"dangerous schema"** of the world, one may be hyper-vigilant, be too cautious and expect the worst. The flip side is the **"totally safe schema"** held by those naïve types who are clueless and don't take normal precautions. The middle-ground schema is the **"reasonably safe schema"** and they take rational precautions and avoid extreme paranoia.

Johnny remarked about his reaction to hearing about "crib death" which indicated he had a **"dangerous schema"** of the world at that time – he spoke about being an uncle:

"My sister Christi had a baby when I was 17, and I had just heard about crib death. The horrible thing was that it wasn't understood. For some unknown reason the baby would stop breathing. So I would sneak into where the baby was sleeping and put my hand in her crib, hold her little finger, and I'd sleep on the floor like that. It was stupid, I'm sure. But I thought the warmth of my hand might help, that maybe if she felt my pulse it would remind her to breathe."

This showed Depp was very vulnerable to negative BPD schemas. It didn't take much to set him off and get him developing a **self-destructive schema**.

2) **Unpredictable versus totally predictable schemas**: BPDs with **"unpredictable schemas"** see the world as chaotic, expect plans to never work out and see themselves as victims or helpless. If a BPD has a **"totally predictable schema"** then he expects his Plan A to always work and will be disappointed when it doesn't because they have no Plan B. A "normal" person with a **"predictable schema"** will expect his plans to work but has a Plan A, Plan B and Plan C just in case.

Depp's Plan A was to be a rock star. Fortunately he had the talent and looks for Plan B (movie star) which he stumbled into while he was in Hollywood aiming to be a rock musician.

Chapter 4

"I see kids who are complete cynics. They're not dreaming. They're out there with high-powered weapons, smoking crack behind the 7-Eleven. They've seen it all. These kids are going to take us into 2000 and beyond. That's scary, man. I wouldn't say I'm pessimistic or optimistic. I'm more realistic, I guess. But not cynical. I look. I watch."

--Johnny Depp

Slow Burn (1986) was Johnny's third film – storyline:

Slow Burn, directed by Matthew Chapman, a well-above average, made-for cable-TV mystery thriller tells the story of a detective and his search for the missing son and ex-wife of his client.

Based on a novel by Arthur Lyons, and well-directed by Matthew Chapman this intelligent thriller follows detective Jacob Ash (Eric Roberts) as he investigates the disappearance of Donnie (Johnny Depp) the missing son of his client Gerald McMurty (Raymond Barry) and his ex-wife artist Laine Fleischer (Beverly D'Angelo) during a routine visit to Las Vegas.

As the investigation continues Jacob discovers an intricate web of deceit and betrayal that leads to a murder which Jacob must solve. D'Angelo, frequently underrated, is top notch in her role of the frightened woman who may have secrets.

Roberts, who can be uneven, is successful in creating an engaging and sexy character who has a good deal of appeal and a good chemistry with D'Angelo. Slow Burn is a surprising, engaging thriller with good performances and an intelligent premise and is highly recommended (*rottentomatoes*).

JOHNNY DEPP'S LIFE BEHIND THE SCENES:

Love and Depp (S. Levitt, *People Magazine*, Oct. 3, 1994):

JOHNNY DEPP DIAGNOSED: UNAUTHORIZED PSYCHOLOGICAL DIAGNOSIS OF HIS SECRET LIFE

No one takes more risks than the Gielgud of grunge. But is this Johnny Depp's year of living *too* dangerously?

After a hotel fracas with girlfriend Kate Moss lands Johnny Depp in jail, the actor one friend calls "the finest human being to step on the earth" can't seem to stay out of trouble.

The star of TV's *21 Jump Street* and the movies *Edward Scissorhands* and *Benny & Joon* has, reportedly, whiled away at least one L.A. evening **hanging by his fingertips from a fifth-story parking garage** at the Beverly Center alongside close friend Nicolas Cage.

And then there is Depp's Bart Simpson-esque penchant for checking into hotels under ribald pseudonyms. Why would a 31-one year old man tell a front-desk clerk that he is "Mr. Donkey Penis"? Because, you see, it makes for such *interesting* wake-up calls. **But maybe it's time Depp got a serious wake-up call.**

Yet these days the chain-smoking, tattoo-festooned, Viper Room-owning movie star seems to be **dancing on the edge of danger.**

At 5:30 a.m. on Sept. 13, a green knit hat pulled down over his forehead, **Depp was arrested on charges of criminal mischief after trashing his $1200-a night room at New York City's tony Mark Hotel.**

Police suspect he was drunk and had been fighting with his girlfriend Kate Moss, 20. After several hours in a holding cell, he was released and told that the charges would be dismissed if he stayed out of trouble for six months and agreed to reimburse the Mark $9,767.12 in damages and guest fees.

That was just the most highly publicized of Depp's recent problems. **One week earlier, visiting Moss in her native London, he reportedly caused a ruckus in a pub when 27-year-old photographer Jonathan Walpole mistakenly picked up Depp's glass from the bar.**

"He pulled my ears very hard, "Walpole told London's *Evening Standard*, adding that "some ape" who was with Depp "leaped on my back, put his arm around my neck and tried to force my head to the floor."

To many of Depp's friends these incidents are, as one put it, "just Johnny being Johnny," the sort of outbursts they have come to expect on occasion from an actor who can be as otherworldly as the character he played in *Scissorhands*. **"I think Johnny obviously has a temper**, but this is a very minor incident," John Waters says of the Mark melee. "The room service must have been bad."

Surely it's time to take stock when you're eligible for counseling from Marlon Brando. Yet Timothy Leary, the '60's LSD guru who is the godfather of Depp's onetime fiancée Winona Ryder, says that **Depp is both "wild** and charitable."

Most friends prefer to focus on the charitable side, offering tales of his kindness and generosity. Driving near the Austin, Texas, set of *Grape* during a downpour, Depp came across a homeless woman; he offered her a lift and gave her every cent he had on him.

He is said to wander, at 4 or 5 in the morning, outside the Viper Room, the Sunset Strip club where 23-year-old River Phoenix died of an overdose last Halloween, and hand out 50 and 100 dollar bills to the destitute huddled on the sidewalk.

But there is a darker side to Depp as well. Before he left the Mark Hotel in handcuffs, he had been arrested on three previous occasions:

1) For getting into a tiff with an L.A. police officer over a jaywalking ticket;

2) For speeding in Arizona;

3) For assaulting a hotel security guard in Vancouver, B.C.

He has engaged since childhood in thrill-seeking escapades that seem downright self-destructive. In a caper that even he, looking back, described as "a really ridiculous thing," **Depp blew on fire with a mouthful of gasoline. His face ignited**, and it was only the quick moves of a friend that saved him from becoming a burn casualty.

His arms bear rows of scars from self-inflicted knife wounds, each one commemorating what Depp considers an important life event. "I have," he once explained, "a funny relationship with my body . . . Ah, it sounds so stupid, but for me there shouldn't be any halfway."

He has certainly been partying full tilt of late. The night after his release from jail, Depp, flanked by leather-clad, heavily tattooed bikers, was at Babyland, a Lower East Side bar filled with cribs and nursery paraphernalia.

Jerry Price, a Manhattan pipe fitter, claims that Depp bumped into him at the club's bar, after which Price says he was pummeled by the biker bodyguards and hit with a rocking horse.

And, at Dan Lynch, yet another hip watering hole, Depp recently directed and starred in a video for Shane MacGowan and the Popes. Their song? "*That Woman's got Me Drinking*."

The woman who would seem to have Depp drinking these days is, of course, the ultrathin Kate Moss, who has appeared topless alongside Marky Mark in Calvin Klein ads. She and Depp met last February at the Manhattan bistro Café Tabac, and Moss has said, "I knew from the first moment we talked that we were going to be together."

Moss and Depp, a friend says, "can't keep their hands, lips, mouths, legs off of each other." Nor are they always successful in keeping their brawls private.

In June they shouted at each other in the dining room of Manhattan's Royalton Hotel. Says a longtime friend of Depp's: "Instead of hitting women, he just gets angry and lets off steam in other ways."

Depp seems to be the kind of passionate fellow who finds scant middle ground between picking someone up and proposing. He married Lori Allison, a make-up artist from Florida, when he was 20 and she was 25; they divorced two years later.

He has since been engaged at least three times—to actresses Sherilyn Fenn, Jennifer Grey, and Winona Ryder—and Tally Chanel, a B-movie actress, also says she got a shot at being Depp's fiancée. They met when she was working as a hostess at the Hollywood premiere of *Die Hard 2* in July 1990.

"I helped him out of his limo," the 27-year-old recalls. "Our eyes locked, and he asked me to marry him." They dated for a year, spending quiet nights at Depp's Hollywood Hills home, ordering in food from a Chinese restaurant.

Even on the night of his recent arrest, **Depp seemed most concerned not with the prospect of doing jail time but**

with the possibility that he had fallen out of favor with a woman, Officer Eileen Perez. "I don't think she likes me," Perez heard Depp say to her partner. Then he brightened up and added, "But I bet if she saw me in a mall, she'd ask for my autograph."

Johnny, meanwhile, started smoking at 12, lost his virginity around age 13 and, **he has said, "Did every kind of drug there was by 14."** At 16, a year after his parents divorced, he dropped out of high school and joined a garage band, the Kids. "Puberty was very vague," he has said. "I literally locked myself in a room and played guitar."

Still, **Depp's own heart throbbed only for Winona Ryder**, whom he first spotted in June 1989 at the premiere of her movie *Great Balls of Fire*.

"There's been nothing in my 27 years that's comparable to the feeling I have with Winona," Depp said.

Five months after their first date, **Depp gave Ryder an engagement ring; three years later they broke up.**

The end of their romance left Depp so desperately in love with Winona," says a friend, **"that when they broke up, he wouldn't admit it was over for the longest time."**

Lately he has focused those same intense affections on Moss—even saying, according to one friend, **"that he wanted to have a baby with Kate."**

Instead the Viper Room became the hippest stop on the Sunset Strip, with block-long lines of young Hollywood types and tourists who want to see **the place where River Phoenix, convulsing on the sidewalk, spent the last moments of his life.**

Are Depp's problems anywhere near as serious? His friends don't think so. "I am not worried at all," says John Waters. **"Johnny is not killing himself. I think he is aware of that pitfall. He has certainly seen it."**

BPD ISSUES, SYMPTOMS & JOHNNY DEPP:

I've included parts of the above article which relate to Depp's BPD symptoms. Parts that are highlighted are particularly relevant to reveal Johnny's BPD mental disorder symptoms in areas such as:

1) Depp's volatile emotions.

2) His unstable, roller-coaster relationships.

3) Johnny's unhinged, self-destructive and impulsive behavior.

4) His insecure identity or self-image.

Some of Depp's friends have pointed out that he's wild but charitable and kind. Some examples include Johnny handing out money to homeless, street people who mostly are active alcoholics-addicts and severe mental cases or psychotic individuals.

What Johnny and his friends don't understand is that Depp is enabling street people to get sicker by handing them money – which will be used to get more alcohol and mood-altering drugs. So what seems like "charity" or "kindness" to naïve people, is really cruel in perpetuating their mental disorders including substance abuse.

By not helping active alcoholics-addicts or mentally ill people, these sufferers are forced to "hit a bottom" and seek help in programs – such as Alcoholics Anonymous, Narcotics Anonymous or other available programs. These street people hustling money, begging and panhandling, are quite aware of soup kitchens and places where they can get free food. They waste money given to them on drugs and alcohol. They're just in denial and don't want to get real help.

Chapter 5

"This is a rumor-filled society and if people want to sit around and talk about whom I've dated, then I'd say they have a lot of spare time and should consider other topics... or masturbation."

--Johnny Depp

Platoon (1986) was Depp's next film. Storyline:

Chris Taylor is a young, naive American who gives up college and volunteers for combat in Vietnam. Upon arrival, he quickly discovers that his presence is quite nonessential, and is considered insignificant to the other soldiers, as he has not fought for as long as the rest of them and felt the effects of combat.

Chris has two non-commissioned officers, the ill-tempered and indestructible Staff Sergeant Robert Barnes and the more pleasant and cooperative Sergeant Elias Grodin. A line is drawn between the two NCOs and a number of men in the platoon when an illegal killing occurs during a village raid.

As the war continues, Chris himself draws towards psychological meltdown. And as he struggles for survival, he soon realizes he is fighting two battles, the conflict with the enemy and the conflict between the men within his platoon (*IMDb*).

JOHNNY DEPP'S LIFE BEHIND THE SCENES:

Johnny Depp has been dating bisexual actress Amber Heard – what's her relationship track record?
Famous hookups reports:

Celebrity Biography

Amber Heard, in 2013, has been dating Marie De Villepin and Johnny Depp. She has been in five celebrity relationships averaging approximately 2.3 years each. She has never been married.

Given Name: Amber Laura Heard

Age: 27 (4/22/1986)

Occupation: Entertainment - Actress

Most Famous For: Role in *All the Boys Love Mandy*

Affairs, Dating & Break ups

Name (Age)	Occupation	Latest Status	Rel. Length	Started	Ended
Johnny Depp (50)	Actor	Dating	5.8 mos.	4/2013	Present
Marie De Villepin	Model	Dating	8.7 mos.	1/2013	Present
Johnny Depp (50)	Actor	Broke Up	7.5 mos.	6/2012	1/2013
Sean Faris (31)	Actor	Broken Engagement			
Taysa van Ree (37)	Artist	Broke Up	4 yrs.	2008	2012

Celebrity Biography

Johnny Depp is currently dating Amber Heard. He has been in 10 celebrity relationships averaging approximately 3.1 years each. His only marriage lasted 2.2 years.

Given Name: John Christopher Depp II

Nickname: Mr. Stench, Colonel

Age: 50 (6/9/1963)

Occupation: Entertainment - Actor

Most Famous For: Captain Jack Sparrow

Marriages, Divorces, Affairs, Dating & Break ups

Name (Age)	Occupation	Latest Status	Rel. Length	Started	Ended

Amber Heard (27)	Actress	Dating	5.8 mos.	4/2013	Present
Amber Heard (27)	Actress	Broke Up	7.5 mos.	6/2012	1/2013
Vanessa Paradis (40)	Singer	Broke Up	14.1 yrs.	5/1998	6/2012
Kate Moss (39)	Model	Broken Engagement	4.2 yrs.	2/1994	4/1998
Holly Robinson Peete (49)	Actress	Broke Up	n/a	1990	1990
Jennifer Grey (53)	Actress	Broken Engagement	n/a	1990	1990
Winona Ryder (41)	Actress	Broken Engagement	3.3 yrs.	8/1989	1993
Sherilyn Fenn (48)	Actress	Broken Engagement	3 yrs.	1985	1988
Lori Anne Allison (56)	Other	Divorced	5 yrs.	3/1981	3/1986
Jennifer Lopez (44)	Singer	Hookup			

Relationship Statistics
Johnny Depp

	Number	Avg. Length
Relationships:	10	3.1 yrs.
Hookups	1	n/a
Dating	9	3.3 yrs.
Engagements	5	0.9 yrs.
Marriages	1	2.2 yrs.
Breakups:		
Dating Breakups	3	
Broken Engagements	4	

Divorces   1

Johnny Depp's Children

Name	Age	Gender	Type	Other Parent
Lily-Rose Melody	14 yrs.	Female	Biological	Vanessa Paradis
John Christopher III	11 yrs.	Male	Biological	Vanessa Paradis

It should be noted that Depp has had sex-love affairs and relationships with other women who are not high-profile celebrities. The B-movie actress was discussed in the last chapter – Depp met her, instantly asked her to marry him and they hung-out for a year.

Johnny has become a bit of a joke in that his SOP (Standard Operating Procedure) is to instantly jump into an intense love affair with a young woman, get engaged to her, have knock-down screaming fights with her, break-up, make-up, break-up – in a yo-yo spiral – and finally dump her yet claim he's still friends with her:

Tally Chanel, a B-movie actress, also says she got a shot at being Depp's fiancée. They met when she was working as a hostess at the Hollywood premiere of *Die Hard 2* in July 1990.

"I helped him out of his limo," the 27-year-old recalls. "Our eyes locked, and he asked me to marry him." They dated for a year, spending quiet nights at Depp's Hollywood Hills home, ordering in food from a Chinese restaurant.

What's the Johnny Depp & Amber Heard relationship significance for diagnosing Depp with BPD? Johnny and Amber have broken-up, made-up and seem to be on Depp's relationship SOP which is a roller-coaster romantic relationship bouncing from idealizing to demonizing the female. He love-bombs her on a pedestal with gifts, then yanks her off his romantic stage and slams her into a demon's dumpster.

Unstable relationships is a symptom of Borderline Personality Disorder which Depp has revealed by this volatile hookups, erratic relationships and sometimes violent breakups.

His romances start with an explosion of "love-at-first-sight" mania, get side-tracked with screaming fights, conflicts, breakups, makeups and eventually a final breakup. Amber is a bisexual half Johnny's age – nearly 25 years younger. She's simultaneously having lesbian affairs. Depp is having a mid-life crisis. What are the odds against it working out with Amber?

Add her bisexual status and Depp's got a lot to overcome. She's obviously high maintenance – he's bought her some expensive jewelry. But how long will it last if Johnny's competing with Amber's girlfriend(s) and has to buy her with expensive gifts?

Apparently Depp and Amber are now in round two after an initial breakup. Johnny appears to be in even more trouble than usual because Amber is a bisexual involved with another woman.

Depp had better take a look at Woody Allen's *Manhattan* which shows what can happen when a guy gets involved with a bisexual or lesbian woman. Here's a report from *Showbizspy* on their recent fights and conflicts which indicates they're headed for a second breakup soon:

Johnny Depp and Amber Heard Are on the Rocks! (*Showbizspy*, Aug. 15, 2013):

JOHNNY Depp**'s romance with** Amber Heard **is reportedly <u>on the rocks</u>.**

According to reports, **Amber resents the 50-year-old actor's controlling nature** — and thinks he's a bit boring.

"**Johnny accepts the fact that Amber has other needs, so he's told her it's OK for her to be with women when she**

has the urge," a source told American tabloid the *National Enquirer*.

"But Johnny and Amber are in a bad place right now.

"When they first started dating, **he promised to help her become the next Angelina Jolie, but Johnny simply hasn't followed through.**

"Instead of finding exciting projects for Amber, or introducing her to Tinsel Town movers and shakers, **he seems to block her from moving forward in her career.**

"Apparently, she was offered the lead in the film version of the raunchy book *Fifty Shades of Grey*, but Johnny told her to say no to it because it would be too smutty."

Johnny has kept Amber cooped up in his Hollywood mansion, and she hates it, according to the source.

"It was cute for a while," noted the source. "Amber liked cooking for Johnny and watching old movies with him. **But now she's bored out of her mind.**"

The pair apparently came to blows when Johnny and Amber were on a press junket in Japan to promote The Lone Ranger.

"**The whole trip was a disaster, and Johnny and Amber got into a huge fight on the flight home**," said the source.

"**She pointed out how much she's given up to be with him and admitted that she misses her old life.**

"**Johnny's been super stressed about the movie and just snapped, telling Amber that she was lucky to be dating him.**

"He promised Amber he'll make things more exciting for her, and he's still dangling the carrot of introducing her to agents and other key players.

"Amber's sticking around, hoping Johnny will be true to his word. But she's not going to wait much longer."

Let's go back to 1998 and see Depp's patterns – do they apply to the present? He admits his breakup with Kate Moss was his fault as reported in *The London Times*:

The Hellraiser's Apprentice (M. Palmer, *The London Times*, Nov. 7, 1998):

Depp blames this commitment to his work for the break-up of his relationship with Kate Moss. Their on-off romance seems to be off for good, and Johnny believes it's his fault.

"I let my career get in the way and I didn't give her the attention I should have done," he says. "We had so much going for us, but I've just been very stupid. I was a horrific pain in the butt to live with. Trust me, I'm a total moron at times."

BPD ISSUES, SYMPTOMS & JOHNNY DEPP:

How could BPD contribute to Depp's unstable relationships? Johnny has admitted, "**I've just been very stupid. I was a horrific pain in the butt to live with. Trust me, I'm a total moron at times.**"

Let's dig deeper than Johnny's excuse that his "career" caused his unstable relationship. He's had at least 10 relationships, hookups, love affairs with celebrity women. And a number of sex-love affairs with other unknown women along the way.

What sets off the up-and-down, yo-yo, roller-coaster relationships? Johnny always flips and falls fast and hard for the woman, then come the breakups, makeups and the final ending.

Borderline Personality Disorder (BPD) sufferers seem to start off idealizing their romantic partner – so Amber heard was at first romanticized, put on a pedestal and venerated through rose-tinted glasses. Then she was demonized, blown off the pedestal and experienced the first breakup with Johnny.

Johnny and Amber were reported to have hooked-up in June of 2012 and then broke-up in January of 2013 – the first relationship lasted seven months. Currently they're into their second relationship which began in April of 2013 and has lasted for six months until October, 2013. Rumors have been reported that they'll soon be breaking-up again.

People with BPD seem to fear abandonment and rejection. Maybe that's why Johnny has such intense starts and endings to his relationships. Fearing abandonment, loneliness or boredom, Depp desperately clings to women he gets involved with – so he breaks-up in a fit of anger and then makes-up and re-starts the relationship with the same woman. He alternates between intense love for the woman and hatred driven by his explosive anger.

Chapter 6

"Novelty boy, franchise boy. Fucked and plucked with no escape from this nightmare…"

--Johnny Depp

***Cry-Baby* (1990) featured Depp** as Wade "Cry-Baby" Walker – storyline:

John Waters does a quirky spin on '50s nostalgia in *Cry-Baby*, his musical homage to Rebel Without a Cause and Romeo and Juliet. Set in Baltimore in 1954 at the birth of rock & roll, the film features Johnny Depp as Wade "Cry-Baby" Walker.

Depp is pure charisma as a juvenile delinquent with a permanent tear slithering down his cheek, a reminder of his state-executed parents.

In the depths of his despair appears goody-goody girl Allison (Amy Locane), who has a sexual crush on Cry-Baby. But Allison's Pat Boone-like boyfriend, Baldwin (Stephen E. Miller), the leader of the squares, is dead set against Cry-Baby and the rest of the juvenile delinquents and leads a revolt against them.

In the resultant riot, the juvenile delinquents are blamed for the chaos, and Cry-Baby finds himself dispatched to reform school (*rottentomatoes*).

JOHNNY DEPP'S LIFE BEHIND THE SCENES:

What clues are there to the secrets behind Depp's relationship breakups? How does Johnny go from "love at first sight" to a breakup? Here are some reports:

Johnny Depp Says It Was Love At First Sight With Vanessa Paradis (*RadarOnline*, Oct. 28, 2011):

With verbiage as vivid and deep as the seven seas, A-list pirate **Johnny Depp** describes the magic moment he met his future partner — and mother of his two kids — **Vanessa Paradis**.

Depp, 48, told the BBC about the instance back in 1998 when he laid his eyes on the beauty at France's Hotel Costes. (He was there filming Roman Polanski's *The Ninth Gate*.)

He said of Paradis: "**She was wearing a dress with an exposed back and I saw that back and that neck, and then she turned around and I saw those eyes, and — boom! — My life as a single man was done**."

"**You have this feeling,**" he said. "**I can't really explain what it was, but I had it when I met her. I saw her across a room and thought, 'What's happening to me?'**"

He said the two met through a mutual acquaintance, and the rest is history.

Depp — who dated **Winona Ryder**, **Jennifer Grey** and **Kate Moss** prior to finding his paradise with Paradis — said the relationship and her clean-living ways finally helped him beat a long-time battle with the bottle, though he slightly indulges every so often to reflect.

"A glass or two of wine before dinner is my favorite thing, watching the sunset and the kiddies playing nearby," he said. "It's perfection."

As RadarOnline.com previously reported, Paradis has also opened up about her and Johnny's relationship in the past, revealing that the two, are as "one."

"I like him very much in all terms and every sense of the way," Paradis said. "He makes me happy. We are many things – we are together and, in a way, one person."

But, despite their perfect relationship, don't expect these two to walk down the aisle anytime soon.

The critically acclaimed actor revealed to Extra why they haven't tied the knot.

 "I never found myself needing that piece of paper," Depp confessed. "Marriage is really from soul to soul, heart to heart. You don't need somebody to say, okay you're married... If Vanessa wanted to get hitched, why not... But the thing is, I'd be so scared of ruining her last name. She's got such a good last name."

Another Hollywood Breakup? Johnny Depp And Vanessa Paradis Are Falling Apart (Margeaux, *celebritydirtylaundry*, Jan. 6, 2012):

Are **Johnny Depp** and his longtime love **Vanessa Paradis** headed for a split? That is what *RadarOnline* is reporting about the couple, who have two children and have been together for more than ten years.

According to the website, **the relationship between the 48-year-old *Pirates of the Caribbean* actor and the French singer, 39, is falling apart, and the two have been constantly arguing in the last few months.**

"Johnny isn't handling anything well right now," said a source to RadarOnline. "People around him are worried about how Johnny is doing because he and Vanessa seem so fractured right now. Their relationship is heading toward the end."

Although the specific source of their fighting wasn't identified, the couple has always had a somewhat unconventional relationship, and *Star Magazine* via Celebitchy.com reported last month that **Johnny was currently going through a "mini mid-life crisis" and drinking a lot and that Vanessa wasn't putting up with it.**

"Johnny has started reaching out to lawyers, probably to quietly discuss how to get out of the relationship. They're not married but they've been together for years and have kids together so it isn't as easy as just breaking up," added the source.

With all of the celebrity breakups as of late, we wouldn't be surprised if Johnny and Vanessa become the next couple to call it quits.

Johnny Depp Denies Breakup Reports, But Where Is Vanessa Paradis? (A. Tereszcuk, *RadarOnline*, May 10, 2012):

Johnny Depp and his long-time girlfriend **Vanessa Paradis have been living separate lives for months**, but he has shot down reports the couple are about to split according to a British publication.

Walking the red carpet for the premiere of *Dark Shadows* in **London Johnny apparently denied that his relationship with Vanessa is on the rocks**.

"The rumors are not true," he reportedly told *The Sun* newspaper. "They are absolutely not true."

RadarOnline exclusively broke the story that **Johnny and Vanessa**, who have been partners for over 14 years and have two children together, **were having troubles.**

""**People around him are worried about how Johnny is doing because he and Vanessa seem so fractured right now. Their relationship is heading toward the end**," a source said about the Oscar winner and his model girlfriend.

**Despite Paradis not being at his side once again, and a growing number of reports emerging that the couple are in trouble, Depp denies there is any friction between the two though.

"No matter what I say about this, people believe the opposite. I can't say enough about it not being over," he told *The Sun*.

The couple, who have a home in France and a jet-setter life, have not been spotted together in months and Vanessa also recently walked the red carpet of her premiere, of Café de Flore in Paris alone.

Johnny Depp Breaks Silence on 'Unpleasant' Breakup with Vanessa Paradis (A. Tereszcuk, *RadarOnline*, June 18, 2013):

Johnny Depp's shocking split with Vanessa Paradis after 14 years and two children together was "unpleasant" he says, for the first time addressing the breakup that RadarOnline.com first reported.

The Lone Ranger star, 50, opened up about the painful breakup, saying "**The last couple years have been a bit bumpy**," after calling it quits with the French actress and the mother of his children.

"**At times, certainly unpleasant, but that's the nature of breakups**, I guess, especially when there are kiddies involved," Depp told *Rolling Stone* magazine and said **being an actor puts an added strain on the situation.**

"Relationships are very difficult. Especially in the racket that I'm in because you're constantly away or they're away and so it's hard. It wasn't easy on her. It wasn't easy on me. It wasn't easy on the kids. So, yeah. The trajectory of that relationship — you play it out until it goes, one thing leads to another."

As *RadarOnline* previously reported, **Johnny and Vanessa separated in early 2012 but they continued to deny the split for months**. He did not address his relationship with Amber Heard in the interview.

Johnny said he will always have a connection to the *Café de Flore* star because of their two children Lily Rose and Jack Depp.

"**So for whatever reason that ceases**, it doesn't stop the fact that you care for that person, and they're the mother of your kids, and you'll always know each other, and **you're always gonna be in each other's lives because of those kids**. You might as well make the best of it."

Despite his friends worrying about him during the beginning of the breakup, **Depp says he was more under control this time than with previous relationships ending.**

"**In terms of the breakup, I definitely wasn't going to rely on the drink to ease things or cushion the blow or cushion the situation**," he said.

"'Cause that could have been fatal. I felt it was my duty to be real clear throughout that. I had something pretty serious to focus on, really, which was making sure that my kids were gonna be cool."

Has Johnny moved on to bisexual Amber Heard?

The Love Diary! Johnny Depp and Amber Heard's Secretly Serious Relationship (J. Boon, *RadarOnline*, April 29, 2013):

Johnny Depp and Amber Heard may have just gone public with their relationship, but the two have been secretly serious since his breakup with Vanessa Paradis, *RadarOnline* is exclusively reporting.

The pair, who was spotted holding hands at a secret Rolling Stones show in Los Angeles this past weekend, **decided to keep their love under wraps** out of respect for Johnny's former partner.

And since then, **Johnny, 49, has been lavishing Amber, 27, with expensive gifts**.

JOHNNY DEPP DIAGNOSED: UNAUTHORIZED PSYCHOLOGICAL DIAGNOSIS OF HIS SECRET LIFE

"Johnny and Amber began dating pretty soon after he split with Vanessa," a source close to the *Pirates of the Caribbean* star tells *Radar*.

"At first, Amber was a little apprehensive, because she didn't want to be seen as the mistress. But Johnny won her over with his generosity and he was constantly giving her gifts."

According to the insider, Johnny was determined to win Amber over — and it worked.

"On a weekly basis, Johnny would send her fresh flowers wherever she was. He also bought her tons of custom-designed jewelry that would cost him up tens of thousands of dollars," the source said.

"He made Amber feel giddy by showing how much he felt for her and, in the end, she slowly fell in love with him."

A second source confirms that the couple has managed to keep their romance under wraps, spending time together outside of Los Angeles.

"They were spending a significant amount of time together in San Diego in the fall and also at his home in the Bahamas, so they wouldn't have to deal with paparazzi and could keep their relationship for under wraps as long as possible," the source told Radar.

As RadarOnline.com previously reported, **Johnny and Amber were spotted looking like loved-up teenagers back in November, 2012.**

"**They were flirty and engaged**," an eyewitness who saw the pair at Hollywood's AV Nightclub in early November told Us Weekly.

A second source told the tabloid that at a Gucci party in October 2012, **Amber was "telling people they were officially together."**

As RadarOnline.com exclusively reported in July**, the couple had briefly cooled off their romance, but can't seem to stay away from each other now.**

"**Johnny and Amber were definitely involved**," a source confirms to Radar about the couple, who first met on the set of *The Rum Diary* when **Johnny was still with Vanessa and Amber had just gone public in her lesbian relationship with photographer Tasya van Ree**.

"**They definitely had chemistry that carried over from the set. Amber quietly split from Tasya around the same time Johnny was secretly separated from Vanessa, so the timing was just right."**

What kind of a woman is Amber Heard?

I've had relationships with men and a wonderful woman: Johnny Depp's new girlfriend Amber Heard opens up about her colorful love life (L. Waterlow, *Mail Online*, Aug. 22, 2013):

1) **Actress said she accepts her love life will be scrutinized**

2) **She says in interview with The Edit starting a new romance can be 'difficult'**

3) **She revealed she's had successful relationships with both sexes**

4) **Smolders in accompanying photo shoot wearing designer outfits**

Actress Amber Heard has admitted she isn't fazed by the scrutiny her love life has been under she it was revealed she's dating the hottest single man in Hollywood, Johnny Depp.

The 27-year-old held hands with her *The Rum Diary* co-star at the premiere of his most recent film, *The Lone Ranger*, and has been pictured with the actor and his two children from his previous long-term relationship with Vanessa Paradis.

'If I didn't want to be scrutinized, I would have just stayed in Texas,' she told *net-a-porter's* digital magazine *The Edit*.

She added philosophically that 'going into relationships is just as difficult as coming out of them. I have never been in the situation where the two have overlapped. I can't imagine how difficult that would be.'

In the interview, the Paranoia star is candid about her past relationships - which she has had with both men and women - but said she did not want her sexuality to be labeled.

She explained: 'I have had relationships, successful relationships, with men, and I had a great relationship with a wonderful woman.

'I will never beg for an easy classification or label for that moment in my life, or assume to know what the future holds for me. I have always been and always will be just who I am and I will never fake anything for anyone.'

Amber revealed how her rise to fame came after she grew up 'in the middle of nowhere with nothing.'

She left home at the age of 16 'curious and hungry' with 'nothing to lose'. After enrolling in acting classes in Austin, Texas, she decided to pursue her acting career seriously.

'I remember my biggest hurdle was that I wasn't yet 18, and it caused some problems - getting a hotel room, for instance,' she said.

'I was on my own. I forged my parents' name to be on set, because I was a minor, but I was working as an adult, I forged a fake ID, too. They (her parents) did not react ideally, as you would expect, but they also couldn't stop me.'

She gained small parts in TV shows such as The *O.C* before breaking into films with roles in *Pineapple Express*, *Zombieland* and *The Rum Diary*.

She has four films currently in the works including *Three Days to Kill* alongside Kevin Costner and *Autobahn* with Zac Efron.

Speaking of her career progression, she said: 'I have been doing this as the only means to sustain myself for 11 years - my entire adult life. People have been calling me an up-and-comer for 10 years. I would rather be called that than a flash in the pan.'

'He lights up the room. He is a wonderful, special person': Amber Heard gushes about Johnny Depp (F. Betiku, *Mail Online*, June 24, 2012):

In the wake of his split from partner of 14-years Vanessa Paradis, it has been claimed Johnny Depp has been romancing Amber Heard.

And the blonde 26-year-old star has been more than a little complimentary about her famous co-star.

The bisexual actress who starred alongside Depp in movie *The Rum Diary* described him as a 'special person'.

The blonde beauty who was been spotted boarding Johnny's private jet back in April of this year, told of how she was keen to bag the role of his leading lady in the film and auditioned four times.

According to a story in *The Sun* Amber complimented the *Pirates of the Caribbean* star, and said that he has the ability to 'light up a room'.

'He looks even better close up', continued the 26-year-old, who then added: 'Johnny is a wonderful, special person.'

Amber's gushing praise for Johnny came shortly after the release of their 2011 film *The Rum Diaries*.

Heard revealed all about the audition process for the role of Chenault.

She said: 'I auditioned four times and was told that Johnny would make the final choice. We've stayed friends, because that's the kind of man he is.'

Last week it was reported that things between Depp and Heard appeared to be 'heating up'.

The Rum Diary co-stars are said to be so close that Heard, 26, has been a 'regular visitor' to the New Mexico set of *The Lone Ranger* where 49-year-old is currently filming.

And **Johnny**, who made an official announcement that he had split from partner of 14 years Vanessa Paradis on Tuesday, **is even said to have bought Heard a horse so they can ride together**, according to a report in *Globe* magazine.

A source claims Depp is smitten by the Hitchcock blonde,

and reportedly said: 'When I first saw Amber, it was like seeing an old-time movie star like Lauren Bacall.'

Whereas Heard described her role as his love interest in the film, *The Rum Diary*, as 'the best experience of my life.'

Speaking about Depp she told *Dazed* magazine: "He's such a wonderful presence; he is enigmatic and compelling and a true artist, seriously intelligent and incredibly sensitive."

'Everybody on set respects and likes him, which says a lot about an actor. It's a grueling job at times and the stress level that everybody feels in the industry is intense – but it doesn't affect Johnny.

'It seems like he has time to look everybody in the eye and I like that, it was wonderful to see.'

Getting adventurous! Johnny Depp clutches girlfriend Amber Heard's hand as they explore German museum with his children (*Mail Online*, July 20, 2013):

He's keeping his loved ones by his side on his *Lone Ranger* promotional tour.

On Saturday, Johnny Depp made a visit to the Pergamon Museum in Berlin, Germany, with his 27-year-old girlfriend Amber Heard clutching his hand and his children Lily-Rose and Jack by their side.

It looks as though Amber is becoming quite well acquainted with her 50-year-old actor boyfriend's family, as she has joined them for a large part of the European tour.

The luckiest girl in the world! Johnny Depp tenderly places a hand on Amber Heard's arm as they dine with The Rolling Stones (I. Kirby, *Mail Online*, May 23, 2013):

Johnny, 49, and his 27-year-old girlfriend may be keeping their relationship under wraps for the most part but their body language gave the game away.

The Dark Shadows star couldn't hide how smitten he is with Amber as he placed a hand affectionately on her arm when they walked out of the eatery.

And it was no surprise that Johnny couldn't keep his hands off his *Rum Diary* co-star as she looked positively stunning.

Johnny stood out in a stone colored hat and violet-lensed spectacles as he kept his lady love close while following her out of the restaurant.

The hot Hollywood couple are clearly big fans of the iconic rock band as they were spotted holding hands while watching them in concert at the end of last month.

But it seems they have also developed a strong friendship as Johnny chatted away to Keith when they stepped outside, while Ronnie happily signed autographs for fans.

According to sources, Johnny and Amber, who dated briefly last summer before reportedly rekindling their romance at the end of 2012, are getting serious.

Johnny already has two children with ex Vanessa Paradis but he is apparently already keen on settling down with his new squeeze.

'They've talked about children - that's how serious it is,' a source told *Grazia*. 'Johnny's like a teenager in love.

'Johnny and Amber have always had an incredible connection. They just couldn't stay away from one another. It has been a rocky road for Amber and Johnny as a couple,' the source added.

'They've been on and off, but this time he really wants to show her that he's in it for the long haul.'

Not such a Lone Ranger: Johnny Depp heads out for dinner with girlfriend Amber Heard after posing without her at latest premiere (K. Dadds, *Mail Online*, July 21, 2013):

He went solo on the red carpet at Sunday night's London premiere of *The Lone Ranger*.

But Johnny Depp wasn't such a *Lone Ranger* afterwards, as he was joined by girlfriend Amber Heard for a late night bite to eat.

The couple, who have so far done their best to keep their relationship away from the red carpet, headed for a celebratory meal at lavish eatery Cipriani.

Johnny led the way as he held his pretty partner's hand, still wearing the same suit he wore to the premiere.

Fans may have been disappointed they didn't get to see him debut his relationship on the carpet with Amber.

But she showed her support by staying out of the spotlight and rejoining him inside away from prying eyes.

Although she still looked red carpet ready despite not getting an official photo opportunity.

It seemed they were stealing some precious moments together after the craziness of the premiere where he faced the fans and press.

Depp is yet to invite Amber on to a red carpet to put their relationship under the limelight so he can put more emphasis on the film.

But Heard has joined Johnny by his side throughout his promotional tour so far.

Just earlier this week they were spotted heading to a museum in Berlin with his children following the German premiere of the film.

'She doesn't like the drama': Amber Heard 'cools down' her relationship with Johnny Depp (S. Bull, *Mail Online*, July 19, 2012):

She hit the headlines earlier this year when it was reported that she had been a pivotal reason behind Johnny Depp and Vanessa Paradis' split.

But now it has been claimed that **Amber Heard's relationship with the actor has 'cooled down', because she is fed up with the 'drama' surrounding their romance**.

A source told *RadarOnline* that while Johnny, 49, and 26-year-old Amber were 'definitely hooking up', Amber is now taking some time to think about what she wants from her relationship with her *Rum Diary* co-star.

The source said: 'Amber has never wanted that sort of attention. She really likes Johnny, but she doesn't like the drama.

'She isn't really sure what is going to happen with them, but just wants the attention to cool down before anything progresses.'

The source added that **Amber and Johnny's relationship began** shortly after they finished filming the movie adaptation of *The Rum Diary*, **before the actor announced his split from long-term partner Vanessa, with whom he has two children, and bisexual Amber revealed she had broken up with girlfriend Tasya van Ree.**

The source continued: 'Johnny and Amber were definitely involved. They definitely had chemistry carried over from the set.

'Amber quietly split from Tasya around the same time Johnny was secretly separated from Vanessa, so the timing was just right.

'They were hooking up for months -- way before he publicly announced that he and Vanessa had split up.

'They did a really good job of keeping their relationship on the down low for a while, especially since many people assumed that Amber was only into girls.'

But it was when Johnny and Vanessa's split was finally made public that the attention on Amber became too much to handle, with reports emerging that she was dating the father-of-two.

The source told *Radar*: **'She prides herself on being free-thinking and independent - not some home-wrecker trying to sleep her way to the top.**

'As soon as the media started publicizing the romance, she told Johnny that she needed some space.

'The crazy thing was that Johnny actually split from Vanessa at the end of last year, so she didn't break them up, but because they didn't announce their relationship was over until June, people were painting her as some kind of scarlet lady, which she is far from being.'

According to the report, **Amber has stepped away from Johnny to concentrate on spending time with her girlfriends, although the pair are still in touch.**

Johnny Depp, 50, takes girlfriend Amber Heard, 27, to mingle with punk rock legends at Ramones tribute (even though she was born a decade AFTER the band's heyday) (S. Dodge, *Mail Online*, August 20, 2013):

Amber Heard was just a twinkle in her father's eye during punk's 1970s heyday, but that didn't stop Johnny Depp from taking her along to mingle with some of his favorite old time rockers over the weekend.

The 50-year-old *Pirates of the Caribbean* star was spotted hand-in-hand with his girlfriend, who is just 27, at the Hollywood Forever Cemetery for the ninth annual tribute for Johnny Ramone, on Sunday.

Amber looked pleased to be in the company of some of the genre's greatest legends despite being born more than a decade after the Ramones enjoyed their glory days at CBGB's in New York in the mid-70s.

The *Fear And Loathing in Las Vegas* star kept a firm grip on his lady's hand for the event, as he arrived in an appropriately chewed up brown leather jacket.

Meanwhile, in the wake of his split from partner of 14-years Vanessa Paradis Johnny has been dating Amber, who he met on set of their 2011 movie *Rum Diaries*.

But the blonde actress took headline news in 2010 with a frank discussion of her bisexuality.

Amber recently told *ELLE* magazine that she made the public disclosure because: **'I didn't want to look like I was hiding anything. I'm not, and wasn't ever, ashamed**.'

Johnny Depp's BPD Relationship Behavior Patterns:

Well, it's clear Depp, age 50, in a shades of mid-life crisis itch, has made the leap from Vanessa Paradis to a younger, 27-year-old bisexual blonde, Amber Heard. I wonder if some interesting triangles will emerge with Johnny, Amber and one of her lesbian girlfriends?

Anyway, let's review the underlying dynamics of Depp's Borderline Personality Disorder (BPD) relationship behavior patterns. I'm not accepting Johnny's usual excuse that he breaks-up with women because he's away on a film shoot too much.

He's been using that alibi for many years. If we dig deeper and peel back the layers, here are the usual BPD relationship behavior patterns that surface which can be identified:

The Projection Game: This "projection" game involves the BPD person projecting his own bad qualities onto his romantic partner. For instance, Johnny might complain to Amber that she's being inconsiderate and selfish by hanging-out with her lesbian girlfriend.

For the sake of this example, let's assume that Johnny is spending time with another young lady he may have met on a film set or at a film promotion event. He'd then be projecting his own selfishness by accusing Amber of doing what he's guilty of.

It's All Your Fault: The "it's all your fault" game is played by BPDs who are using the defense mechanism of continual faultfinding, criticism and sarcasm aimed at their lover or significant other.

For example, Johnny put down Amber's interest in playing the lead in *Fifty Shades of Grey* – it was "too smutty" to play. Of course, this is a mild example. But let's pretend Depp continually finds fault with parts Amber is offered. Since nobody knows anything in Hollywood, he could be hurting her career and lowering her self-esteem.

Johnny's Needs Are Most Important: Because of Johnny's tendency to have a sense of entitlement as a movie superstar, he could easily stress with women lovers that his needs take priority. So when he was dragging Amber around with him to promote *The Lone Ranger*, he found himself getting into fights with her – according to reports.

Amber is supposed to be available at Johnny's convenience. As a superstar Hollywood player, Depp can narcissistically demand that the world revolves around him. Rumors have surfaced that she's gotten very bored hanging-out at Depp's house waiting for him to come home from film shoots or whatever.

No-Win Situations (Heads I Win, Tails You Lose): No-win situation games include a kind of "heads I win, tails you lose" thread. Johnny, for instance, always uses the excuse that his problem in relationships with the "loves of his life" is his career and demands to be on location.

So he claims he can't give them the attention they demand. Of course, when he spends time with Winona Ryder or Kate Moss or Vanessa Paradis, he ends up trashing hotel rooms, in knock-down screaming fights and bickering with his girlfriends.

One of the major reasons why a BPD like Depp gets into fights is that he could be playing no-win games, criticizing women no matter what they do. They can't win. It's Winona's fault if Depp can't get his way. If Kate Moss won't agree with him, he'll tear up the hotel room – trash it because it's all Kate's fault.

Vanessa Paradis sticks her nose into Depp's movie casting and is wrong to tell him not to attach to a script. If she ignores Johnny's acting decisions, it's her fault because she doesn't care. I'm just making up these examples based on reported rumors.

Closer – No, Keep Your Distance: It's normal for Depp's women to want to be close to him. However, with a BPD guy like Johnny, closeness scares him on some level. Underneath he feels worthless and wears a mask to seem confident.

Depp may feel overwhelmed when a woman gets too close because he has a weak self-identity. The BPD individual swings back and forth between a need for closeness out of fear of abandonment and a creeping fear of engulfment.

He can't see things from Winona's or Kate's or Vanessa's or Amber's viewpoint. Minutes ago Johnny was threatening to walk out on her and now he suddenly needs her and wants to cuddle or have sex.

Verbal Abuse Methods ("I'm doing you a favor – yelling at you to make you a better woman."**):**

1) **Domination:** The BPD person uses threats to get his way.

2) **Verbal Assaults:** A BPD sufferer will use yelling, screaming, reprimanding, humiliating, criticizing, name-calling, threatening, excessive blaming and using sarcasm in a cutting way. It also involves exaggerating other people's faults and making fun of them in front of others. Self-confidence and self-worth is eroded by this over time.

3) **Abusive Expectations:** A BPD guy will put down or discount his female partner's needs for attention and support. But he demands to be her first priority no matter what.

4) **Unpredictable Responses:** Crazy mood swings, sudden emotional outbursts are common with a BPD individual. A woman will get very anxious if living with a BPD man – she'll be frightened, unsettled, off-balance and hyper-vigilant (constantly on guard or jumpy over expected attacks which can lead to psychosomatic illness on her part).

5) **Gaslighting:** This "gaslighting" term came from the movie, *Gaslight*. It refers to denying a person's perceptions of events and conversations which are known to be true.

6) **Constant Chaos:** A BPD guy will often be a "drama-king" – starting arguments, creating drama and being in constant conflict with others.

The above discussed BPD relationship behavior pattern dynamics would be expected to more likely be the real factors leading Johnny Depp to have stormy relationships with women and sooner or later leave them or split.

Chapter 7

"I guess I still feel a little bit outside it all...ish. I mean, not so much outside as just not inside..."

--Johnny Depp

Edward Scissorhands (1990) was Depp's next film – storyline:

Tim Burton's *Edward Scissorhands* opens as an eccentric inventor (Vincent Price) lovingly assembles a synthetic youth named Edward (Johnny Depp).

Edward has all the essential ingredients for today's standard body, with the exception of a pair of hands. For what is initially thought to be a temporary period, he is fitted with long, scissor-like extremities that, while able to trim a mean hedge, are hardly conducive to day-to-day life. When the kindly inventor dies, however, Edward is left lonely and cursed with some very heavy metal for hands.

He is eventually taken in by Peg Boggs (Dianne Weist), an Avon lady who takes pity on him after seeing his bleak existence. Edward, in spite of his inherent ability to slay anyone he comes across, is a gentle soul whose only wish is to be loved. His impromptu family has, at best, a limited understanding of Edward, but he finds himself drawn to Peg's weary but sympathetic daughter, Kim (Winona Ryder), who is dating Jim (Anthony Michael Hall), the neighborhood bully.

Meanwhile, Edward finds himself a local celebrity after the town realizes that his talents include creative hedge trimming and an unrivaled ability to cut hair. His so-called friends are proven fair-weather when Edward is accused of a crime, after which his only supporters are Peg and Kim (*rottentomatoes*).

JOHNNY DEPP'S LIFE BEHIND THE SCENES:

In *Edward Scissorhands* Johnny worked with Winona Ryder with whom he had an off-screen relationship. **Why was his relationship with Winona so rocky after starting off so hot?**

It was via *Edward Scissorhands* that Ryder, at 17, met her first real boyfriend, co-star Johnny Depp. **It was a stormy relationship, lived in the public eye.**

Depp had "Winona Forever" tattooed on his arm (columnist Liz Smith recently reported that in deference to his current girlfriend, supermodel Kate Moss, Depp has had the tattoo altered to read "**Wino Forever**").

When they broke up three years later, Ryder reflected, **"I was just really young. I don't know what his excuse is, but that's mine"** (*tripod*).

Winona has reflected on her life including Johnny Depp (*celebitchy*):

I don't really think Winona's a bad person, she just comes across as screwed up in this interview – **screwed up and drowning in self-pity. She talks about her "first real break-up" and how it sucked really hard**. She doesn't say the name "Johnny Depp" but who else could she be talking about?

Ryder, who was engaged to Johnny Depp after co-starring with him in 1990's *Edward Scissorhands* (they split when she was 19), says one of her first big challenges was dealing heartache during the height of her fame.

"I had just done *Dracula* and *Edward Scissorhands*. **I had just had my first real break-up, the first heartbreak**," she tells Pippa Lee director Rebecca Miller, who interviewed her for the U.K. edition of *Elle*, out Wednesday.

"**And I think it was really ironic because, like, everybody else just thought I had everything in the world, you know, I had no reason to be depressed, everything was sort of at its peak, but inside I was completely lost**."

Oh, Johnny. I think he's one of those guys who is really difficult to get over. Neither Winona nor Kate Moss seemed to ever be the same after they had a taste of Johnny and his magical age-defying non-existent beer gut.

Apparently **Winona was very stressed-out and anxious at the time she was engaged to Depp and at 19 entered a psychiatric ward of a hospital** according to this report (*freelibrary*):

ACTRESS Winona Ryder has confessed that she has grim, first-hand experience of the role she plays in her current movie - a **tortured psychiatric patient**.

She once checked herself into a hospital's psychiatric ward because she felt so frightened. Winona, aged 27, says the crisis came nine years ago.

She declares: "**I really thought I was losing my mind. I was really, overworked and not sleeping.**"

Friends believe it was **Winona's stormy relationship with actor Johnny Depp that pushed her over the edge** and that it was Oscar-winning actress and singer Cher who saved her sanity.

When Winona admitted herself to the hospital's mental wing, aged 19, a doctor said she had **severe anxiety conditions.**

The actress, starring as a mental patient in the movie *Girl Interrupted*, was at the time engaged to Johnny.

A friend says: "**They had knock-down, screaming fights. Winona was the hottest young movie star in America. She couldn't handle that pressure and the demands of the relationship with Johnny.**"

This relationship pattern revealed between Depp and Winona was not in conflict simply because of Winona's youth or that Depp was away at movie locations – and so he couldn't pay attention to his romantic partner. Winona's excuse was that she was too young. Depp's usual break-up excuse is that he could not provide his wife or fiancée or girlfriend at the time with the "attention" she wanted.

Depp appeared to have provided too much attention to Ryder in the form of:

1) **Knock-down, screaming fights between Depp and Winona.**

2) **Pressure on Ryder to comply with Johnny's demands in their relationship.**

It appears that **Winona, then 19, was able to temporarily leave Depp, took a break at a psychiatric ward in a hospital and was found to be suffering from "a severe anxiety condition."**

As I've theorized, if Depp suffers from **Borderline Personality Disorder (BPD), he's likely to inappropriately explode in intense anger or difficulty controlling anger, frequent displays of temper, constant anger and recurrent physical fights**. While, Depp and Ryder have made an effort to keep their stormy relationship conflicts a secret, some reports have surfaced.

When one adds **Johnny's impulsivity such as substance abuse – abusing alcohol and mood-altering drugs – to the mix along with uncontrolled anger and

temper tantrums, it will lead to major relationship stress-outs or a break-up sooner or later.

Depp looks to his romantic partner to fill up the empty spiritual hole inside himself. He makes extraordinary demands on a romantic partner to provide him with never-ending love, compassion and attention. Johnny looks to his lovers and others to enhance his self-esteem, deliver approval, rally his confidence and intensify his sense of identity.

Johnny's **BPD psychological substructure** – below his surface charm and movie superstar looks – is built on **low self-esteem**. Like other BPDs, **Depp may be hyper-vigilant, looking for clues that his romantic partner doesn't really love him and will soon abandon him.**

BPD people desperately want a close relationship and the warm benefits of intimacy. Ironically, they often panic and do things to drive their lovers and close friends away. So when Depp sensed Ryder was not showing him enough attention or he perceived clues that she didn't love him enough, he'd go off like many BPDs do by:

1) **Exploding in a rage – get into "knock-down, screaming fights..."**

2) **Make unsupported accusations, express jealous suspicions.**

3) Maybe seek revenge – e.g., have an affair, cheat on his romantic mate.

4) Mutilate or cut himself – Johnny frequently did that in his youth at least.

5) Act-out with destructive behavior.

In the beginning, **Depp seems to over-idealize, romanticize and view his lover through rose-tinted glasses. He got a tattoo that said "WINONA FOREVER"** – and later changed it to "WINO FOREVER" after they split. So it may have been a shock to Winona when **suddenly Depp flipped, fought with her and devalued her.**

BPDs such as Depp get into what's called "splitting" or all-or-nothing, black-and-white thinking. When Johnny got mad at Winona, he'd devalue, degrade and diminish her at an unrealistic, unfair level. So she'd go from his fairy godmother to the wicked witch. Ryder went from a saint to a demon.

Johnny's "splitting" results in his labeling his lover either all "good" or completely "evil" – there is no balance, no in-between, no gray area, no nuances or shadings mixing positives and negatives. Depp perceives her as being at one extreme or the other – black or white, good or evil, angel or demon.

How does Depp explain away his extremes? Here's a quote from him:

"**We're all a mishmash of extremes. I know that I have demons. I don't know if I want to get rid of them altogether, but I would like to experience them in a different way. Maybe go face to face with them. I've never really had the time to go to therapy. Well, here and there. But not enough to help me**."

BPD ISSUES, SYMPTOMS & JOHNNY DEPP:

In this chapter I've reviewed Johnny Depp's background with a focus on his relationship with Winona Ryder. They were reported to have had a roller-coaster relationship which would yo-yo from one extreme to another from Depp's viewpoint.

He seems to idealize or romanticize women in his romances, then Ping-Pong to the opposite extreme by demonizing his former "angel" who is evaluated as a monster or evil spirit when he's in a rage. This black or white, all-or-nothing thinking is called "splitting."

At first Johnny found Winona "the love of my life" and registered it with a tattoo: "Winona Forever" on his arm. Then the "loving" relationship broke-up at times, they then made-up.

There were "knock-down screaming fights" reported, Winona flipped-out and entered a psychiatric ward of a hospital to recover from the "pressure of a relationship with Depp."

The dynamics of this indicate some Borderline Personality Disorder symptoms including:

1) A pattern of unstable, intense, and stormy relationships where the BPD person may shift between idealizing and devaluing his partner.

2) Persistent and strong efforts to avoid real or imagined abandonment by others.

3) Lack of a cohesive identity or a poor or unstable self-image or sense of self. For example, is Johnny Depp a screaming, demanding maniac from *A Nightmare on Elm Street* or a sweet, thoughtful movie-star dreamboat every girl dreams of?

Chapter 8

"I despise those prick actors who say, "I was in character," and "I became the character," and all that stuff. It's hideous. It's just masturbation at the highest level."

--Johnny Depp

In *Arizona Dream* (1992) Depp played Axel – storyline:

An Inuit hunter races his sled home with a fresh-caught halibut. This fish pervades the entire film, in real and imaginary form. Meanwhile, Axel tags fish in New York as a naturalist's gofer.

He's happy there, but a messenger arrives to bring him to Arizona for his uncle's wedding. It's a ruse to get Axel into the family business.

In Arizona, Axel meets two odd women: vivacious, needy, and plagued by neuroses and familial discord. He gets romantically involved with one, while the other, rich but depressed, plays accordion tunes to a gaggle of pet turtles (*IMDb*).

JOHNNY DEPP'S LIFE BEHIND THE SCENES:

Why did Johnny Depp break-up with Winona Ryder?
Here are some possible answers from *Fanpop*:

She was the one who broke up with him sadly because at the time many people were judging their relationship and she couldn't handle it. She was 18 and he was 27. Winona said she was very immature at the time.

After she broke up with Johnny she started to have health problems like insomnia and depression. She said that it was the darkest time of her life because she really loved him.

Another fan agreed: He did not break up with her, she broke up with him. Her parents thought she was too young to get married (they were engaged when she was 18, she was 17 when they started dating and he was 26). They were still friends afterward. Johnny mentioned in an interview (can't remember which) that they had dinner with the family afterward, so no hard feelings.

Here's more on the **Depp-Ryder love affair** and breakup – their relationship was from 1989 to 1993:

Johnny Depp and Winona Ryder – a couple known by most people as one of the most publicized couples of the 90's. When their eyes first met at the *Great Balls of Fire!* Premiere in New York, **they knew it was love at first sight**.

Johnny couldn't help but notice the dark brown velvet eyes that flickered adorably, or the gorgeous bopped black hair that was swept away from her forehead to offset the pale porcelain skin that he thought echoed visages of a young Elizabeth Taylor with an equally enviable body.

"It was a classic glance," raved Johnny, "like that zoom lens in West Side Story when everything else gets foggy."

"It wasn't," Winona said, "a long moment, but it was suspended."

A couple of months later, Josh Richman, a mutual friend, dragged Winona into Johnny's hotel room. She watched entranced by the charm that had caused much of American girlhood to fall for him, and was even more enamored of the intelligence that his smart, sensitive *21 Jump Street* role had seemed to imbue him with.

"I thought maybe he would be a jerk. I didn't know," said Winona, "but he was really, really shy."

Almost before they even knew what was happening, they arranged to meet each other again.

"When I first met Winona and we fell in love, it was absolutely like nothing before. We hung out the whole day and night, and we've been hanging out ever since. I love her more than anything in the world."

Winona made it clear, however, that she wouldn't be diving in too quick, saying she had "read horror stories about what happens when you do."

But she underestimated the strength of her own emotions. Five months after they met, Johnny gave Winona an engagement ring, and a month later, the couple were living together, even if it was in a succession of hotels and rented apartments.

"I have beds, tables, chairs, a TV set," said Johnny, "And they're mine, and **I have Winona. That's all I need.**"

Johnny Depp and Winona Ryder - it was a relationship made in tabloid heaven. Winona was young, sweet, charming, a child. **Johnny, on the other hand, was a hell-raising party monster.** Well, according to the press he was.

All the same, the gossip columnists couldn't go wrong. Even Timothy Leary would later describe Johnny as both "wild and charitable" and although Winona focused on the charitable side, the Hollywood insiders found Johnny's apparent past and presumably future indiscretions of considerably greater interest.

There was the fact that he had been married and divorced, engaged twice more, and would even spread his engagement to Winona into a trilogy of breakups and reconciliations, affirmed by the number of times Winona's engagement ring came off and went back on again.

Indeed, it was Johnny's romantic past and presumably future that was the number one concern. Manhattan was even stricken by a brief craze after the announcement of his betrothal to Winona, in which car bumper stickers appeared demanding, HONK IF YOU'VE NEVER BEEN ENGAGED TO JOHNNY DEPP. Not that it bothered him - or did it?

"**I'll just answer that I was engaged to Sherilyn, I was engaged to Winona, and I was engaged to Jennifer Grey.** But a lot was written about that shit, and it was taken to another level and it was turned into some kind of horrible joke."

"I've never been one of those guys who goes out and screws everything that's in front of him. When you're growing up, you go through a series of misjudgments. Not bad choices, but wrong choices. **People make mistakes. We all fuck up. I was really young for the longest time. My relationships weren't as heavy as people think they were**," said Johnny.

"**I don't know what it is, possibly I am trying to rectify my family's situation, or I was just madly in love.** There's been nothing throughout my 27 years that has been comparable to the feeling I have with Winona. There's something inside me that knows really well, that no one else has ever known, or will ever know. **Life is trial and error, but** when you find the one who's really it, there's no mistaking it," Depp disclosed.

That, Johnny explained, was why he was going to get **Winona's name tattooed on his arm** for $75. When Winona heard that news, her initial response was excitement and pride.

"I was thrilled when he got the tattoo," Winona sighed. **"Wouldn't any woman be?"** It was only later that her interest turned to apprehension. As she waited at Sunset Strip Tattoo joint – "Tattooers of the Stars Since 1971" - while Johnny's 'Winona Forever' double-banner tattoo was engraved into his right bicep to match the tribute to his mother on his left, those feelings grew stronger.

At the same time, "I was sort of in shock," Winona freely admits. Besides, "I'd never seen anyone get a tattoo before so I was pretty squeamish, I guess." Even as she repeatedly removed the bandage to stare at the engraving that Mike Messina had so perfectly etched, "I kept thinking it was going to wash off or something. I couldn't believe it was real. I mean it's a big thing because it's so permanent."

Johnny himself had no doubts. "I love Winona. I'm going to love her forever. Putting her on my arm solidified it. The truth is very powerful, believe me this is not something I took lightly."

But according to Messina, **"It was no big deal for him, mainly because he's had tattoos done before."** Even if the process did hurt. But that was all part of the allure. **"Yeah!" Johnny yelped. "I liked the pain. It was electric, kind of nice."**

They broke up in 1993 because Winona's father said "at 19, Winona is too young to marry."

"To have the tattoo removed, or erase it, is to try and say it never happened. If I alter it in some way, make it funny - put her next boyfriend's name on top of it, say - it would still be honest," said Johnny.

"She's a sweet kid, man. It's always a little weird, you're like 'We used to do this and that, we used to have fun and hang out together.' But at least we were able to feel that for each other. I feel real lucky that we got that," revealed Johnny.

"I think Johnny Depp's great and I have nothing but kind things to say about him," Winona said.

"When we broke up, it was horrible. I mean it was so hard to get over and we had everything out for the wedding. So that was difficult to tell people that the wedding was off, but what can I do now. Just move on. But I still think about all those good times we had," recalled Winona.

"**When I hear our song**, I get all these memories from when we went out together. Or any song from 1989 to 1993, it **makes me think of her and that can suck but half of it makes me really happy**," Johnny remarked.

"**Our song was playing when I first laid my eyes on her and that was *Take My Breath Away* by Berlin** and every time it comes on anywhere I think of her eyes," **Johnny exposed sentimentally.**

"**Johnny has always protested that he still loves Winona**, while she has always held a special place for him in her heart because he was her first real love. So they might get back together but I don't know," said a friend of Johnny and Winona.

"Well, we went out to dinner, just as friends, a couple days ago and we talked about what's going on in life. It's really great that we can just sit and enjoy each other's company. Right now it's hard for us, I just broke up with Matt and he just broke up with Kate. So we can both relate," Winona explained.

"We had a nice chat and just hung out after nothing big. **I hope maybe in the future something could happen**

again. Maybe, we'll have to see. But I would like that. I'm going to Paris to shoot *The 9th Gate* **so maybe after I'll call her again and we can go out sometime**," Johnny said in May 1998.

"He was so desperately in love with Winona, that when they broke up, he wouldn't admit it was over for the longest time," Tim Burton commented.

"The split in 1993 was during the filming of *Ed Wood* and there were days he would come crying, I felt so bad. I asked him why it happened but all he said was, 'It wasn't her fault, it was mine.' And when he met Kate in January of '94, it wasn't the same as Winona. I felt weird to be around him like he wasn't acting like Johnny anymore. It's almost like Winona took Johnny's soul, Johnny's love," a friend disclosed.

"Winona kept him calm. Kept him cool. Not like out of control. **I feel Johnny got arrested because Kate couldn't stop him from being wild and free. Winona could**," an insider divulged.

"I believe he never really loved Kate. I mean, I love Johnny like a son, but he never was the same. I believe, also know, he belongs with Winona. So many people try to tell him (and Winona) they should just talk. They never say anything. I know Christina Ricci also told Johnny (during filming of *Fear and Loathing in Las Vegas*) to call Winona.

Christina is very, very, very close to Winona. They're like sisters," said a friend.

"I know them both so well. Even if he's with Vanessa now and has two kids, I think he'll return to Winona someday. Not today, maybe not tomorrow, but soon. Don't tell him I said that!" Christina Ricci said.

When Winona got arrested, Johnny Depp (her former boyfriend) got her a dozen pink roses to make her feel better and wrote a note himself stating, "Don't worry hon, it happens to the best of us. Good luck in court! I got faith in you!"

"When I met Johnny, I was pure virgin. He changed that. He was my first everything. My first real kiss. My first real boyfriend. My first fiancé. The first guy I had sex with. So he'll always be in my heart. Forever. Kind of funny that word," Winona disclosed.

People reported (The Insider, M. Fink, June 21, 1993):

GROWING UP (TOGETHER) IS HARD TO DO

Stick a fork into the relationship of Winona Ryder and Johnny Depp, and you will discover...it's done. Ryder's representative confirms, after months of press speculation, that Ryder and Depp are a couple no more. The two young movie stars have called off their engagement and gone their separate ways.

The reason? "**They're young, and they grew apart**," says Ryder's spokeswoman.

We hear from other sources that Ryder is now seeing David Pirner, lead singer of the rock group Soul Asylum. Pirner apparently left his girlfriend of 11 years to be with Ryder. As to Depp's love life, not to mention his "Winona Forever" tattoo, his rep says she won't comment on Depp's personal life.

Now that Winona has turned 40, she's recently revealed that she's finally ready to "bag a husband." I guess Johnny Depp and those other guys in her serial dating weren't really serious candidates.

Winona Ryder: "I Gotta Bag Me a Husband!" (US Weekly, Dec. 2, 2010):

She's dated everyone from **Johnny Depp** to **Matt Damon** and, most recently, Rilo Kiley guitarist **Blake Sennett**.

As she approaches her 40th birthday next year, **Winona Ryder** says she is finally ready to settle down. In a USA Today interview, the iconic 90s actress - who returns to the big screen this month with a supporting role in the thriller *Black Swan* - says during her non-working time she lives in San Francisco, where she hangs with other artists.

"There's a lot of cute writers up there," she says. "I gotta bag me a husband!"

Though she has been MIA for the last decade since she was arrested for shoplifting $4,760 worth of goods at Saks Fifth Avenue in Beverly Hills, she has a few buzzed-about upcoming projects -- including *The Dilemma* (out Jan. 14), costarring Vince Vaughn.

What's really behind these stormy relationships?

Winona couldn't marry Depp because she was too young at 19 and now she's over 40 and she still can't find a guy to marry. Of course there are other reasons why Depp and Ryder can't seem to marry and settle down with kids. But **the usual socially-acceptable reasons are offered by Depp, Ryder and Hollywood P.R. people.**

BPD ISSUES, SYMPTOMS & JOHNNY DEPP:

If we clear away or scrape off all the sentimental gossip about Johnny Depp's behavior such as in relationships, we can begin to understand a side of him from a unique psychological viewpoint. Let's take a **cognitive approach to Depp's Borderline Personality Disorder (BPD):**

In graduate school in New York I got some training in CBT (cognitive behavior therapy) from Dr. Albert Ellis who was the first psychologist to create, research and apply cognitive psychotherapy. Dr. Ellis called his system RET – Rational-Emotive Therapy. He first introduced it at RT – Rational Therapy in 1955.

His early training was in psychoanalysis but he found it was not effective. Dr. Ellis told me that psychoanalysis – he'd trained in Jungian psychoanalysis – might help clients feel better but they didn't get any better.

Ellis had his own institute in Manhattan where he practiced and held workshops using his cognitive psychotherapy (RET). Let's pretend we are going to help Johnny Depp using a cognitive approach to treating his BPD.

What are common maladaptive "schemas" (BPD attitude & belief systems) characteristic of those with BPD? Beck (1990) came up with a list of schemas:

1) **Abandonment/Loss Schema:** "I'll be alone; no one will be there for me..."

2) **Unlovability Schema:** "No one would love me if they really got to know me..."

3) **Dependence Schema:** "I can't cope on my own; I need someone to rely on..."

4) **Subjugation/Lack of Individuation Schema:** "If I don't do what others want, they'll abandon me or attack me..."

5) **Mistrust Schema:** "People will hurt me, attack me, or take advantage of me. I must protect myself."

6) **Inadequate Self/Discipline Schema**: "I can't control myself..."

7) **Fear of Losing Emotional Control Schema:** "I must control my emotions or something terrible will happen..."

8) **Guilt/Punishment Schema:** "I'm a bad person. I deserve to be punished..."

9) **Emotional Deprivation Schema:** "No one is ever there to meet my needs or to care for me..."

In Beck's theory there are three basic assumptions underlying the perceptions and interpretations of a person with BPD such as Johnny Depp:

1) **"The world is dangerous and malevolent."** This cognitive perception of BPD individuals implies that taking risks is dangerous. Some risks include letting down your guard, revealing a personal weakness, or being "out of

control." These feelings lead to chronic feelings of tension, tiredness, suspicion and guardedness.

2) **"I am powerless and vulnerable."** BPD people with this perception or thinking believe they can't deal with the dangerous world they view. The result is that they then become dependent on someone they see as capable of taking care of them. However, BPDs feel this dependence is unacceptable because they believe they are inherently unlovable and unacceptable.

3) **"I am inherently unacceptable."** BPDs fear that when people get to know them they can't trust them. Another cognitive distortion is that "I am a fake; someday, they will find me out." This latter view overshadows high-achieving activities.

I'll address cognitive psychotherapy treatment goals and strategies in the next chapter.

Chapter 9

"I'm not a Blockbuster boy, I never wanted to be. I just don't want to look back in 30 or 40 or 50 years and have my grandkids say, 'You did a lot of stupid shit, Granddad. What an idiot you were, smiling for the cameras and playing the game...'"

--Johnny Depp

Ed Wood (1994) starred Depp as Wood – storyline:

Hollywood visionary Tim Burton pays homage to another Hollywood visionary, albeit a less successful one, in this unusual fictionalized biography.

The film follows Wood (Johnny Depp) in his quest for film greatness as he writes and directs turkey after turkey, cross-dresses, and surrounds himself with a motley crew of Hollywood misfits, outcasts, has-beens, and never-weres.

The real story, however, is his friendship with aging, morphine-addicted Bela Lugosi (Martin Landau), whom he tries to help stage a comeback. Landau's unforgettable Oscar-winning performance must be seen to be believed, as must Rick Baker's Oscar-winning makeup.

While it would have been easy to make a film simply ridiculing the bumbling director, Burton instead focuses on his driving passion for filmmaking and his unwavering persistence in the face of ridicule and failure.

Possibly the most surprising aspect of the film is the genuine sentiment with which Burton treats the relationship between Wood and Lugosi; his devotion to Lugosi is touching, as is Lugosi's final soliloquy -- an inane bit of dialogue from the hilariously bad Bride of the Monster that grows into a poignant metaphor for the actor's life and ultimate triumph of his spirit.

Even the look of the film is right; it manages to preserve the air of one of Wood's own films while retaining a sense of artistry in much of the composition on screen (note the scene at the drug rehab where Lugosi endures a horrifying night of detox).

In all, Ed Wood is a unique film -- at times side-splittingly funny; at others, tragic or even frightening -- and a heartfelt tribute to the love of movies, good and bad alike (*rottentomatoes*).

JOHNNY DEPP'S LIFE BEHIND THE SCENES:

Depp shot to the top of the Hollywood superstar A-list with the success of *Pirates of the Caribbean: The Curse of the Black Pearl*.

In 2004 he received Oscar and Golden Globe nominations. The Screen Actors Guild recognized him as Best Actor. He continued to get praise for other films such as *Secret Window*, *Finding Neverland* (second Best Actor Oscar nomination), and *The Libertine*.

He also scored with some comic roles in *Charlie and the Chocolate Factory* and *Corpse Bride*. In 2006, the sequel to Pirates of the Caribbean: Dead Man's Chest earned more than $1 billion worldwide – the third film in movie history to make over $1 billion.

What's the significance of this success? Okay, Depp has shown he has range, is versatile and can score commercially at the box-office. But is there a psychological downside to all these accomplishments and productivity?

I'd submit a theory that Johnny's BPD has been aggravated by the success – his ego has been inflated and he has even more of a sense of entitlement as a celebrity. This will impact his volatile relationships, unstable emotions, erratic behavior and shaky self-identity.

What happened to break-up Depp and Paradis?

How resentment and 'blazing fights' tore Johnny Depp and Vanessa Paradis's relationship apart... TWO years ago (A. Proud, *Mail Online*, July 5, 2012):

Johnny Depp's relationship with Vanessa Paradis crumbled because she grew to resent the success SHE inspired the actor to achieve.

And the couple are said to have called it quits in 2010, after Paradis decided that she could not go on, but decided not to announce it.

According to a source, the former model and singer, 39, urged the actor to take mainstream roles, such as 2003's *Pirates of the Caribbean: The Curse of the Black Pearl*.

Until then, despite being a huge name, Depp had been inclined to more obscure and cult-like roles. But his step into the world of blockbusters paid off handsomely.

The film hauled in more than $300 million and turned Depp into one of the world's most profitable leading men. But Vanessa grew unhappy, it is claimed in *Us Weekly* despite the fact she was reaping the rewards of his $20-million-a-film career.

It didn't help that Vanessa, who had a huge hit in Europe with *Joe Le Taxi*, was watching her singer career lie dormant.

A source told the magazine: **'Vanessa started to feel like she'd sacrificed her career for his.'**

Depp, who earned more than $75 million in 2010, reacted to the enmity by becoming resentful himself.

The source said: **'Nothing Johnny did was ever good enough for Vanessa. When he was working, she wasn't happy.**

'And when he wasn't working, he was called a slob for not doing enough for the kids and her family.'

The former couple are parents to Lily-Rose, 13, and Jack, 10.

'They'd have blazing fights,' says the friend. **'Vanessa would take her frustrations out on him.'** And he **'started to drink heavily.'**

Though they continued to drift apart, Depp and Paradis always put their children's needs first. **"It broke Johnny's heart that the family he loves so much was becoming fractured**," said the friend.

So in 2010, it is claimed, the singer decided to pull the plug, but they agreed to keep the split under wraps.

'Johnny was heartbroken,' the friend told *Us*. 'But they agreed the kids' lives shouldn't be affected. That's why they didn't announce it.'

Since then, Depp, 49, has found love again with his Rum Diary costar, Amber Heard, 26. 'They are 100 percent dating,' a source revealed. 'He treats her really well.'

The *Mirror* reported:

Johnny Depp 50th birthday: He's still looking for his true love (Mirror, June 9, 2013):

JOHNNY DEPP DIAGNOSED: UNAUTHORIZED PSYCHOLOGICAL DIAGNOSIS OF HIS SECRET LIFE

The actor, 50 today, enjoys mega riches and is hailed as the world's sexiest man but still has not achieved the - stable home life he longed for.

He has fabulous wealth and fame but as a little boy Johnny Depp wanted nothing more than to stop his parents fighting.

Today, his 50th birthday, he enjoys mega riches and is hailed as the world's sexiest man. **But still he has not achieved the stable home life he longed for.**

Pals told *The Sunday People* part of it is that Johnny always acts like a teenager with women, rather than a middle-aged dad of two.

And his psyche must owe a lot to a childhood in which his volatile parents uprooted him 30 times in 15 years.

The Pirates of the Caribbean superstar has loved and lost some of the world's most beautiful women, including British supermodel Kate Moss.

He was shattered when his 14-year relationship with sexy French singer Vanessa Paradis, 40, ended last June.

Yet Johnny soon fell into the arms of bombshell actress Amber Heard, 27. **He is already calling the bisexual beauty his soul mate and talking of marriage.**

But friends are saying it is a relationship that won't last. Old schoolmate Yves Bouhadana said: **"Johnny falls in love at first sight. When he falls for a girl he really falls for her."**

Yves, who was in a teenage band with Johnny and is still friends with him, added**: "He wears his heart on his sleeve. He's is a genuinely nice guy."**

"He doesn't act around his friends. What you see is what you get."

The actor is worth more than £225million and his agents can command £15million for a film role.

But his childhood was far from idyllic. **He was the youngest of four and witnessed constant rows between his dad John, an engineer, and waitress mum Betty Sue.** When the family moved from Kentucky to Florida all of them lived at first in a single motel room.

They moved on average every six months and the future star constantly changed schools. **The marriage unraveled slowly and painfully and by the time Depp was 13 he was**

smoking dope, drinking heavily and deliberately cutting his arms to hurt himself.

Talking later about his marks, he said: "My body is a journal, in a way. Every important event is marked there." His parents' marriage ended when he was 15.

Johnny's first and most lasting love was music. His mother bought him a guitar for his 13th birthday and he spent hours learning to play.

He made friends with a group of like-minded boys, including Yves, and they formed heavy metal bands.

They discovered groupies and Johnny lost his virginity in the back of a van after a concert at a school.

He described it as "forgettable" and it even put him off casual sex.

While band mates picked up all the girls, Johnny concentrated on his music. **Then he fell head over heels in love with make-up artist Lori Allison after a 1980 gig in Florida. He was 17 and she was 22. He proposed marriage almost immediately but they did not tie the knot until Christmas Eve 1983, in Miami. Johnny was 20.**

Yves, now a 49-year-old sales executive living in Ohio, recalled: "She was absolutely beautiful. Still is."

"Lori was his first serious relationship and he couldn't wait to marry her. She is a very private person and doesn't like to talk about the marriage. They are still friends.

"That's the great thing with Johnny. He hasn't changed since we were at school. We all still get together."

Johnny wanted to make it as a rock guitarist and Lori supported him as a make-up artist when they moved to Hollywood with his band The Kids.

But musical success and happiness eluded him. The Kids opened for the Ramones, Iggy Pop, The Pretenders and Talking Heads but the band failed to get a record deal and his marriage fell apart within two years. Biographer Cristopher Heard said: **"It ended just simply because of the stress of failure."**

The couple were evicted from several apartments and were divorced in 1985. But Lori had introduced him to actor Nicolas Cage and the two became mates. Cage persuaded him to get an agent.

Success came quickly with a memorable role in 1984's *A Nightmare on Elm Street*, which became an unexpected hit.

Soon Johnny was engaged to *Twin Peaks* beauty Sherilyn Fenn **but they split after two years**, blaming work commitments.

Never on his own for long, Johnny dated Dirty Dancing's Jennifer Grey and – following a familiar pattern – proposed.

But that relationship also lasted only two years and **Johnny quickly hooked up with fiancée Number 4, Winona Ryder**, his co-star in 1990's *Edward Scissorhands*.

Work got in the way again and after splitting from Winona he **moved on to Kate Moss**. She was 23, a supermodel, and he was a 33-year-old film star. **The relationship was volatile. Johnny once caused £7,000 damage to his New York hotel room after a row with Kate.**

And he was devastated when they broke up in 1998 after four years together.

Johnny said: **"I cried for a week after we split. I didn't give her the attention I should have done. I was a horrific pain in the butt to live with. I'm a total moron at times. I let my work get in the way."**

"I will never let it happen again. I think you could say I have truly discovered the meaning of loneliness."

But within weeks he was spotted out with Vanessa. And three months later she was pregnant. Their daughter Lily-Rose Melody Depp was born in 1999 and the couple's son John Christopher "Jack" Depp III came along in 2002.

With homes in France and the Bahamas, they looked settled. But in the later years he started to spend more time working in Hollywood and the split from Vanessa was announced 12 months ago.

True to form he quickly sought solace with Amber. Pals said **Johnny was once again acting like a teenager in love. The pair had two bust-ups in the early stages but have since calmed down.**

One friend said**: "Johnny always goes overboard with women. He has whisked Amber off to his island in the Bahamas and has already introduced her to his children. When they're apart he sends her poetry. It is very sweet but everyone worries about him getting hurt again."**

"Despite his fame and incredible good looks, Johnny is very vulnerable."

Another report from Vanessa's viewpoint on the breakup with Depp:

Vanessa Paradis Talks Johnny Depp Split: You Can Be "Unhappy" and "In Love" (A. Toomey, *Eonline*, Aug. 17, 2012):

Break-ups are hard to handle, and no one knows that better than **Vanessa Paradis.**

The stunning French actress and longtime love of **Johnny Depp** officially announced their separation in June, after two kids (**Lily-Rose**, 13, and **Jack**, 10) and 14-years together.

Paradis previously told French *Elle* that she didn't "want to talk about him [Johnny Depp]," but she has since shed light on the demise of her relationship with the 49-year-old actor in the September issue of *Harper's Bazaar*.

Keep in mind, the magazine sat down with Vanessa just two days before the split was officially announced to the media.

"Love is the strongest and most fragile thing we have in life," the 39-year-old beauty says. **"Nothing is ever for sure, but when something in love doesn't work from the beginning, it's never going to work. Don't push it."**

She continues, explaining that it is indeed possible to be in love and unhappy:

"When you meet the love of your life, it's just obvious and natural and easier," she says before adding, "You keep learning all the time. **Sometimes you could be in an unhappy relationship; you are very much in love with someone, but it's making you unhappy and you think things can change and you can work it out."**

Although Johnny and Vanessa seemingly tried to make it work (rumors were brewing for months before they officially called it quits), both are moving on and leading single lives.

Johnny has since been romantically linked to his *Rum Diary* costar **Amber Heard** and has even been spotted jamming with Aerosmith in his spare time.

As for Vanessa? Well, she seems more than ready to find a new man.

"My type is obviously creative," she reveals. "Creative, with burning eyes and a pretty mouth."

Amber Heard tells her side:

Amber Heard Says Johnny Depp Relationship Is "Not Part of My Professional Life" (S. Webber, US Weekly, July 31, 2013):

In a very rare moment, Amber Heard opened up to *Flare* magazine about dating Johnny Depp in its September 2013 issue.

Amber Heard speaks! The *Playboy Club* actress --who's kept mum on her relationship with **Johnny Depp** thus far -- has now opened up about her love life in *Flare* magazine's September 2013 issue.

"It's not part of my professional life. I want to be an artist. I don't want to be a celebrity," she said of wanting to keep the relationship private.

"You can find pictures of me on the Internet pumping gas, picking up dry cleaning, walking my dog, but nowhere are you going to find pictures of me hanging around at some nightclub…Can you ever imagine yourself in a situation like Brad Pitt and Angelina Jolie or Kim Kardashian and Kanye West, where the world feels like they have a stake in your private life? I would never want it."

Adding, "I guess I could not hold hands with who I want to, but what kind of life would that be? I don't want to change just because people are watching."

And tight-lipped is exactly how the 27-year-old and Depp, 50, have kept their relationship -- at least when it comes to talking about it.

The duo recently stepped out holding hands while walking the red carpet together at Depp's latest flick *The Lone Ranger* in June.

The actors first met on the set of *Rum Diary* in 2009, and **their relationship was confirmed in June 2012**. "**They are 100 percent dating**," a source told *Us Weekly* at the time. "He treats her very well." Adding a pal of the actress, **"They started sleeping together during the press tour."**

Heard was last linked to girlfriend **Tasya van Ree**, after four years of dating. Depp announced his split with longtime love **Vanessa Paradis** in June 2012 after 14 years together.

"The last couple years have been a bit bumpy," Depp told Rolling Stone in its July 2013 issue about the split. **"At times, certainly unpleasant, but that's the nature of breakups, I guess, especially when there are kiddies involved."** The two are parents to Lily-Rose, 14, and Jack, 11.

Amber Heard and Johnny Depp – breaking-up already?

Johnny Depp and Amber Heard Are on the Rocks! (*Showbizspy*, Aug. 15, 2013):

JOHNNY Depp's romance with **Amber Heard** is reportedly on the rocks.

According to reports, Amber resents the 50-year-old actor's controlling nature — and thinks he's a bit boring.

"**Johnny accepts the fact that Amber has other needs, so he's told her it's OK for her to be with women when she has the urge**," a source told American tabloid the *National Enquirer*.

"But Johnny and Amber are in a bad place right now."

"When they first started dating, he promised to help her become the next Angelina Jolie, but Johnny simply hasn't followed through."

"Instead of finding exciting projects for Amber, or introducing her to Tinsel Town movers and shakers, he seems to block her from moving forward in her career."

"Apparently, she was offered the lead in the film version of the raunchy book *50 Shades of Grey*, but Johnny told her to say no to it because it would be too smutty."

Johnny has kept Amber cooped up in his Hollywood mansion, and she hates it, according to the source.

"It was cute for a while," noted the source. **"Amber liked cooking for Johnny and watching old movies with him. But now she's bored out of her mind."**

The pair apparently came to blows when Johnny and Amber were on a press junket in Japan to promote *The Lone Ranger*.

"The whole trip was a disaster, and Johnny and Amber got into a huge fight on the flight home," said the source.

"She pointed out how much she's given up to be with him and admitted that she misses her old life."

"Johnny's been super stressed about the movie and just snapped, telling Amber that she was lucky to be dating him."

"He promised Amber he'll make things more exciting for her, and he's still dangling the carrot of introducing her to agents and other key players."

"Amber's sticking around, hoping Johnny will be true to his word. But she's not going to wait much longer."

Can Johnny buy Amber's love?

Johnny Depp Buys $50k Necklace for Amber Heard (*Showbizspy*, Sept. 21, 2013):

JOHNNY Depp spares no expense when it comes to pleasing his girlfriend, **Amber Heard**.

According to America's *Life & Style* magazine, the actor has bought the actress a $50k pair of earrings.

"**Johnny recently surprised her with $50,000 Neil Lane diamond drop earrings**," a source said.

The pair met on the set of their 2011 film, *The Rum Diary*, and began dating shortly after.

"It's not part of my professional life. I want to be an artist. I don't want to be a celebrity," she recently said of wanting to keep their relationship private.

"You can find pictures of me on the Internet pumping gas, picking up dry cleaning, walking my dog, but nowhere are you going to find pictures of me hanging around at some nightclub."

Will Amber's bisexuality interfere with her Depp romance?

Amber Heard Not Ashamed of Her Sexuality (*Showbizspy*, Aug. 14, 2013):

AMBER Heard has opened up about her sexuality.

The actress — who's currently dating **Johnny Depp** — has **revealed why she came out as bisexual.**

"I didn't want to look like I was hiding anything," she said. "I'm not, and wasn't ever, ashamed."

Heard is anything but predictable, and that's the way she likes it.

"I don't imagine myself, my work, or my life, fitting into any kind of standardized path," she explained.

"In fact, the idea of there even being a standard freaks me out a lot."

Depp buys Amber a $40,000 gift because she's lonely?

Johnny Depp Spends $40k on Present For Amber Heard (*Showbizspy*, July 22, 2013):

JOHNNY Depp bought girlfriend **Amber Heard** a $40,000 gift because **she complained she's been terribly lonely because he's spent so much time away from her promoting his new movie**, *The Lone Ranger*.

Depp apparently got Amber a beautiful diamond and emerald-encrusted platinum brooch that had once belonged to European royalty.

"Johnny set up a romantic dinner and put the brooch into a red balloon tied to a bottle of expensive champagne," a source told American tabloid the *National Enquirer*.

"Some guys just have the cool to know that sometimes, love does mean saying, 'I'm sorry!'"

Depp ended his 14-year relationship with **Vanessa Paradis** last summer. He recently confessed that the split was difficult for their children, Rose, 14, and Jack, 11.

"The last couple years have been a bit bumpy," he said adding, **"At times, certainly unpleasant, but that's the nature of break-ups**, I guess, especially when there are kiddies involved."

Meanwhile, **Paradis has begged Depp not to marry Heard.**

"Vanessa doesn't care for Amber at all," said a source.

"She's convinced that Amber's trying to get her hooks into Johnny and his money by getting him to propose."

"But Vanessa doesn't believe it's going to last, and that's why she's against Johnny marrying Amber. She thinks their kids will be crushed when the relationship goes south."

"Vanessa thinks he's smitten because Amber's so exotic and says he'll grow tired of her."

"But before he does, he just might pop the question – and that's the last thing Vanessa wants."

Is Amber a gold-digger – just out for Johnny's money?

JOHNNY Depp and **Amber Heard** have been spending quality time together in Moscow.

Johnny, 50, is busy promoting his new film, *The Lone Ranger*, abroad, but now he has his 27-year-old girlfriend to keep him company, according to *New York Post* gossip column *Page Six*.

The pair — who have rarely been seen together since they were first romantically linked last year — reportedly looked close as they held hands in front of photographers.

Depp ended his 14-year relationship with **Vanessa Paradis** last summer. **He recently confessed that the split was difficult for their children, Rose, 14, and Jack, 11.**

Depp helps Amber with some Hollywood movie star perks:

Johnny Depp Gets Amber Heard a Better Movie Trailer (Showbizspy, June 16, 2013):

JOHNNY Depp makes sure his girlfriend, **Amber Heard**, gets what she wants!

The actress — who's filming her new movie *Paranoia* in LA's hot, dusty, downtown industrial area — complained to Depp that her dressing trailer was too small and hotter than hell because its air conditioner was on life support.

Depp snapped his fingers in some exec's face — and when Amber hit the set next morning, she was thrilled to find her teeny trailer replaced by a state-of-the-art caravan the size of a locomotive.

Amber's costar, **Gary Oldman**, reportedly said "How do I start dating Johnny Depp?"

Meanwhile, Depp's ex, **Vanessa Paradis**, has begged the star not to marry Amber.

Johnny Depp: An Outlaw Looks at 50

Single, sober and still wondering what it's all about (B. Hiatt, Rolling Stone, June 18, 2013):

"I'm kicking 50 right up the ass," he says, just a couple of weeks before the end of his forties, dragging on one of his fat, brown, proficiently self-rolled cigarettes. "I can't say that I'd want to be doing this for another 10 years."

"And then, at a certain point, just take it down to the bare minimum and concentrate on, I guess, living life. Really living life. And going somewhere where you don't have to be on the run, or sneak in through the kitchen or the underground labyrinth of the hotel. **At a certain point, when you get old enough or get a few brain cells back, you realize that, on some level, you lived a life of a fugitive."**

Then again, getting older opens up some interesting roles – look at his late drinking buddy Marlon Brando. And he isn't good at laying back. **"I don't know if I can relax," he says. "Relax, I can't do. My brain, on idle, is a bad thing. I just get weird. I mean, not weird. I get, I get antsy."** He stubs out his cigarette in an ashtray set on a wooden coffee table with a roulette wheel built into its top.

"He has a lot of interests and a great sense of humor. You get drawn to guys like that. He's basically the same as I am – a shy boy that you get a lot from. Also, we know that we have something we have to do . . . and we don't know what that is," Keith Richards has remarked on Depp.

Depp is, at the moment, dressed like a hobo whom other hobos would worry about. On his head is a battered, ancient brown fedora with a big tear on top, like Indiana Jones' post-refrigerator-ride.

He's thrown a shapeless brown canvas jacket over a blue denim shirt that's open to reveal a bonus shirt, an orange-striped Henley, beneath. His jeans are huge, carpenter-cut, shredded practically to bits, with white paint splattered up the legs and duct tape covering some of the worst holes at the rear.

He's wearing a bunch of skull rings on his fingers. His brown leather boots (worn over white socks) are the only faux-distressed element of his outfit – a gift from their manufacturer, A.S. 98., they're brand-new but look 30 years old. He has a goatee and a mustache and many, many tattoos, some of them very recently acquired. "I'm running out of real estate," he says.

As for the duct tape on his jeans: "I realized one morning as I was going to a thing my boy had at school – one of those things where, you know, they get up and sing a song? I had to be there at a certain time, and, of course, I was running late and I was reaching back to check and see if I had my wallet and passport and stuff. I always have a passport for some reason."

He takes the passport out from his back pocket and shows it off – it's nearly as battered as his hat. "Fugitive," he says, again. "And so I reached back and I thought, 'Jesus Christ!'

There was this really long tear – and there were no undergarments involved."

At this point, he must be interrupted – this is important stuff, cover of *Tiger Beat*-circa-1988 stuff. Johnny Depp doesn't wear underwear?

"That's the general approach," he says, possibly blushing a little under the shadow of his awful hat. "And so, yeah, I just immediately looked for duct tape. I know, it's pathetic. And then I continue to wear them."

Johnny Depp Talks 'Bumpy,' 'Unpleasant' Breakup with Vanessa Parades (S. Byrne, *omg! yahoo*, June 19, 2013):

One year after Johnny Depp confirmed the end of his romance with the mother of his two children, French singer-actress Vanessa Paradis, he's ready to talk about the end of that 14-year coupling.

"The last couple years have been a bit bumpy," the 50-year-old "Lone Ranger" star tells Rolling Stone. **"At times, certainly unpleasant, but that's the nature of breakups, I guess, especially when there are kiddies involved."**

He hinted that his and Paradis's careers were to blame, which, sadly, has become a fairly standard line in celebrity breakup stories.

"Relationships are very difficult, especially in the racket that I'm in because you're constantly away or they're away and so it's hard," Depp shares. "It wasn't easy on her. It wasn't easy on me. It wasn't easy on the kids."

But they rode it out until the end, he says with Depp confirming their split on June 19, 2012 — though rumors of trouble first surfaced six months before that.

"**The trajectory of that relationship — you play it out until it goes, one thing leads to another. So for whatever reason that ceases, it doesn't stop the fact that you care for that person**, and they're the mother of your kids, and you'll always know each other, and you're always gonna be in each other's lives because of those kids," says the father of Lily-Rose, 14, and Jack, 11. "You might as well make the best of it."

As for the kids, "They've been incredibly understanding. Incredibly strong throughout the whole ordeal. And it's hard on every side. You know, Vanessa's side, certainly not easy. My side, not easy. The kids are the most complicated."

Depp also talks about how he recovered from the breakup, spending time with his rocker pal Marilyn Manson (who jokes about their "bromance" in the article), but making a point not to drown his sorrows.

"In terms of the breakup, I definitely wasn't going to rely on the drink to ease things or cushion the blow or cushion the situation," he tells the magazine "'Cause that could have been fatal. I felt it was my duty to be real clear throughout that. I had something pretty serious to focus on, really, which was making sure that my kids were gonna be cool."

Something else that probably helped him cushion the blow has been his new girlfriend, Amber Heard. While he doesn't open up about his 27-year-old "The Rum Diary" co-star in the interview, he's been spending time with her over the past year. In recent months we've watched them slowly take their romance public — first with a little PDA at a Rolling Stones concert and then a dinner out at a Los Angeles hot spot with Depp pal Keith Richards.

BPD ISSUES, SYMPTOMS & JOHNNNY DEPP:

The information in this chapter seems to document Depp's BPD signs and symptoms including:

1) **Unstable relationships** (Depp's tempestuous hookups, breakups, makeups, screaming fights with Winona Ryder, Kate Moss, Vanessa Paradis – and apparently also with his current bisexual girlfriend,

Amber Heard; Depp and Heard have fought, broken-up and now appear to be into a turbulent-second relationship).

2) **Fiery, frenzied emotions** (most of Johnny's negative press has revealed his volatile emotions connected with his up and down, blustery romantic life).

3) **Unbalanced, impulsive behavior** (excessive drinking, drugging which Depp is mostly in denial about; prior self-mutilation – cutting in his teen years which seems to have transformed into the pain from tattoos; trashing hotels, assaulting photographers, several arrests and police conflicts, using bodyguards to assault people, etc.).

4) **Unstable, wobbly self-identity or variable self-concept** (Depp has transformed from bad-boy-delinquent teenager and twenty-something terror, party-monster maniac into dreamy-rich superstar and quirky-phantom actor; his shaggy-dude act with uneven-facial hair, torn-ragged clothing patched with duct tape seems to reflect an unconscious or shaky self-image based on low self-esteem and guilt).

What psychotherapy might help Depp cope with his BPD?

What **cognitive psychotherapy goals and strategies** might help Johnny Depp to overcome his self-defeating, underlying cognitive distortions and irrational thinking which seems to perpetuate his track-record of unstable relationships?

Here are eight intervention strategies for treating BPD people using a cognitive theoretical approach (Beck):

1) **Develop trust in the relationship and use a collaborative strategy:** Establish a patient/therapist relationship of trust by acknowledging that the patient has had painful experiences in the past like those with BPD. Then clearly set consistent limits, only making promises that can be kept and defining the relationship so patients know what to expect.

2) **Choose an initial focus of therapy with the patient that will lead to some immediate felt progress:** Set some simple behavioral goals which will take the focus off maintaining trust and intimacy.

3) **Reduce or eliminate dichotomous thinking early in therapy:** As dichotomous thinking – black-and-white or good-bad or idealizing-demonizing – occurs the therapist should point it out and suggest more adaptive, nuanced responses. This should reduce extreme mood swings and dilemmas faced by those with BPD.

4) **Deal with transference issues in the session:** "Transference" refers to patients responding to generalized beliefs about clinicians or therapists or relationships based on particular images of themselves or therapists or relationships, and emotional reactions that connect the two – and not how the therapist behaves as an individual. When strong emotional reactions occur, the therapist should get at the irrational thinking underlying it, resolve misunderstandings and misconceptions clearly and convey that the patient will not be rejected or attacked because of emotional reactions.

5) **Address the patient's fear of change directly by examining the risks involved in trying things a new way:** The therapist needs to clarify that decisions will be collaborative including ending therapy.

6) **Help patients increase control over their emotions by acknowledging their emotions and modeling appropriate ways to respond to them:** The therapist should talk to BPD patients about more adaptive ways to express emotions. For example, many BPD people believe expressing anger will lead to immediate rejection or attack by the recipient.

7) **Improve impulse control by acknowledging and dealing with the patient's initial response to changing behavior, "Why should I?"** The therapist should discuss alternatives to acting on impulses. For instance, in self-mutilation, cutting type impulses, discussing the motivation behind it

can lead to alternatives. Self-mutilation acts may be based on a desire to punish others, obtain relief from guilt, or as a distraction from more aversive thoughts and feelings. Sometimes self-mutilating BPD people aim to escape feelings of emptiness and boredom.

8) **Strengthen the patient's sense of identity:** The therapist can help the BPD patient to identify their positive characteristics and accomplishments and provide positive feedback about their coping decisions. The clinician can help patients evaluate their own actions to get them into providing positive self-reinforcement.

Chapter 10

"America is dumb. It's like a dumb puppy that has big teeth that can bite and hurt you, aggressive. My daughter is four, my boy is one. I'd like them to see America as a toy, a broken toy. Investigate it a little, check it out, get this feeling and then get out."

--Johnny Depp

Depp played Don Juan DeMarco in *Don Juan DeMarco* (1994) – storyline:

A psychiatrist treats a most unusual patient, only to find that the doctor is the one who gains the most from their sessions in this philosophical romantic comedy. A young man in a mask and cape (played by Johnny Depp) is standing atop a billboard, threatening to jump.

When the potential suicide is finally talked down, he's brought to a psychiatric facility where after one doctor washes his hands of the case, he's placed under the supervision of Dr. Jack Mickler (Marlon Brando), an aging psychiatrist soon to retire.

The patient informs Mickler that he is actually the great lover Don Juan, who has seduced over 1,500 women, but has fallen into a deep depression after being unable to win the hand of the woman of his dreams. Mickler has ten days to work with "Don Juan," after which he will either be released on medication or committed to a long-term stay in a mental hospital.

As Mickler talks with the young man, who speaks rapturously of the art of love, the doctor finds that his philosophies are helping to kick start his failing relationship with his wife (Faye Dunaway), and he slowly becomes convinced that his patient might really be Don Juan after all.

Don Juan DeMarco's theme song, "Have You Ever Really Loved a Woman," became a major hit for singer and songwriter Bryan Adams; after working with Marlon Brando on this film, Johnny Depp cast the legendary actor in a key supporting role in his directorial debut, The Brave (*rottentomatoes*).

JOHNNY DEPP'S LIFE BEHIND THE SCENES:

What kind of woman does Depp go for? Let's take a look at Kate Moss and consider her relationship with Johnny:

Hooked on hedonism... Inside the dark and disturbing world of Kate Moss – by the people who really know her (L. Collins, *Mail Online*, Oct. 13, 2008):

Love or loathe her, Kate Moss is one of the most influential women of our age. **Now a riveting new book reveals how a failed affair with a Hollywood legend triggered her descent into a spiral of self-destruction.**

Jason Lake's recollection of the previous day was hazy. **There had been drink and drugs and the wild rave** on the Ibiza beach, and his friend Jade Jagger had introduced him to the girl who now shared his bed. The model.

What was her name? Kate Moss, that was it. She had told him she had just split up from someone called Johnny Depp, another apparent celebrity of whom Jason had never heard...

...Yet on a personal front her life had never been so empty. In Johnny Depp, the film star with whom she had

started a passionate relationship in 1994, Kate thought she had found 'the one'.

She was convinced fate had brought them together and, **three years later, when the grand romance started to run out of steam for all the usual reasons - work pressures, conflicting schedules, lack of time together - they were devastated**.

Kate's reaction was to begin living at an unsustainable pace, physically, spiritually and emotionally, and abandon herself to partying.

She demonstrated an iron constitution and a capacity for alcohol that earned her the nickname 'The Tank'. She would later admit she had been 'bang into drugs'.

Her appetite for the 'sex, drugs and rock 'n' roll' ethos was reflected in the fact that she was often seen at high-profile events such as Rolling Stone Ronnie Wood's 50th birthday party, a Wild West-themed affair to which she wore tiny Daisy Duke hotpants and a cream hide top that was little more than two ragged strips of material stitched together at the front and tied at the back.

In May 1998, she went to the Cannes premier of *Fear and Loathing in Las Vegas* with her former lover, exciting speculation that they were reunited.

Afterwards though, **Depp was categorical in his assertions that he and Kate were no longer together and that both knew there was 'no going back'.**

Though he had been married before, and engaged to actress Winona Ryder, **Johnny claimed never to have really loved before the age of 30 - the age when he met Kate - and gave every impression of being a man who was far from over her.**

How difficult it must have been for Kate to hear the heartfelt expressions of regret for the end of their romance. **In later years, she would seem to try to recapture a fraction of what she had with Depp many times over.**

He asked her what she did. 'I'm a model,' came the bemused reply. Then, perhaps hoping to prompt some realization of the scale of her celebrity, she added: **"I've just split up with Johnny Depp."** That name also meant nothing to Jason.

...'She spoke about Johnny a bit. She was upset about it, really upset. We'd talk about relationships and she'd say, "Isn't it hard? Aren't they s*?"** And I'd say how life was a mixture of joy and pain. I was trying to console her, I suppose.

In November, Kate learned that Vanessa Paradis was pregnant with Depp's child. Any hopes she harbored of a reconciliation with Depp ended.

Later that month she made a difficult admission. **Something was terribly wrong. She needed help. She no longer felt in control of her life. It was a dizzying, fearsome realization.**

Over dinner at The Ivy with Meg and Noel Gallagher and Scottish music mogul Alan McGee, during which **Kate ate nothing, she tearfully shared her anxieties.**

The following morning she checked herself into The Priory in Roehampton.

Kate intended to stay for two weeks but ended up staying for five (the Priory recommends a stay of 28 days for the treatment of addictions).

Not once, she claimed, did she crave a drink, though she couldn't remember a time in the past decade when she had walked down a catwalk sober or woken without a hangover.

For several months she attended Alcoholics Anonymous and Narcotics Anonymous meetings and saw a psychiatrist once a week.

For a time she enjoyed a relatively stable and conventional relationship with magazine editor Jefferson Hack, with whom she had a child, Lila Grace.

But unfortunately for Kate, her stint in The Priory was not her last brush with rehab.

In the first week of 2005, her friend Mick Jones, a former member of The Clash, invited Kate to watch Pete Doherty working in the studio with his band, Babyshambles.

Draw up a list of habits and character traits that no mother would want to find in her daughter's boyfriend and Doherty would tick every box.

He was five years younger than Kate. By the time she met him, he had fathered an 18-month-old son, Astile - born to Lisa Moorish, former flatmate of Meg Mathews and mother to a child by Liam Gallagher.

He had spent four weeks of a six-month sentence in prison for burglary. He was addicted to heroin, with three failed attempts at rehabilitation to his name. His drug use made his behavior unpredictable and his moods violently changeable.

He had little to recommend him as a partner. Kate fell for him instantly.

Escaping into fantasy

Johnny Depp gave Kate an appreciation of writers such as F. Scott Fitzgerald, Jack Kerouac, Truman Capote and Hunter S. Thompson.

Kate has read and re-read the works of F. Scott Fitzgerald. **She makes no secret of the extent to which she relates to the American author's tales of desperate, destructive decadence, and just as she has been drawn to the books again and again, so she has returned to the lifestyle many times over.**

Fitzgerald was the inspiration for the theme of her 30th birthday party: The Beautiful and Damned.

When Kate was in The Priory, Marianne Faithfull sent her C.S. Lewis's *The Chronicles of Narnia*. Kate had read the stories as a child, but she read them again, gratefully escaping into their fantasy world.

'I just loved them ... it would completely be the whole heavy day and then go back and get into bed and read these books. It was such a treat.'

She is also a fan of mystical bestseller *The Celestine Prophecy*, by James Redfield, which convinced her that her meeting with Johnny Depp was predestined.

Kate is, by nature, flirtatious and tactile, and drink and drugs are great inhibition removers.

How did Kate Moss see the Depp-Moss split? *Eonline* reported:

Yes, **Kate Moss** is a supermodel. But she's also human, and when she and **Johnny Depp** broke up, she reacted how any woman of sound mind would.

She turned into a crying mess. For years. Yes, years.

"There's nobody that's ever really been able to take care of me," *Vanity Fair*'s December cover girl told the magazine of the one-time *It* couple's split. **"Johnny did for a bit."**

She added, **"I believed what he said. Like if I said, 'What do I do?' he'd tell me. And that's what I missed when I left. I really lost that gauge of somebody I could trust. Nightmare. Years and years of crying. Oh, the tears!"**

Meanwhile, she didn't feel quite the same way about all her leading men, and admitted that she had mixed feelings about her infamous 1992 Calvin Klein campaign that skyrocketed her profile as a model.

"I had a nervous breakdown when I was 17 or 18, when I had to go and work with Marky Mark **and** Herb Ritts**," she said. "It didn't feel like me at all. I felt really bad about straddling this buff guy. I didn't like it. I couldn't get out of bed for two weeks. I thought I was going to die."**

She turned down a doctor's offer of Valium following the incident, after she was advised not to start pill-popping.

"It was just anxiety. Nobody takes care of you mentally. There's a massive pressure to do what you have to do. I was really little, and I was going to work with Steven Meisel. It was just really weird—a stretch limo coming to pick you up from work. I didn't like it. But it was work, and I had to do it."

Being beautiful can be an ugly business. Still, it's a tough job, but someone's got to do it.

Is Johnny Depp over Kate Moss? Did the relationship split back-up on him?

Johnny Depp 'Still Not over Kate Moss Romance' (R. Merriman, *entertainmentwise*, Nov. 9, 2012):

Actor reportedly reached out to former girlfriend over split in 1998...

Johnny Depp might have split with girlfriend of 14 years Vanessa Paradis earlier this year, but according to insiders it's his romance with Kate Moss, who he dated for four years in the 90s that he is struggling to get over.

The secretive model recently opened up about her romance with the smoldering hunk, which ended in 1998 and claimed **she "cried for years" over the split** in an interview with *Vanity Fair*.

It wasn't just Kate who struggled with the split, those close to the '*Pirates of The Caribbean*' actor claims **he never really "got over" how their relationship ended.**

"Back in the '90s, Johnny never took responsibility for how the split broke Kate's heart," a source told *Look* magazine.

"Their life was about parties and alcohol-fuelled antics, and Johnny moved on before he even had time to mourn their relationship."

According to insiders her confession touched Johnny forcing him to get in touch with the now married star to apologize for ever hurting her.

"When Johnny heard this it really made him sit up and take notice," the source added.

"He had no idea how much he hurt Kate all those years ago, so he gave her a call out of the blue. He mainly wanted to say sorry."

Depp has previously admitted he wasn't a good match for the fashion icon.

"**I was not good for Kate**," he told the *Mail Online* in 2007, "but she's a strong girl and a great girl and very smart."

Depp split with his partner of 14 years Vanessa Paradis in June. Despite reports of a romance with his '*Rum Diaries*' co-star Amber Heard, Paradis has claimed no-one knows the truth about their split, and because of her family, she would never "sell" her personal life.

What's Johnny's viewpoint?

Johnny Depp: My family is my treasure (C. Illey, *Mail Online*, May 18, 2007):

In a highly personal interview, Johnny Depp explains why

playing the pirate Captain Jack Sparrow has helped him finally find the reason he wants to live.

When I first met Johnny Depp, he was not bankable, certainly not box-office gold. He ticked all the bad-boy boxes. Edgy, dark, an outsider who was attracted to the strangely gothic - the sad-eyed *Edward Scissorhands*, the transvestite director Ed Wood, the drug dealer in *Blow*.

He ripped up hotel rooms, and when the paparazzi lurked outside the Mirabelle restaurant in London to get a shot of his girlfriend Vanessa Paradis's pregnant tummy, **he walloped them with a plank of wood.**

Depp says that the birth of his daughter Lily-Rose, now seven, "was not only the greatest thing that's ever happened - it's the only thing that's ever happened to me."

It was that pregnant tummy that changed everything. It caused a seismic shift.

When Depp became a dad, he became the person he always wanted to be: calm, happy, loving and loved.

That manifested itself in his most iconic role: Jack Sparrow in the blockbuster trilogy *Pirates of the Caribbean*, the final installment of which -*Pirates of the Caribbean: At World's End* - opens here next Thursday.

The character he created took its inspiration from raddled Keith Richards and cartoon skunk sexpot Pepe Le Pew: mischievous rather than villainous, all glittering gold teeth and high-polished camp.

When we meet this time, in a sterile hotel room in Los Angeles, Depp's charisma and teeth sparkle.

He's still filming a few scenes for *Pirates*, and the teeth are still on, but now they look as if they belong.

Johnny Depp, the man, has merged with Jack Sparrow, the character.

He is no longer miserable, dark, anaesthetized with drugs. He is bright, sparky and children-friendly.

...It's also difficult, looking at Depp the family man, to remember **Johnny the serial fiancé. When he was with a woman, he was all about being only with that woman.**

When he had a relationship with Winona Ryder, he had her name tattooed on his arm.

Once it was over, he had it changed to **"Wino Forever"**.

Then, of course, there was his turbulent on-off relationship with Kate Moss.

Sometimes he was filling her hotel room with daisies, other times he was **throwing the television out of the hotel window**.

Now, though, he's marketing gold and he is clear and profound about what caused this transformation: "Meeting Vanessa and fatherhood."

Depp says that the birth of his daughter Lily-Rose, now seven, "was not only the greatest thing that's ever happened - it's the only thing that's ever happened to me.

"I helped give our daughter life and I feel she gave me life.

"Suddenly, you meet your reason to live, meet the future. It was like my birth in a way. I was born that day."

Dramatic words, but **he says them almost in a whisper. He has stopped drinking spirits and taking drugs.**

"I quit drinking spirits because I couldn't stop."

"I would just keep going until a black screen came down, where you can't see anything anymore."

"Trying to numb and medicate myself was never about recreation, it was existing without living."

"Now I have a solid foundation to stand on."

His eyes twinkle some more when he talks about his kids, Lily-Rose and five-year-old Jack.

He is so devoted to Vanessa that even a screen kiss with co-star Keira Knightley upset him.

He says he could never love anybody else.

"I'm old fashioned. It's my Kentucky mentality - seems I can't escape it after all."

Despite his reputation, pre-Vanessa, as a man who loved women, Depp was never a womanizer.

His relationships were long and monogamous, even if some of them were, to put it mildly, tumultuous.

His relationship with Kate Moss in the mid-Nineties was intense and passionate, but not quite as in the legends.

He denies the story about filling a bath with champagne at the Portobello Hotel in which he and Moss supposedly bathed.

"I wish it was true," he says, with a sad little smile.

He is clearly uneasy talking about Kate, whom he's not spoken to since they split up.

One feels this is more out of loyalty to Paradis than lack of love for Moss.

"I was not good for Kate," he says. "But she's a strong girl and a great girl and very smart."

He says he was shocked at her treatment by newspapers, who nicknamed her **Cocaine Kate**.

"Dragging her through the mud like that - they are weird and two-faced."

"Let her be! I have never met Pete Doherty, but I think he has talent and him and Kate could be great together."

"She's got a great brain on her and she's a good mummy."

Depp met Paradis, whom he touchingly refers to as "my girl" - possibly the only man in the world who could use this term of endearment without it sounding ridiculous - in France in 1998.

He was filming the Roman Polanski movie *The Ninth Gate* at the time.

It was one of those instant connections.

"You have this feeling - I can't really explain what it was, but I had it when I met Vanessa."

I saw her across a room and I thought: "What's happening to me?"

"I had no way of knowing how great a person she was or how great a mother she would be."

"I can remember thinking the last thing in the world I wanted was a relationship, but it was impossible to escape. I was gone."

Paradis, despite her pop star background and having a hit with *Joe Le Taxi* when she was 14, came from a very stable, sensible background.

She still looks like a luscious Lolita, all angular cheekbones and big eyes.

She is now 33, but has always said she wanted to be a mother, and there's nothing that makes her happier than carrying a child.

Which brings us back to that block of wood and the paparazzi. Depp doesn't even attempt to look contrite.

"I told them: 'I know the photograph you want and you're not going to get it! I don't want to be a novelty tonight.'"

"They were rude and said: 'We are going to get the picture!'"

"Vanessa got in the car and they were trying to pull the door open."

"There was a block of wood on the ground, so I grabbed it and smacked the hand of the guy who was trying to open the car door."

Johnny was born in Owensboro, Kentucky and had a peripatetic childhood.

The family moved to Florida and shifted more than a dozen times between motels and homes.

His high-school career was colorful - he was once suspended for mooning at his gym teacher - and he dropped out at 15.

"I felt completely and utterly confused by everything that was going on around me," he admits.

"I always wanted to know why, and it really annoyed the teachers."

That year, his parents split up.

"I was pretty much ready to leave myself and did so not long after that."

"So on the one hand it was a release, and on the other it was a radical change for Mom and she got very ill."

"There was never any time for me, as a kid, to feel bad at the parents splitting up because the kid had to go straight to the mom and look after her and make sure she was OK."

"There was never any time for mourning the loss of family."

Now he has found the family he missed for so long.

He still has a base in the South of France, but has bought his mother a house next door to his Hollywood Hills home. Whatever was lost is now complete.

Depp says when growing up he used to love the *Pirates of the Caribbean* ride at Disney World in Florida.

Now he enjoys taking his kids on it, too.

Meanwhile, in each *Pirates* film, his character has become archer, more over the top.

The *World's End* features spectacular swashbuckling scenes - and a Captain Jack who is more comedic, and nimble, than ever.

A bit like the man himself. Somehow Captain Jack and Johnny Depp seem set to continue to evolve together, and perhaps they are not ready to let go of each other yet.

BPD ISSUES, SYMPTOMS & JOHNNY DEPP:

Johnny has been drawn into intense, erratic relationships with a series of celebrity women – famous ladies who were often wild, zany alcoholic-addicts like Kate Moss; possible BPD victims like partying, shoplifting Winona Ryder or exotic, off-beat types like his current girlfriend, bisexual Amber Heard.

Some of these women – like Kate Moss - have admitted to rehab for drug and alcohol addiction. Winona Ryder ended up in a psychiatric ward for "anxiety" while involved with Depp.

Johnny's already broken-up with bisexual Amber Heard and re-started a second relationship with her. Meanwhile Amber has had relationships simultaneously with two lesbian women.

Vanessa seemed to have been the most stable woman and since they had kids, Depp hung-out with her for over a decade.

Johnny's extreme, roller-coaster BPD relationship pattern is a merry-go-round of:

1) Falling hard and fast in love with a sexy, pretty woman.

2) Stressing-out when she seems to get too close, engulfing or smothering him and his shaky self-identity.

3) Becoming outrageous, silly and bizarrely outraged when he perceives that she will abandon him.

4) Throwing temper tantrums, trashing hotel rooms and assaulting photographers when things don't go his way with women.

5) Splitting up, separating, and breaking-up with women when Depp gets into his stupid-crazy stage – breaking off his engagement to marry her.

6) Making-up, patching-up, salvaging his relationship after a break-up – sentimentally reclaiming his lost love and getting engaged to be married again.

7) Repeat these steps several times – more break-ups, more engagements.

8) More knock-down screaming fights and finally an end, Depp's done with her.

9) Johnny then makes socially-acceptable comments about the woman – how he'll always love her; how his career interfered with the attention she needed; how he couldn't "love" before he was 30 – oops! He's had unstable relationships after 30!

10) Depp then casts his line and reels in another cute babe who has no chance of a stable relationship with Johnny because of his BPD. Amber Heard is the current example now experiencing Depp's roller-coaster relationship ride as part of his 10-steps to love which I've just outlined.

The signs and symptoms of Depp's BPD – based on his eccentric relationship patterns - include:

1) **Uncontrollable emotions**: Depp, as a BPD sufferer, has difficulty managing his emotions revolving around his relationships with women – emotions such as sadness, shame, loneliness, fear and anger toward himself.

2) **Unsound, quaking relationships**: I've outlined above my theory of the 10 stages Depp experiences in his romantic relationships.

3) **Unstable, impulsive behavior**: Depp has claimed he's cutting down on drinking alcohol and has just used it to self-medicate – which sounds like an active alcoholic making rationalizations. He's also had a drug addiction in the past. But drugs and alcoholic issues must be treated by Twelve-Step programs such as A.A. (Alcoholics Anonymous) or N.A. (Narcotics Anonymous) – they don't just go away become of remarks in a P.R. interview. Also, it's the reckless behavior patterns and moral issues behind alcohol and drug addiction that must be addressed. Putting down a bottle of booze or saying "no" to mood-altering drugs will not solve deep-seated mental disorder issues connected to an addictive personality.

4) **Dubious, uncertain self-image**: Johnny would need long-term psychotherapy to come to both conscious and unconscious factors related to his poor self-concept, his shuddering self-identity or self-image.

Chapter 11

"I smoked with Jesus Christ! Jesus is a Marlboro man!"

--Johnny Depp

Dead Man (1995) featured Johnny Depp playing William "Bill" Blake – storyline:

A dark, bitter commentary on modern American life cloaked in the form of a surrealist western, Jim Jarmusch's Dead Man stars Johnny Depp as William Blake, a newly-orphaned accountant who leaves his home in Cleveland to accept a job in the frontier town of Machine.

Upon his arrival, Blake is told by the factory owner Dickinson (Robert Mitchum) that the job has already been filled. Dejectedly, he enters a nearby tavern, ultimately spending the night with a former prostitute.

A violent altercation with the woman's lover (Gabriel Byrne), also Dickinson's son, leaves Blake a murderer as well as mortally wounded, a bullet lodged dangerously close to his heart. He flees into the wilderness, where a Native American named Nobody (Gary Farmer) mistakes Blake for the English poet William Blake and determines that he will be Blake's guide in his protracted passage into the spirit world (*rottentomatoes*).

JOHNNY DEPP'S LIFE BEHIND THE SCENES:

Let's take a look at Amber Heard, Johnny's new bisexual girlfriend – Depp has already broken-up with her at least once. He's since made-up with Amber, rekindled the relationship and currently is in round two of their romance. What has the press been reporting?

Amber Heard Addresses Privacy Issues with Johnny Depp Relationship! (*Perez Hilton*, 7/31/2013):

As one half of the year's sexiest couple, **Amber Heard** is feelin' the media's heat when it comes to her relationship with the desirable and impeccable **Johnny Depp**.

As their love becomes more serious, curious reporters want to know what everyone wants to know:

EVERYTHING!!

But despite the questions, Amber stands firm in her decision to keep it private.

In the September 2013 issue of *Flare*, she declares:

"It's not part of my professional life. I want to be an artist. I don't want to be a celebrity. You can find pictures of me on the Internet pumping gas, picking up dry cleaning, walking my dog, but nowhere are you going to find pictures of me hanging around at some nightclub..."

"Can you ever imagine yourself in a situation like Brad Pitt and Angelina Jolie or Kim Kardashian and Kanye West, where the world feels like they have a stake in your private life? I would never want it. I guess I could not hold hands with who I want to, but what kind of life would that be? I don't want to change just because people are watching..."

Uh well...as much as she has a point, WE have to point out the fact that Johnny *was* a part of her professional life —

back when they sparked during the filming and promotion of *The Rum Diary* — and it was that seed that began to sizzle!

If you'll recall, it was *PerezHilton* that first speculated that a legit romance had blossomed back when we saw her board his private jet months after the premiere tour.

But alas, they're not filming a movie together now...well, at least no professional ones anyways. Wink wink. And as much as we'd love to be a fly on their private island, we have to wish what's best for their growth. Enjoy your love, you two!

BPD ISSUES, SYMPTOMS & JOHNNY DEPP:

I'm afraid the Depp unstable, shuddering relationship merry-go-round will continue with bisexual Amber aboard. The precarious nature of Johnny's relationships is already in evidence because we are in round two of the Amber-Johnny coupling. Actually it's a triangle since Amber simultaneously keeps up a bisexual romance with her current lesbian girlfriend.

They've already broken-up once and experienced angry verbal brawls, hostilities over conflicts, disputes over Amber's career choices and other clashes over other issues. One of Depp's BPD problems is a lack of perspective in his relationships. **Three skills Johnny lacks include:**

1) The ability to understand the needs, feelings, and beliefs of other people.

2) Ability to see how other people perceive them.

3) Ability to see how their own behavior affects others.

Chapter 12

"The only gossip I'm interested in is things from the Weekly World News - 'Woman's bra bursts, 11 injured.' That kind of thing."

--Johnny Depp

Nick of Time (1995) starred Depp as Gene Watson – storyline:

A stranger pulled into a deadly scheme races against time to save his daughter in this thriller. Gene Watson (Johnny Depp) is an accountant who comes to L.A. with his ten-year-old daughter Lynn (Courtney Chase) to attend a funeral. On the street, Gene and Lynn are pulled aside by Mr. Smith

(Christopher Walken) and Ms. Jones (Roma Maffia), who flash what look like police badges and usher them into a van.

Gene soon discovers that he's been kidnapped, and his captors have an unusual demand -- if Gene does not murder Gov. Eleanor Grant (Marsha Mason) within 75 minutes, his daughter will be killed. Gene now has just an hour and a quarter to tip off the authorities, spare Gov. Grant, and find out what Smith and Jones are trying to do, along with saving his daughter's life.

He finds a much-needed ally in one-legged shoe-shine man Huey (Charles S. Dutton). Most of the action in Nick of Time occurs in "real time," meaning that the passage of time on screen matches that of real life, as the frequent shots of clocks and watches will attest (*rottentomatoes*).

JOHNNY DEPP'S LIFE BEHIND THE SCENES:

Let's see if Depp has really "opened-up" in a meaningful way about his split with Vanessa Paradis:

Johnny Depp: "Vanessa Paradis split was unpleasant"

(Glamour, June 19, 2013):

JOHNNY DEPP DIAGNOSED: UNAUTHORIZED PSYCHOLOGICAL DIAGNOSIS OF HIS SECRET LIFE

Johnny Depp has opened up about his split from his longtime lover Vanessa Paradis, describing the last few years of the couple's 14-year-old relationship as "unpleasant".

Speaking in an interview with Rolling Stone, the 50-year-old actor said: "**The last couple years have been a bit bumpy. At times, certainly unpleasant, but that's the nature of break-ups**, I guess, especially when there are kiddies involved."

The *Dark Shadows* star revealed that **he and Paradis's work as actors also put an added a strain on the relationship, as they spent less time together.**

He added: "**So for whatever reason that ceases, it doesn't stop the fact that you care for that person**, and they're the mother of your kids, and you'll always know each other, and you're always gonna be in each other's lives because of those kids. You might as well make the best of it."

The *Pirates of the Caribbean* actor, who has two children with the French actress, also revealed that daughter Lily-Rose, 14, and son Jack, 11, have been "incredibly understanding, incredibly strong throughout the whole ordeal".

The couple split in June 2012.

On 24 September 2012, we wrote...

Vanessa Paradis is reportedly moving on from ex-boyfriend Johnny Depp with Carla Bruni's former flame, Benjamin Biolay.

Singer Biolay, 39, was reportedly introduced to Paradis by Chanel designer Karl Lagerfeld.

Speaking about Lagerfeld's match-making, a source revealed: "They're the same age and have similar backgrounds in music, so Karl was keen for them to meet."

The mole added: "They have even recorded a duet called Enjoy on Benjamin's latest album... They plan to promote and tour the album together next spring."

News of the two's reported romantic liaison comes after they were first snapped enjoying a meal at Paris restaurant, Ralph's, in April this year. At the time, **Depp and Paradis were subject to intense media speculation that the long-standing couple had ended their 14-year relationship**, after the pair hadn't been seen at a public event together since 2010.

It was then revealed in June that the Hollywood actor and the French star - who have two children together - had indeed separated.

In a joint statement via their publicist, the two said that they had "**amicably separated**", adding: "Please respect their privacy and, more importantly, the privacy of their children."

Meanwhile, Depp has since been linked to his *Rum Diary* co-star Amber Heard.

On 13 August 2012, we wrote...

Vanessa Paradis has talked about her split from partner Johnny Depp for the first time.

Talking to a French magazine, the actress said **she had no qualms about the break-up.**

"**I don't have the recipe for happiness, but I think the engine is simply having the desire,**" she said. "**It's not feeling obliged or forced or repeating yourself."**

"I hate, for example, whenever you hear someone say, 'You have to work at being a couple'," she explained. **"No, you have to want to be there."**

"And for me, I want to be right where I am right now," she added.

Vanessa Paradis and Johnny Depp announced that they were separating in June this year.

On 21st June, we wrote...

Vanessa Paradis may be in line to receive up to £100m in an out-of-court settlement, following her separation from partner Johnny Depp.

The actor is thought to have offered the French actress this large lump sum, following the announcement of their split on Tuesday, in order to keep the break-up amicable.

Hollywood lawyer Robert Nachshin said the fact that the pair, who have been together 14 years, never married makes the situation more complicated.

"If the couple had been married, Mr. Depp's wife would be able to simply claim 50%, child support payments and alimony."

"However, because they are not married this does not apply. The partner Paradis would have to file a civil suit and go to court."

Johnny Depp is reputed to be worth £225m so giving Vanessa £100m would avoid a long (and no doubt public) legal battle. "Litigation is expensive, and could run into extremely high figures. This won't be a monthly payment plan - he will make a lump sum payment as a settlement."

As well as the settlement, it is thought Vanessa will retain the house the couple shared with their two children in Southern France.

On 20th June, we wrote...

Just hours after announcing that they have separated, reports have emerged that **Johnny Depp and his long-term partner Vanessa Paradis had been trying to save their relationship for months.**

Speaking to *People* magazine, a source revealed: **"They've tried for months to save the relationship... but have known for weeks that it couldn't be saved."**

The mole also revealed that the timing of the couple's announcement of their split purposefully coincided with Paradis' recent trip to France, where she was promoting her upcoming flick *Je Me Suis Fait Tout Petit*.

"It was all decided before she got on that plane." The source added.

News of the couple's split came after months of speculation as to the state of their relationship and amid reports that they had been living separate lives.

On 19th June 2012, we wrote...

Johnny Depp and Vanessa Paradis have confirmed that they have split after 14 years together.

The couple have two children, Lily-Rose, 13, and nine-year-old Jack, but have not been seen at a public event together for two years.

They have been plagued by split rumors for several months but, though Johnny has been linked to actress Amber Heard, it was thought that they were working through their issues.

A source said of the star: "For the first time in a long time, he is talking about her. They both want to make it work."

As recently as last month, the *Pirates of the Caribbean* actor denied that they had broken up.

"The rumors are not true. They are absolutely not true. No matter what I say about this, people believe the opposite. I can't say enough about it not being over," Depp claimed.

Johnny and Vanessa got together in 1998; the *Rum Diaries* actor has previously dated Winona Ryder and Kate Moss.

On 11th May, 2012, we wrote...

Johnny Depp has slammed reports that he and Vanessa Paradis have split.

The couple - who have been together for 14 years - have been the subject of a numerous split rumors since January, even though Paradis deemed the rumors "false" earlier this year.

However, Depp has now spoken on the subject. When asked if he and Paradis were still an item at the *Dark Shadows* London premiere on Wednesday, Depp said: **"The rumors are not true."**

"They are absolutely not true. No matter what I say about this, people believe the opposite."

The 48-year-old actor then added: **"I can't say enough about it not being over."**

On 25 January 2012, we wrote...

Vanessa Paradis has denied rumors that she and her long-term boyfriend Johnny Depp have separated.

Appearing on French chat show *Le Grand Journal*, Paradis refuted the claims that she and Depp are no longer together, although she refused to go into detail on the subject.

When quizzed by the show's panelist Arianne Massanet on how she dealt with such rumors, Paradis responded: **"It depends which rumor... Here, this is one which could hurt my family**. After that...they say that we have 52 houses in France, we separate in winter, and we get married every summer. Me, I'm in my 12th pregnancy."

"All this is, I don't know, because the Queen of England didn't lose her teeth this week and there's nothing happening," she later quipped.

However, despite not being drawn on the claims, when asked to clarify whether the reports were untrue, Paradis said: "Yes it's false - of course it's false."

On the 18 January 2012 we wrote:

Angelina Jolie is helping Johnny Depp and Vanessa Paradis get through their alleged relationship troubles, according to reports.

Earlier this month it was claimed that the Hollywood couple, who have been together for 14 years and have two children, were on the verge of splitting up.

It has now been rumored that their Hollywood pal Angelina Jolie has stepped in to play marriage counselor, offering advice to help them work things out.

A source revealed: "They, Johnny and Angelina, stayed in touch after *The Tourist*. When she heard what was going on she reached out to him to see how he was coping and urged him to work it out."

There has been no official word from the Depp-Paradis camp on the rumors yet.

On the 9 January 2012 we wrote:

Johnny Depp and Vanessa Paradis are rumored to be on the brink of splitting up after 14 years together.

The pair are thought to be on the verge of breaking up because of their constant bickering.

"People around him are worried about how Johnny is doing because **he and Vanessa seem so fractured** right now," a source told the *RadarOnline*. "**Johnny isn't handling anything well right now.**"

The *Pirates of the Caribbean* star is also rumored to be seeking legal advice on the relationship, despite the fact the pair were never married.

"**Johnny has started reaching out to lawyers, probably to quietly discuss how to get out of the relationship**," the unnamed source continued. "'They're not married but **they've been together for years and have kids together so it isn't as easy as just breaking up.**"

Vanessa and Johnny have two children - Jack, nine, and Lily-Rose, 12 - but the problems in their relationship are thought to have started in April, when **Johnny was photographed appearing to kiss another woman**, who turned out to be the actor's publicist, Robin Baum.

"Whenever Johnny and Vanessa are rumored to be having relationship problems, it's Robin who as his press officer has to deny them."

BPD ISSUES, SYMPTOMS & JOHNNY DEPP:

Johnny typically goes through a phase or stage of denial as his relationship boat sinks, water is rushing over the decks and yet Depp denies the romance is going down.

His BPD blocks Depp from seeing himself through his romantic partner's eyes. **What are the behaviors Johnny exhibits that his girlfriends find controlling or outrageous which causes a break-up?**

1) **Jealousy**: Johnny gets anxious when he senses his romantic partner may be abandoning him. He then becomes intensely jealous. For instance, he may call her excessively, demand constant reassurance, and check-up on his girlfriend's every move. His anger and jealousy backfires on him and drives her away.

2) **Seductiveness**: Sometimes BPD individuals engage in seductive gestures, sexualized behavior, facial expressions and touching – Depp may do this with other women. Then when other women respond, he may act shocked and his girlfriend gets angry when she

finds out. He may have affairs when he suspects his girlfriend is cheating on him – while he's guilty of what he fears.

3) **Anger**: Johnny's BPD temper tantrums and explosive anger causes others including his girlfriend to avoid him. He can't understand why.

4) **Hysteria**: BPD people such as Depp are drama kings – they over-react to situations or people. So when a normal person is irritated, Johnny flies into a rage. His sadness turns into profound dysphoria (generalized feeling of distress) or deep depression. His pleasure feelings transform into ecstasy or manic bliss. Depp goes from worry to terror, panic and horror. He responds to far higher or lower levels than the situation warrants.

5) **Impulsivity**: Depp has a track-record of reckless, impulsive behavior including substance abuse (active alcoholic-addict – abusing alcohol and narcotic drugs), burglary, vandalism, theft, trashing hotel rooms, fights with police and several arrests, fights with photographers, assaulting people or using his bodyguards to assault others; self-mutilation such as cutting himself and even getting off on the pain from getting tattoos.

Chapter 13

"Tim Burton can ask me everything. If he wants me to have sex with an aardvark in one of his next movies, then I will do that."

--Johnny Depp

The Brave (1997) showcased Johnny Depp as Raphael – storyline:

Johnny Depp made his debut as a director and screenwriter with this allegorical tale of the plight of Native Americans. Raphael (Depp) is an alcoholic American Indian who lives in a hovel near a junkyard with his wife Rita (Elpidia Carillo) and his children Frankie (Cody Lightning) and Marta

(Nicole Mancera); he scrapes together a meager living rescuing potentially salable items from the rubbish.

Desperate to raise money, Raphael arranges to meet a wealthy man named McCarthy (Marlon Brando), who makes him an unusual offer: he'll pay Raphael $50,000 to appear in a film in which he's beaten to death by a gang of rednecks. The murder in the film will not be faked; if he takes the role, Raphael will suffer a painful demise in front of the camera.

Raphael accepts, hoping the money will help Rita build a better life for their children. For the next seven days, Raphael tries to enjoy his last week on Earth and teach Frankie something of his new responsibilities as the man of the house.

The Brave received decidedly mixed reviews in its initial screenings at the 1997 Cannes Film Festival; it had a limited release in Europe but has yet to appear in the United States, either in theaters or on home video. Punk rock icon Iggy Pop composed the film's score (*rottentomatoes*).

JOHNNY DEPP'S LIFE BEHIND THE SCENES:

Here's some more research on Johnny's relationships:

Kate Moss Dishes On Her Dreamy Relationship With Johnny Depp in US Vogue (J. Vince, *Grazia Daily*, March 21, 2012):

Here at *Grazia Daily*, we don't need much of a reason to look through old photos of Kate Moss and Johnny Depp. Weren't they just dreamy together? Yes, the uber-hot supermodel is now a happily married woman and the hunky Hollywood actor is a family man, but we can still indulge now and again, right? And lucky for us, today a veritable excuse has arisen for us to collate a gallery of the beautiful pair. Hurrah!

Yes, Mossy has been talking about her ex-man candy in the April issue of US *Vogue*, giving us a tantalizing insight into their ridiculously cool relationship. Kate and Johnny met at the Cafe Tabac in New York City back in 1994 and dated on and off until their final public appearance at the 1998 Cannes Film Festival for the premiere of *Fear and Loathing in Las Vegas*. During that time, **Kate reveals Mr. Depp was nothing but gentlemanly, often whisking her away to his glam hotel room whenever they were in Paris.**

'When I was with Johnny Depp, he always stayed at the Ritz,' the 38-year-old reveals in the interview. 'I had an apartment in Paris at the time, but he said, 'No, we're staying at the Ritz,' so **he came by and swept me up to the Ritz - he didn't want to slum it in my apartment!'**

Oh, could he BE any more perfect? Understandably, such an offer didn't take much persuading and Kate admits **to loving the swanky hotel's cocktails. 'I drink the French 76: vodka, sugar, lemon juice topped up with**

champagne,' she says. 'It's the best drink ever, but it only tastes like that in the Hemingway Bar. Colin Field, Ritz Paris head bartender, made it for my wedding. **It doesn't taste at all strong - and then, whoa, whoops-a-daisy!**' Ah, that's our Kate...But what we'd give to see Johnny back on her arm. We can but dream...

Bio (*People*):

1970-1979:

Not Exactly Neverland

Depp's family settles in Miramar, Fla., when Depp is 7, living in a hotel until his father finds work. **Prone to self-inflicted knife wounds – his arms still bear the visible scars** – Depp starts smoking at 12, loses his virginity at 13, **starts doing drugs at 14 and eventually drops out of high school** at 16 to join the garage band, The Kids.

1983:

The Marrying Man

Months after moving to L.A. with his bandmates, Depp, 20, marries makeup artist Lori Allison, 25, in Miami. The relationship lasts two years and leads to one important connection. Through her friend Nicolas Cage, Depp is introduced to the agent who lands him his first film role, as a teen swallowed by his bed in 1984's *Nightmare on Elm Street*.

1986:

Reporting for Duty

Depp gets his first taste of Oscar-quality work with a small role as a Vietnamese-speaking GI in Oliver Stone's *Platoon*. The film will receive eight Oscar nominations the following year, taking home statues for Best Picture, Best Director, Best Sound and Best Film Editing.

1987

Undercover Bother

With the successful premiere of high school cop drama *21 Jump Street*, one of the first shows on the new FOX network, Depp becomes a teen heartthrob, receiving 10,000 fan letters a month.

Although he signed a six-year contract with the show, not believing it would last a season, Depp begins to rebel against his heartthrob status and by 1990 negotiates his way out in order to pursue movie work. "He didn't make any secret of the fact that he didn't particularly care about being on that show," recalls cast mate Holly Robinson to *PEOPLE*.

1989

Depp Dates Winona

Depp meets actress Winona Ryder at a film premiere and is immediately smitten. "**There's been nothing in my 27 years that's comparable to the feeling I have with Winona**," he tells *PEOPLE* at the time.

Five months after their first date, the couple is engaged; three years later they split. **Depp**, who alters the "Winona Forever" tattoo on his right biceps to read "Wino

Forever," **seems to have a fiancée fetish: before Ryder, he was also briefly engaged to actresses Sherilyn Fenn and Jennifer Grey**

1990

Total Cutup

In an extreme contrast from his *21 Jump Street* persona, Depp takes on the eccentric title role in *Edward Scissorhands*. It is his first collaboration with director Tim Burton, whom he works with on many other films, including *Ed Wood* (1994) and *Sleepy Hollow* (1999).

1993

Art-Film Confidential

Depp passes on big-budget roles for films like *Benny & Joon*, where he plays an eccentric who models himself after silent-movie star Buster Keaton. He'll continue the trend with *What's Eating Gilbert Grape* (opposite Leonardo DiCaprio) and *Ed Wood*.

"I was so uncomfortable being a product, I swore to myself that I would choose my own path," Depp says on *Inside the Actors Studio*. "I figured I could always go back to playing guitar or pumping gas or something."

Death of a Friend

Fellow actor and pal River Phoenix collapses outside the Viper Room, the Sunset Strip club Depp co-owns until 2003. **An autopsy shows that Phoenix's body had toxic levels of cocaine and heroin, as well as marijuana and Valium.**

Depp faces accusations that his nightspot is one of the centers of Hollywood's drug trade. "To pinpoint one club or one street is really ridiculous," he tells *USA Today*. "There's a tragic loss of a very gifted, very sweet, nice young man."

1994

Up-and-Down Relationship

Depp meets model Kate Moss at the Manhattan bistro Café Tabac, and from the beginning **their union is one of tremendous highs and lows. "They can't keep their hands, lips, mouths, legs off each other**," a friend says to *PEOPLE*.

The passion often turns the other way as the pair are frequently seen shouting at each other in public. **"Instead of hitting women, he just gets angry and lets off steam in other ways**," a longtime friend says to *PEOPLE*.

Charge It to the Room

Suspected of being drunk and fighting with Moss, Depp is arrested on suspicion of criminal mischief after trashing his $1,200-a-night room at New York City's Mark Hotel. Charges are dismissed after Depp pays nearly $10,000 in damages and fees.

Ironically, legendary-hotel trasher Roger Daltrey of The Who was trying to sleep next door. "On a scale of 1 to 10," Daltrey says to *PEOPLE*, "I give him a 1. It took him so bloody long. The Who could've done the job in one minute flat."

1998

Going Gonzo

After becoming friendly with journalist Hunter S. Thompson, Depp portrays him in the film adaptation of Thompson's novel *Fear and Loathing in Las Vegas*. In August 2005, six months after the author's suicide, Depp pays for an invitation-only memorial where Thompson's ashes are shot out of a 15-foot cannon over his Aspen ranch.

Paradis Found

In Paris filming the supernatural mystery *The Ninth Gate*, Depp meets French model-singer Vanessa Paradis, 26. "**She walked towards me, directly at me, and just said 'Hi.' And then I just knew, you know, it's over with**," he tells Oprah.

Meeting Paradis, he says, "**changed my life completely**." **Within months, the pair move into a $2 million villa in a rural village on France's Cote d'Azur**.

1999

Little Flower

Depp and Paradis welcome their first child, Lily-Rose Melody Depp, in Paris. They have a son, John Christopher Depp III, whom they call Jack, in April 2002. "Johnny is the perfect father."

He dresses the children, he changes them, he makes them laugh," Paradis says in French *Elle* in 2002. Her one complaint? "Well, he does give Lily-Rose too many potato chips."

2003

Ahoy, Mate

Depp steals the show from Orlando Bloom and Keira Knightley in Disney's blockbuster *Pirates of the Caribbean: The Curse of the Black Pearl*. Modeling his character, Captain Jack Sparrow, after Rolling Stones guitarist Keith Richards, Depp's oddball portrayal earns him his first Oscar nomination. The film grosses $654 million during its theatrical run, and Depp reprises the role in 2006 and 2007.

He's Too Sexy

Depp lands the cover of *PEOPLE*'s Sexiest Man Alive in 2003, beating such handsome faces as Brad Pitt, Russell Crowe, Nick Lachey and George Clooney. With the popularity of *Pirates of the Caribbean*, Depp gains a new generation of fans.

Lasse Halstrom, who directed Depp in *What's Eating Gilbert Grape*, talks of the leading man's charm: "**He's a little dangerous, he has a secret, and he has great warmth – all those things you can see in his eyes. That's the key to his appeal**."

2004

Panning for Accolades

Depp goes two for two, giving another Oscar-nominated performance as *Peter Pan* author J.M. Barrie in *Finding Neverland* with Kate Winslet.

"Johnny is at the pinnacle of his career," *Neverland* producer Harvey Weinstein says to *PEOPLE*. "He is the most versatile actor in the industry. He is a leading man, a character actor, and he has the courage of his convictions."

2005

Candyman

Delivering his own version of the Willy-Wonka character popularized by Gene Wilder in 1971, Depp once again caters toward a younger audience in *Charlie and the Chocolate Factory*.

Filming in London, Depp flies home to France every weekend until the last month of shooting, when he brings his family with him. "He wanted Lily-Rose to see him playing with the Oompa Loompas," producer Richard Zanuck says to *PEOPLE*.

2007

A Mighty Trilogy

Pirates of the Caribbean: At World's End opens at No. 1 at the box office, grossing $153 million its first week. Days later, the previous *Pirates* installment wins the MTV Movie Award for Best Movie and Depp takes home the popcorn for Best Performance.

"I want to thank the producers and Disney for not firing me first," Depp says during his acceptance speech.

Singing in *Sweeney Todd*

Depp appears on the cover of *EW*, where he discusses his sixth collaboration with director Tim Burton in the adaptation of the musical, *Sweeney Todd*. "He makes Sid Vicious look like the innocent paper boy," Depp says of his character. "He's beyond dark."

Despite the singing (which "couldn't be more foreign to me in a lot of ways"), the actor says, "After certain takes, Tim would just howl with laughter and go, 'I think this is my favorite character.'" After winning a lead actor Golden Globe for the dark role, Depp earns a Best Actor Oscar nomination.

2009

Two-Timing Johnny

Depp is named *PEOPLE*'s Sexiest Man Alive for the second time. "Johnny Depp has magical powers. He's unlike anyone else," says actress Isla Fisher. "He's funny, generous and clever. It's just a shame he's so hard on the eyes."

2010

Welcome to *Wonderland*

Depp reunites with director Tim Burton for the seventh time to play the Mad Hatter in *Alice in Wonderland*, costarring Anne Hathaway. "He's a fascinating character," says Depp, who sports green eyes and fiery red hair for the part. "He's mad. He's unpredictable. To play the Mad Hatter and breathe life into Tim's vision is a dream come true."

2012

Back on the Market

Multiple sources tell PEOPLE that Depp, 48, and longtime love Paradis, 39, are all but officially finished. "**It's so sad**," says an insider of the couple, whose 14-year union produced two children, daughter Lily-Rose, 12, and son Jack, 9.

Though both Deep and Paradis initially deny the reports, a rep for the couple confirms on June 19 that they "**have amicably separated**".

BPD ISSUES, SYMPTOMS & JOHNNY DEPP:

Why do Depp's relationships always fail? **What factors could be leading to his unstable, volatile, erratic relationships for decades?** My theory is that he suffers from BPD which, besides those I've mentioned, includes these problems:

1) **Johnny causes unintended hurt**: Depp, like other BPD people, fails to see how his romantic partners feel about him and how his behavior impacts them. He gets so caught up in his emotional turmoil and distress, Johnny can't step back and see what pain, fear and hurt he's causing his lovers. He can't see his girlfriend's perspective and so that leads to the destruction of the relationship.

2) **Depp crashes her boundaries**: BPD people don't understand or respect other people's boundaries.

Johnny then awkwardly crosses the personal limits of his girlfriend or lover. He doesn't get her rules, limits or personal space. Depp, for example, has been heard to scream and fight with Kate Moss in public.

3) **He disrespects his romantic partners and lovers**: BPD people don't respect their partners' boundaries. For example, if Johnny fears being abandoned, he could demand to know where his partner is at all times. He might ask her to cut herself off from her friends. I'm wondering how long Johnny will tolerate bisexual Amber having a lesbian lover while she's involved with him.

Chapter 14

"I sat there snarling at him in that deeply expressive way that only teens possess, decompressing too fast back into reality..."

--Johnny Depp

Donnie Brasco (1997) starred Depp as Donnie Brasco/Joseph D. Pistone – storyline:

This drama about an undercover cop who learns the hidden dangers of working his way inside the mob was based on a true story. Joe Pistone (Johnny Depp) is an FBI agent who is given an assignment to infiltrate the Mafia; calling himself Donnie Brasco, he befriends Lefty Ruggiero (Al Pacino), a low-level mob hit man whose personal life is in tatters.

Lefty's romantic relationship is falling apart, his son is a junkie, and his health is failing, which only adds to his growing disillusionment about having spent 30 years with the Mafia (and killing 26 people) with little to show for it.

But in Donnie, Lefty sees someone who can succeed where he failed; he takes the young man under his wing, and under Lefty's tutelage Donnie quickly rises through the ranks of organized crime; however, the longer he plays the role of the gangster, the more Joe Pistone finds himself becoming Donnie Brasco in his increasingly rare off hours; it drives a wedge between himself and his wife (Anne Heche) and children, and Joe realizes that a break in character among the hoodlums he's come to know could mean a death sentence for himself and his family.

Just as importantly, Joe has come to regard Lefty as a close and trusted friend, and Joe realizes that when the day comes where he has to turn in his Mob associates, he'll be ending Lefty's life as surely as if he put a slug in his head himself. The supporting cast includes Michael Madsen as Sonny, Lefty's boss, and Bruno Kirby as Nicky, one of Sonny's henchmen. The real-life Joe Pistone today lives under an assumed name with a 500,000-dollar contract on his life still in effect (*rottentomatoes*).

JOHNNY DEPP'S LIFE BEHIND THE SCENES:

Further research on Depp's relationships reveals more about his BPD:

Johnny Depp & Vanessa Paradis' Constant 'Blazing Fights' May Have Ruined Their Relationship (S. Brown-Worsham, *Cafemom*, July 13, 2012):

Relationships can be a wonderful **slog fest** at times and I mean that in the best possible way. When we first meet and fall in love, it's all wine and roses and bliss and love, but a few years down the road and a few kids in the mix, and it changes. Suddenly that which was once endearing about your beloved becomes difficult and hard to take. We can often find ourselves **fighting the same old tired fight** again and again.

It turns out celebrity couples are no different. According to reports **Johnny Depp and Vanessa Paradis** didn't fall out of love after spending more than a decade together. **Instead, they got sick of fighting the same fight we all do.**

It seems career resentment and fights over who does more at home built and built until the two could no longer take it. We have all been there.

The fact is, most relationships have that one (or two or three) sticking point that just never stops nagging at us. No one is perfect and most of us can point to at least one thing our partner does that just sets our teeth on edge it is so annoying.

But fighting the same fight, the same way, year after year, is not only damaging to our psyches, it's also

damaging to the health of our relationships. We need to move past them.

But how do we do that? We have to change the record, therapists would say. **That means we try to find a way to see things from the other's perspective.**

In my own marriage, that means trying (and not always succeeding) to see how my husband feels instead of just how I feel when he comes home from a long day. Usually by that time, I have been alone with the kids for a couple hours while cooking dinner and putting out fires (both literal and figurative) and I need a break. Meanwhile he needs a break from the office and the commute.

It's hard and it doesn't always work and that isn't the only fight in our marriage. But with most marriages, if you can even knock out one regular fight, you can knock them all out.

No one wants to end up splitting over the dishes. But it can quickly become a rut. **It's up to us to fight that constantly, stay vigilant, and change the way we discuss our issues.**

How do you and your partner keep from fighting the same fights?

BPD ISSUES, SYMPTOMS & JOHNNY DEPP:

The writer of "**Johnny Depp & Vanessa Paradis' Constant 'Blazing Fights' May Have Ruined Their Relationship**" makes the mistaken assumption that all relationships are the same – "...**Instead, they got sick of fighting the same fight we all do.**"

The writer offers some common sense observation which is supposed to explain why Johnny Depp and Vanessa Paradis split: "**No one is perfect and most of us can point to at least one thing our partner does that just sets our teeth on edge it is so annoying.**"

Some of the advice is partly correct but comes from a vague understanding of the dynamics Depp sets in motion with his romantic partners. The writer suggests: "**That means we try to find a way to see things from the other's perspective.**"

First, my theory is that Johnny Depp is afflicted with BPD – Borderline Personality Disorder. BPD is a specific syndrome of signs, symptoms and predictable behavior. As I warned in the last chapter, Depp lacks perspective concerning his romantic partner's viewpoint – here's what I said:

Johnny causes unintended hurt: Depp, like other BPD people, fails to see how his romantic partners feel about him and how his behavior impacts them.

He gets so caught up in his emotional turmoil and distress, Johnny can't step back and see what pain, fear and hurt he's causing his lovers. He can't see his girlfriend's perspective and so that leads to the destruction of the relationship.

The writer offers a sort of catchphrase or therapy slogan as a solution: **"It's up to us to fight that constantly, stay vigilant, and change the way we discuss our issues."**

The problem with this "common sense" or "logical" advice is that it is not specific enough and it is not tied to a diagnostic evaluation of Depp. **Depp's BPD makes handling him a counter-intuitive, challenging and difficult task.** Here are some examples of behavior I'd expect from Johnny:

1) **Depp at the extremes – "splitting"** or relying on black-or-white thinking: He'll perceive his girlfriend as either an angel or a demon. She's all good one day and all bad the next – he may have no memory of a nasty, insulting outburst against her the day before.

2) **Silent treatment:** Johnny might use the silent treatment to abuse his partner – make her upset, angry or hurt. He is then refusing to communicate and will not tell what is bothering him or what the complaint may be. The problem he's mad about can be very minor and petty. The silent treatment used against someone who loves Johnny is very cruel – it can make them feel helpless, powerless, discounted, diminished and confused.

3) **Gaslighting:** Depp might use "gaslighting" which means providing false or distorted information with the intent of disrupting someone's ability to trust her own senses, reasoning ability and memory of events. It's named after the 1940 film *Gaslight* – which presents a character who manipulates a woman's home gas lights to try to make her feel like she's going insane.

There are other dirty tricks Johnny could be playing to drive his girlfriend crazy – I'll get into more BPD behavior later in this book. As a BPD person, Depp may not be acting consciously or intentionally to sadistically hurt his girlfriend. These negative behaviors may be his standard coping style.

How should Depp's girlfriend cope with his BPD-related negative qualities such as "splitting", using the silent treatment to punish her or even "gaslighting"?

1) **To combat verbal or non-verbal (e.g., silent treatment) abuse from a BPD guy** like Depp, his girlfriend or romantic partner should inhibit her own anger. If she expresses her anger – trades explosive outbursts – it will escalate the conflict.

2) **You (girlfriend/lover) should not argue** or try to reason.

3) **Don't fight back – but don't agree** that you deserve the abuse.

There are other techniques to cope but these are some examples. Later, don't accept apologies. Just tell him that he hurt you and you want him to minimize such incidents or behavior.

I know you want to kick him in the balls, throw things at him or scream back at him. You can try various ways to punish him or fight back and see what works if you don't want my advice.

Chapter 15

"I watched Rebel Without a Cause (1955), and I thought, 'Wow, this guy really has something', and I was hooked. I wasn't really into acting at the time - but James Dean was the catalyst."

--Johnny Depp

Fear and Loathing in Las Vegas (1998) presented Depp as the character Raoul Duke – storyline:

Terry Gilliam (Brazil, Twelve Monkeys, The Fisher King) directed this colorful, stylized, pseudo-psychedelic $21-million adaptation of the 1971 Hunter S. Thompson classic, Fear and Loathing in Las Vegas: A Savage Journey into the Heart of the American Dream, about stoned sportswriter Raoul Duke, Thompson's alter ego, on a wild drug-crazed road trip, a paranoid plummet into the belly of the beast, with his pal, lawyer Oscar Zeta Acosta.

Originally serialized in Rolling Stone (November 1971), the book catapulted Thompson headfirst toward the Kerouac-Mailer-Capote pantheon and jump-started the entire movement of "gonzo journalism." Carrying a suitcase of drugs, Raoul Duke (Johnny Depp with shaved pate) and his attorney Dr. Gonzo (Benicio Del Toro) drive a red convertible across the Mojave from L.A. to Vegas, where Duke has an assignment to cover the Mint 400 desert motorcycle race.

As the drugs kick in, Duke ventures into voiceover, filling in the blank spots and narrative gaps. "This is not a good town for psychedelic drugs," says Duke, but even so, they consume vast quantities, eventually escalating to ether. Duke notes that with ether "you can actually watch yourself behaving this terrible way, but you can't control it."

The two trash their hotel room, and Gonzo goes back to L.A. Thinking the hotel room holocaust will lead to an arrest, Duke begins a drive back to L.A., but after an odd encounter with a highway patrolman (Gary Busey) and a telephone conversation with Gonzo, he returns to Vegas to cover the District Attorney Convention on Narcotics and Dangerous Drugs in the glitzy Flamingo Hotel. This time the drugged-out duo trash their Flamingo room.

The crazed carnival atmosphere segues into a carney casino, Bazooko's Circus, where a barker (Penn Jillette) spiels amid aerialists, clowns, and a rotating carousel bar. Gonzo worries over runaway teen Lucy (Christina Ricci), who paints portraits of Barbra Streisand. Soon the hallucinations begin: Duke sees Gonzo transmogrify into a demon with breasts on its back, and an acid vision of a Vegas bar features large legit lounge lizards (courtesy of monster makeup man Rob Bottin). Flashbacks depicting Duke's intro to the drug scene jump back to love-Haight relationships in San Francisco's Summer of Love.

Cameos and guest stars include Mark Harmon, Cameron Diaz, Flea, Lyle Lovett, Harry Dean Stanton, Ellen Barkin, Tobey Maguire, and Hunter S. Thompson himself. The film features a Geffen Records soundtrack mixing rock of the period with Vegas lounge tunes.

Over the years, various script adaptations came and went as did numerous talents; people connected with past efforts to film Thompson's book include Martin Scorsese, Jack Nicholson, Dan Aykroyd, John Belushi, and writer-director Alex Cox. Shown in competition at the 1998 Cannes Film Festival (*rottentomatoes*).

JOHNNY DEPP'S LIFE BEHIND THE SCENES:

Kate Moss Admits Breakdown, 'Years of Crying' Over Johnny Depp (E. Koonse, *Christian Post*, Nov. 1, 2012):

Following her launch into stardom, supermodel Kate Moss has admitted to suffering an **emotional breakdown** in a recent interview.

...Moss also recalled her four-year relationship with actor Johnny Depp, as well as "years and years of crying" following their split.

The pair met when Moss was 20-years-old. **During their romance, Depp once trashed a New York City hotel room after reportedly having a fight with Moss. Despite their turbulent relationship, Moss said Depp offered her unprecedented stability.**

"There's nobody that's ever really been able to take care of me," said the model. "Johnny did for a bit. I believed what he said... and that's what I missed when I left."

Over the years Moss has earned a reputation for being a party girl, including the 2005 cocaine scandal. However, today she is married to Jamie Hince and is busy raising her 10-year-old daughter from a previous relationship, Lila Grace.

The Love Diary! Johnny Depp and Amber Heard's Secretly Serious Relationship (J. Boon, *RadarOnline*, April 29, 2013):

Johnny Depp and Amber Heard may have just gone public with their relationship, but the two have been secretly serious since his breakup with Vanessa Paradis, *RadarOnline* is exclusively reporting.

The pair, who was spotted holding hands at a secret Rolling Stones show in Los Angeles this past weekend, decided to keep their love under wraps out of respect for Johnny's former partner.

And since then, Johnny, 49, has been lavishing Amber, 27, with expensive gifts.

"Johnny and Amber began dating pretty soon after he split with Vanessa," a source close to the *Pirates of the Caribbean* star tells *Radar*.

"At first, Amber was a little apprehensive, because she didn't want to be seen as the mistress. But Johnny won her over with his generosity and he was constantly giving her gifts."

According to the insider, Johnny was determined to win Amber over — and it worked.

"On a weekly basis, Johnny would send her fresh flowers wherever she was. He also bought her tons of custom-designed jewelry that would cost him up tens of thousands of dollars," the source said.

"He made Amber feel giddy by showing how much he felt for her and, in the end, she slowly fell in love with him."

A second source confirms that the couple has managed to keep their romance under wraps, spending time together outside of Los Angeles.

"They were spending a significant amount of time together in San Diego in the fall and also at his home in the Bahamas, so they wouldn't have to deal with paparazzi and could keep their relationship for under wraps as long as possible," the source told *Radar*.

As *RadarOnline* previously reported, Johnny and Amber were spotted looking like loved-up teenagers back in November, 2012.

"They were flirty and engaged," an eyewitness who saw the pair at Hollywood's AV Nightclub in early November told Us Weekly.

A second source told the tabloid that at a Gucci party in October 2012, Amber was "telling people they were officially together."

As *RadarOnline* exclusively reported in July, the couple had briefly cooled off their romance, but can't seem to stay away from each other now.

"Johnny and Amber were definitely involved," a source confirms to Radar about the couple, who first met on the set of *The Rum Diary* when Johnny was still with Vanessa and Amber had just gone public in her lesbian relationship with photographer Tasya van Ree.

"They definitely had chemistry that carried over from the set. Amber quietly split from Tasya around the same time Johnny was secretly separated from Vanessa, so the timing was just right."

BPD ISSUES, SYMPTOMS & JOHNNY DEPP:

Depp picks women who will provide him with headaches and who are not appropriate as romantic partners. If she's pretty, sexy and stimulates him with some kind of chemistry, that's enough.

The fact that she's a crazy, active alcoholic-addict like Kate Moss or a bisexual with a lesbian girlfriend like Amber Heard doesn't matter to Depp. Then add Johnny's BPD syndrome to the equation of the relationship and the outlook is impossible.

He kind of falls for women like a teenage boy, falling hard and fast, showering them with expensive gifts and promising to help their careers.

Both Kate Moss and Amber Heard have broken-up with Johnny after fights, conflicts and stressful situations. **What are examples of Depp's BPD behavior that could have driven these women away?**

1) **Isolation tactics**: Depp might try to isolate his girlfriend from her friends or family. Or put down your friends and family. He may suffocate you. Does he cross-examine you about where you're going, with whom and how long you'll be gone?

2) **Emotional explosions**: He may fly into rages, act-out like a drama king, maybe he's addicted to danger and takes you on an emotional roller coaster. If you challenge his risky behavior, he may explode with anger.

3) **Demanding based on a sense of entitlement**: Particularly with a Hollywood movie superstar, one can expect an inflated sense of entitlement – he may demand special treatment and to be waited on. He is not aware of the impact of his demands on his romantic partner.

Chapter 16

"Kids write to me and say they are having these problems or they want to commit suicide or something. It's scary. I have to say, Listen, I'm just an actor, not a professional psychologist. If you need help, you should go and get it."

--Johnny Depp

The Source (1999) featured Johnny Depp as Jack Kerouac – storyline:

The Source is based on Jack Kerouac's legendary classic *On the Road*. Kerouac (Depp) was an icon of the Beat-hipster sensibility – he traveled around and wrote it up in *On the Road*.

Director Chuck Workman, who documented the life of pop culture icon Andy Warhol in his 1990 film Superstar, here explores the lives, works and influence of four leading lights of the "Beat Generation" of the 1950s: William S. Burroughs, Allen Ginsberg, Jack Kerouac and Neal Cassady.

Cutting back and forth between archive footage of his subjects, readings of selections from the three authors by Johnny Depp, Dennis Hopper and John Turturro (Cassady was an associate and inspiration to the Beats), and film clips that in both serious and farcical fashion document the impact the Beat culture had on American society, Workman creates a fast-paced collage of sounds and images that attempts to show how the Beats became the dominant counter-cultural movement of the last half of America's 20th Century (*rottentomatoes*).

JOHNNY DEPP'S LIFE BEHIND THE SCENES:

Johnny Depp finally talks about that big breakup (C. Goddard, *Sheknows*, June 18, 2013):

Johnny Depp Talks Split

Johnny Depp is finally breaking his silence over his split from Vanessa Paradis. What happened to the glamorous jet-setting couple?

Other than a brief confirmation over a year ago, Johnny Depp hasn't publicly spoken of his breakup from longtime love and baby mama Vanessa Paradis — until now.

The Lone Ranger star broke down the breakup and its aftermath in an interview with *Rolling Stone*.

"The last couple years have been a bit bumpy," Depp told the magazine. "At times, certainly unpleasant, but that's the nature of breakups, I guess, especially when there are kiddies involved."

"Relationships are very difficult. Especially in the racket that I'm in because you're constantly away or they're away and so it's hard. It wasn't easy on her. It wasn't easy on me. It wasn't easy on the kids. So, yeah..."

"**The trajectory of that relationship — you play it out until it goes, one thing leads to another," the 50-year-old actor explained. "So for whatever reason that - ceases**, it doesn't stop the fact that you care for that person, and they're the mother of your kids, and you'll always know each other, and you're always gonna be in each other's lives because of those kids. You might as well make the best of it."

Famous hookups reports:

Johnny Depp's Celebrity Relationships

Johnny Depp is currently dating Amber Heard. He has been in 10 celebrity relationships averaging approximately 3.1 years each. His only marriage lasted 2.2 years.

Marriages, Divorces, Affairs, Dating & Break ups

Name (Age)	Occupation	Latest Status	Rel. Length	Started	Ended
Amber Heard (27)	Actress	Dating	5.7 mos.	4/2013	Present
Amber Heard (27)	Actress	Broke Up	7.5 mos.	6/2012	1/2013
Vanessa Paradis (40)	Singer	Broke Up	14.1 yrs.	5/1998	6/2012
Kate Moss (39)	Model	Broken Engagement	4.2 yrs.	2/1994	4/1998
Holly Robinson Peete (49)	Actress	Broke Up	n/a	1990	1990
Jennifer Grey (53)	Actress	Broken Engagement	n/a	1990	1990
Winona Ryder (41)	Actress	Broken Engagement	3.3 yrs.	8/1989	1993
Sherilyn Fenn (48)	Actress	Broken Engagement	3 yrs.	1985	1988
Lori Anne Allison (56)	Other	Divorced	5 yrs.	3/1981	3/1986
Jennifer Lopez (44)	Singer	Hookup			

Johnny Depp's Dating History Is Pretty Impressive (L. Blickley, The Huffington Post, July 18, 2013):

Johnny Depp is one of the most handsome men in Hollywood -- and one of the most beloved.

And considering he's never gone a year without a lady on his arm, it's obvious he has no problem picking up women. (Well, *duh*).

Depp, 50, recently ended his 14-year relationship with Vanessa Paradis and has since reportedly been romancing 27-year-old Amber Heard. But let's not forget that he also dated some other stunning starlets, including Winona Ryder and Kate Moss.

Girl fight! Vanessa Paradis calls Amber Heard a "nobody" (M. Morris, *SheKnows,* July 11, 2012):

Vanessa Paradis Blames Amber Heard

Vanessa Paradis doesn't blame Johnny Depp for their breakup -- she blames Amber Heard. Read the "special message" Paradis allegedly gave to the sexy blonde actress.

Vanessa Paradis is reportedly none too pleased that her former love, Johnny Depp, is dating his blonde *Rum Diary* co-star Amber Heard. **The French pop singer, 39, blames Heard for the breakup, calling her a "man-stealing, two-bit nobody and has vowed to not let her anywhere near**

their children Lily-Rose [13] and Jack [10]," a source told the U.K. tabloid *Now*.

Isn't that how it works? Women end up blaming "the other woman" instead of the man. Hey Vanessa: It takes two to tango, you know. Plus, sources told *US Weekly* that Paradis and Depp had fiery rows in the final weeks of their relationship.

"Nothing Johnny did was ever good enough for Vanessa. When he was working, she wasn't happy. And when he wasn't working, he was called a slob for not doing enough for the kids and her family," the source said.

"They'd have blazing fights. Vanessa would take her frustrations out on him," the source continued, adding that **it influenced Depp to "drink heavily.**" Of course, no one in the **love triangle** is talking about anything, so we're left to speculate. One thing we do know for sure: Heard definitely likes Depp.

"I mean who isn't a fan of Johnny's? He's been a cultural icon and a talented actor since I can remember," Heard told *SheKnows* while promoting *Rum Diary*.

"I have such a strange job," she continued. "It puts me in the most interesting circumstances and I certainly wasn't complaining about this one. I'm in the middle of an Aaron Eckhart/Johnny Depp sandwich. I was just fine."

What do people think about the Vanessa-Amber girl fight?

Should Vanessa Paradis be upset with Amber Heard? Or, should her anger be directed toward her ex?

Comments on "Girl fight! Vanessa Paradis calls Amber Heard a 'nobody'":

Ha! She has a lot of nerve calling Amber a *nobody*...if Vanessa and Johnny had never met, Vanessa would surely be a *nobody*. She is 5'3" and perhaps average looking - her singing is mediocre at best. **It sucks to get dumped honey**, we've all been there. But you made out with a fat bank account in the end.

The writing has been on the wall for a long time with these two. Vanessa got pregnant within a month of hooking up with Depp when he was still embroiled with Kate Moss. I think he never resolved the Kate Moss relationship.

He was in lust with Vanessa's looks (as in she looks a lot like Kate Moss). Johnny has longed for a family since forever and boom he got it. Vanessa got pregnant with their second child almost immediately.

Now the kids are nearing and in their teens and what is left is the original couple, their foundation. Well Depp-Paradis never had one. There connection was the children, and that is really all there will ever be now between them. I saw this coming years ago!

Amber is special if she slept with Johnny Depp. He was only with Vanessa because she got pregnant. Amber is so womanly maybe he isn't into the boyish look anymore and wants a chubby girl for a change. He has so many addictions. I have an addiction to him since I want him for myself.

I blame Johnny. He never married Vanessa - I think she tolerated that to cover up for him and his career. As they got older, there was no turning back and he did whatever he wanted. I blame Mr. Depp. He got off too easily.

I don't see anything good coming out of this one. I say he lost some of his fans. And I think his international appeal will drop too. **Depp's your typical white trash, and he does look awful. He looked better when he was younger, he looks like a dirty old man with tattoos and dresses too young for his age - definitely a mid-life crisis.** Feeling sorry for his kids. They really lose.

It definitely does take two to tango! **But there should also be a mutual respect among women to not get involved with a taken man**, and unfortunately that isn't always upheld.

It is easy to get mad at the other woman because as women we know what they are capable of. And I'm sure she is just as mad at Depp too. It is disappointing.

I don't know who to blame but it seems to me **Vanessa first blamed Angeline Jolie now she is blaming Amber. Why isn't it Vanessa's fault they've been separated for two years and that is before Johnny met Amber.**

I also don't think she has the right to say who her children can meet because they are Johnny's children too and he has a right to say who they can see and can't see. He is their father. And as far as custody goes they should share them 50/50.

BPD ISSUES, SYMPTOMS & JOHNNY DEPP:

Johnny's "opening-up" about his relationship conflicts seems like nothing more than superficial, socially-acceptable excuses which he's used in the past to explain his break-ups. Depp claims:

1) "**The last couple years have been a bit bumpy**," Depp told the magazine. "At times, certainly unpleasant, but that's the nature of breakups, I guess, especially when there are kiddies involved."

2) "**Relationships are very difficult. Especially in the racket that I'm in because you're constantly away or they're away and so it's hard**. It wasn't easy on her. It wasn't easy on me. It wasn't easy on the kids.

3) "**The trajectory of that relationship — you play it out until it goes, one thing leads to another**," the 50-year-old actor explained. "So for whatever reason that - ceases, it doesn't stop the fact that you care for that person, and they're the mother of your kids, and you'll always know each other, and you're always gonna be in each other's lives because of those kids. You might as well make the best of it."

Compare Johnny's excuses for breaking-up with Vanessa with the deeper BPD-related behavior patterns I've been discussing. Amber has been ducking the "home-wrecker" bullet. Vanessa has jealously complained about Angelina Jolie and also Amber Heard – that these women have interfered with her relationship with Depp.

My best assessment is that Depp follows an unconscious-BPD pattern of unstable relationships. If you look at the table in this chapter, you can see woman after woman who have been on Johnny's relationship merry-go-round. He's already broken-up with Amber Heard at least once and is now in the second-round relationship with her.

Chapter 17

"I'd been in high school three years, and I may have just walked in yesterday. I had, like, eight credits. I was in my third year of high school and I didn't want to be there. I was bored out of my mind and I hated it."

--Johnny Depp

The Ninth Gate (1999) starred Johnny Depp as Dean Corso – storyline:

An authority on rare books is drawn into a confrontation with the forces of darkness in this thriller directed by Roman Polanski. Dean Corso (Johnny Depp) is a rare book broker who makes his living tracking down valuable items for rich bibliophiles.

Corso is hired by Boris Balkan (Frank Langella), a millionaire New Yorker with a vast collection of occult literature and a keen interest in "The Nine Gates to the Kingdom of Shadows." Legend has it that the book was co-written by Satan in the 17th century, and only three copies are known to exist; the owner of one recently sold the book to Balkan a few days before killing himself.

Balkan wants Corso to find the other two copies (one owned by a Mr. Fargas in Portugal and the other by a French collector named Kessler) and examine them to determine if they are forgeries. Corso is told to be thorough and spare no expense.

He begins by visiting Liana Telfer (Lena Olin), the widow of the man who once owned Balkan's copy of the book, who has an unusually strong desire to get the book back, and confers with his friend Bernie (James Russo), who soon turns up dead, in a manner much like an illustration from the book. Corso learns that the book contains clues to a puzzle that will allow people to call up the devil, and certain people will stop at nothing to find the missing parts of the formula (*rottentomatoes*).

JOHNNY DEPP'S LIFE BEHIND THE SCENES:

| JOHNNY DEPP DIAGNOSED: UNAUTHORIZED PSYCHOLOGICAL DIAGNOSIS OF HIS SECRET LIFE |

Keith Richards, cheating death, my fear of camera phones and Vanessa Paradis: A surreal evening with Johnny Depp (M. Palmer, Mail Online, Nov. 5, 2011):

At the recent GQ Men of the Year awards he presented an award to his good friend Keith Richards, but **spent most of the time in his own private room nursing an expensive bottle of wine.**

'I was all over the place and always the new kid at school, which is never easy,' said Johnny.

We walk through a lounge littered with six or seven guitars, books and computer equipment, and into a dining room heavy with abstract art and African sculptures, where Robinson is waiting for us. **A bottle of Château Haut-Brion 1996 (£364) and three glasses are on the table**. One of his assistants brings some sandwiches as Depp sits down at the table.

'At some point, it became more honest for me on set. I understand it – everything is defined. Here are the lights, here's the scene I have to do. It has become very natural, while the outside world has become unnatural. It's bizarre, because I've done interviews where there's a camera on and I still feel uncomfortable. Yet if it's a scene and I'm in character, then I'm not.'

Depp has always felt like a misfit. His Kentucky-based family relocated to Florida when he was seven, and subsequently moved houses over 20 times.

'**I was all over the place and always the new kid at school, which is never easy**,' he says.

'**If someone is being bullied or feels like an outsider and they relate to something that I've done, even if it's just igniting a spark, that's great. I had that feeling as a kid. I was messed with no end. And then you fight back – and that's the rage that's just under the surface, and in the end it comes out.**

On filming *Pirates*... with Richards, he says, '**I'd have my glass of wine** and he would have his usual. I've no idea what that is, because it looks like nuclear waste. We'd just hang out.

The actor and author first met in December 1994. There was an instant connection – two eccentric, kindred spirits who **bonded over a bottle of Chivas Regal.**

The clock is inching towards midnight, some four hours since **we began sampling the delights of Johnny Depp's fine wine cellar. As the empties stack up** and the ashtrays fill, the conversation becomes unpredictable, ranging from smoking (Depp blames Robinson for starting him smoking 'horrible little cigars' again after two years' abstinence) to **drinking** (**Robinson blames Depp,** or more specifically writing the script for *The Rum Diary*, **for causing him to fall off the wagon after six years of being teetotal**) to ghosts (Robinson has had the Dean of Hereford Cathedral perform two exorcisms on his 16th-century manor house).

'There's the wind and the sea, and you're thinking about nothing. On the island I can be at base level. **A little wine** and maybe a guitar. It's the best place.'

Respite from rage and the real world, with a **glass of Haut-Brion.**

BPD ISSUES, SYMPTOMS & JOHNNY DEPP:

I cut parts of the above interview with Depp that were irrelevant to BPD. Depp complained about being a misfit as a child and teenager because of the many moves his family made.

It could be argued that Johnny's fear of abandonment, unstable, stormy relationships and his precarious self-image could have partly resulted from his family turmoil and constant moving from place to place – which led to Depp ending up in many different schools and no stable peer group.

Woven throughout the interview were references to alcoholic drinks. In later interviews Johnny has claimed he's stopping or cutting down on drinking booze.

Signs and symptoms of BPD are reflected in his interview including:

1) Fear of abandonment.

2) Unstable relationships.

3) Poor self-image or sense of self.

4) Impulsive and self-destructive behavior such as substance abuse of alcohol and drugs.

Chapter 18

"On fame...They say, 'It's you!' But you don't know them. That's bad for an actor because the most important thing you can do is observe people. And now you can't because you're the one being observed."

--Johnny Depp

The Astronaut's Wife (1999) starred Depp as Commander Spencer Armacost – storyline:

Depp was cast as an astronaut who returns from a space mission to his wife Jillian (Charlize Theron) and is suspected of having carried back a dangerous extraterrestrial presence from space.

His astronaut partner appears to die from a questionable heart attack and his wife commits suicide. Jillian finds her husband has changed. He takes a corporate position in business. Jillian is surprised that her husband has become cold, strange, impenetrable and withdrawn.

Science fiction blends with domestic horror in this thriller. Spencer Armacost (Johnny Depp) is an astronaut on a routine mission in space when something goes horribly wrong and it looks as if he's doomed. However, Spencer is rescued at the last moment and returns to earth a hero. He soon announces that he's retiring from space exploration to spend more time with his wife Jillian (Charlize Theron).

Jillian has suffered from depression in the past and would like to start a family, so she's initially thrilled with Spencer's decision. Jillian soon finds herself pregnant, but she starts to notice something odd about her husband, as if the man who returned isn't quite the same person who went away.

As her pregnancy advances, Jillian's anxieties increase, but has something really happened to Spencer, or have Jillian's old demons merely resurfaced? The Astronaut's Wife marked the directorial debut of Rand Ravich, who previously penned screenplays for such films as The Maker and Candyman: Farewell to the Flesh (*rottentomatoes*).

JOHNNY DEPP'S LIFE BEHIND THE SCENES:

By 2010 Johnny Depp's had several more box office hits including *Alice in Wonderland* (over $1 billion worldwide) and another *Pirates of the Caribbean* sequel – the fourth installment subtitled *On Stranger Tides* (over $1 billion worldwide). Some of his other films did less well: *The Tourist* ($278 million worldwide) and *Rango*, an animated Western ($243 million worldwide). In 2012 came *Dark Shadows* – a new version of the classic Gothic soap opera *Dark Shadows*.

As *On Stranger Tides* hit theaters, Johnny reported for work on Tim Burton's new version of the classic Gothic soap opera *Dark Shadows*. Johnny plays the iconic vampire Barnabas Collins, leading an impressive ensemble that includes Eva Green, Michelle Pfeiffer, Helena Bonham Carter, Jackie Earle Haley, and Chloe Moretz. *Dark Shadows* appeared in theaters on May 11, 2012. The *Lone Ranger* was released in 2013 but was a disappointment at the box office.

Let's consider a French interview of Depp:

Le Musée Imaginaire de Johnny Depp (F. Ferney, France5 TV, Aug. 25, 2002):

FRÉDÉRIC FERNEY: [*reading the opening passage of* The Catcher in the Rye *by JD Salinger*] "If you really want to hear about it, the first thing you'll probably want to know is where I was born, what my lousy childhood was like, and how my parents were occupied and all before they had me, and all that *David Copperfield kind of crap.* But I don't feel like going into it, if you want to know the truth." All right. We're not going to dwell at length on that, but just give us a few landmarks about your family background and childhood years. Early years, say. Johnny.

JOHNNY DEPP DIAGNOSED: UNAUTHORIZED PSYCHOLOGICAL DIAGNOSIS OF HIS SECRET LIFE

JOHNNY: I'm from the bellybutton of nowhere, y'know? Which is a beautiful place to be from, in fact. Kentucky. My earliest memories are of my brother, in fact, who—we were very close when I was growing up, and he's a writer and has always been a writer. And from a very young age, even when I was doing horribly in school, my brother turned me on to great books and great writers and things like that, so . . . Yeah, well, I'm a gas station attendant who got lucky. That's what I am.

FRÉDÉRIC FERNEY: [*finishing the quote*] "No man's guilt is not yours, nor is any man's innocence a thing apart. Despise evil and ungodliness, but not men of ungodliness or evil. These, understand. Have no shame in being kindly and gentle, but if the time comes in the time of your life to kill, kill and have no regret. In the time of your life, live—so that in that wondrous time you shall not add to the misery and sorrow of the world, but shall smile to the infinite delight and mystery of it." William Saroyan.

JOHNNY: Fantastic! Unbelievable! Just . . . crazy. Beautiful. And perfect. And a kind of—for me, like a bible. A bible because, yeah: 'The time of your life'— which is tiny—live! And don't hold anything against others. But if someone comes in and you have to take care of it, you have to take care of it. Take 'em out.

FRÉDÉRIC FERNEY: Why Artaud? For many people, he was just a crazy poor bastard, who went crazy.

JOHNNY: Well, I think that's easy, y'know? I think that's easy for people to say—certainly now, but probably as easy in fact at that time to say—'Bah, he's just crazy, you know? Fucking leave him alone,' y'know? Artaud was, I think, a guy who cared probably too much for his own good and it landed him in the—as NICK eloquently puts—the bug house. The crazy house. But he wouldn't conform.

FRÉDÉRIC FERNEY: The loony bin.

JOHNNY: The loony bin.

FRÉDÉRIC FERNEY: Kerouac calls it 'the loony bin.'

JOHNNY: He wouldn't conform, you know? He wouldn't conform to what was expected of him. And he spilled everything out of his—like Nick says, to just open your rib cage and let it out. And that is freedom. He did it. And was called crazy and sick and whatever.

FRÉDÉRIC FERNEY: JOHNNY, what do you like in Antonin Artaud? Is it not the disgraced bastard; the loser?

JOHNNY: Not at all! That's the definition that he's been given; that he's been disgraced and everything. I *never* see Artaud as disgraced. *Ever*. Any more than I see Ed Wood—you know, the filmmaker that I played in the film *Ed Wood*—as disgraced. I don't see these people—certainly not Artaud—as disgraced. I see him as a winner.

FRÉDÉRIC FERNEY: Tell me about Basquiat.

JOHNNY: What I like about Basquiat was his sense of immediacy. He had a great respect for art, but in fact went so below that level. He just went for the immediate. His sense of immediacy. He just spewed onto the canvas what was in his brain at that moment. Whether it was a childish design, or a few words that he might have been obsessed with that day . . . And that— which in a way was a great 'Fuck you' to art at that point in the late '70s-early '80s—that I appreciate.

FRÉDÉRIC FERNEY: Do you think it's still meaningful now, today? Now? 20 years after?

JOHNNY: Very much so. As much or more than Warhol. Warhol's statement in the early '60s. Yeah. Definitely. Basquiat in a way was the Warhol of the '80s.

FRÉDÉRIC FERNEY: What did you like? The drawings? The poems? What did you like about Jean Cocteau?

JOHNNY: First of all, the drawings he made for the book *Opium* were . . . staggering, for me. Staggering. Because here was a guy who was writing about his cure, or coming off the drug, you know? Getting the bug off his back. He also had one of the greatest quotes that I think defined opium or opiates. He talks about a guy who says 'You really have to quit doing opium, you know,' and the guy says: 'Yeah, I know, I know.' Says: 'If you don't, you may as well jump off of a building.' He says: 'Yeah, I'll jump off a building and my body will arrive slowly, after I do.' [*smiling*] Really amazing. Perfect sense, y'know?

FRÉDÉRIC FERNEY: Tell me the one you feel the closest. Keaton?

JOHNNY: Keaton is for me—I'd like to quote NICK Tosches—"a great unsung hero," Buster Keaton. Everybody praises Charlie Chaplin; salutes Charlie Chaplin; gives him Oscars and awards up the ass, y'know? And Keaton walked away with essentially nothing, y'know? A drunk.

FRÉDÉRIC FERNEY: What do you think of France and the French? Anything to say about that? Do you like France?

JOHNNY: No . . . France for me, France has been the greatest gift for me, y'know? France has been very kind to me; it's been a very welcoming place for me. For me it's the first time in my life I've been able to in fact call a place 'home.' So, France gave me that.

BPD ISSUES, SYMPTOMS & JOHNNY DEPP:

The quotes that I've left from the French interview portray Depp's identification with artists who were often alcoholic-addicts, considered losers by society. I think the reason these people have meaning for Johnny is that he has BPD which involves instability in various parts of Depp's life such as:

1) **A lack of a cohesive identity or a poor and unstable self-image or sense of self.** Remember, Johnny's fragmented childhood and teen years resulted in him leading a bad boy lifestyle. Scrape off the Hollywood movie superstar trappings and his underlying psyche is still haunted by his childhood family life which was dysfunctional, unstable, angry, explosive and unpredictable.

2) **Depp's pattern of intense, hot-tempered, capricious, fickle romantic relationships.** He's been married, engaged to or seriously involved with over a dozen women – all his romantic partners break-up with Johnny. His pattern is to go from "love at first sight", clinging to the woman, getting engaged, and then breaking-up with her several times until the final split.

3) **Impulsive behavior which is self-destructive** such as substance abuse of alcohol and drugs. He's also engaged in self-mutilation, cutting himself out of anger,

guilt or a chronic sense of boredom and feelings of emptiness.

Chapter 19

"If you love two people at the same time, choose the second. Because if you really loved the first one, you wouldn't have fallen for the second..."

--Johnny Depp

Sleepy Hollow (1999) starred Depp as Constable Ichabod Crane – storyline:

Depp played Ichabod Crane as a well-intentioned but kind of pathetic man committed as an intellectual – but now out of his league in a space of passionate action.

Washington Irving's tale of Ichabod Crane and the Headless Horseman gets a few new twists in a screen adaptation directed by Tim Burton. In this version, Ichabod (Johnny Depp) is a New York City detective whose unorthodox techniques and penchant for gadgets make him unpopular with is colleagues.

He is sent to the remote town of Sleepy Hollow to investigate a series of bizarre murders, in which a number of people have been found dead in the woods, with their heads cut off. Local legend has it that a Hessian ghost rides through the woods on horseback, lopping off the heads of the unsuspecting and unbelieving.

Ichabod refuses to believe in this legend, convinced that there must be a logical explanation for the murders. In time, Ichabod becomes smitten with a local lass, Katrina Van Tassel (Christina Ricci), who is the sweetheart of the burly Brom Bones (Casper Van Dien), and he becomes determined to capture the murderer to prove his bravery and win her heart.

Christopher Walken, Jeffrey Jones, and Christopher Lee highlight the supporting cast; Lee's appearance is particularly apt, since Burton has cited the Hammer films of the 1960s as a major influence in making this film. Andrew Kevin Walker and Tom Stoppard contributed to the screenplay (*rottentomatoes*).

JOHNNY DEPP'S LIFE BEHIND THE SCENES:

Once a troublemaker, Johnny Depp of *21 Jump Street* is now admired for his cool and his part in a series about teen problems. (E. Warren, TV Guide, Jan. 23, 1988):

It comes from years of real-life experience. Depp, 24, grew up in Miramar, Fla., where he wasn't exactly on the road to becoming a National Merit scholar. **"I hung around with bad crowds," he admits.**

"We used to break and enter places. We'd break into the school and destroy a room or something. I used to steal things from stores." And, like some of the kids Officer Tom Hanson has busted on *21 Jump Street*, **Depp was into drugs.** "Pretty much any drug you can name," he says, "I've done it." At 13 he lost his virginity, and at 16 he dropped out of high school.

Fast-forward eight years to Vancouver, where *Jump Street* is shot. **Depp has acquired a taste for $80-a-shot cognac** and is a fan-magazine star, routinely mobbed by adoring teen-age girls.

How cool is Johnny Depp? **He's so cool that he orders a $75 bottle of wine without blinking** as he sits down in his favorite Italian restaurant (weird white rag still around his head) to explain how he got that way.

Back in blue-collar Miramar, where **Depp's father was director of public works and his mother was a waitress, Johnny and Sal were into drugs, girls, petty crime and, most of all, music. Music was how they kept the faith within their isolated teen-age world of angry parents and threatening teachers.**

He also got married, got divorced and met actor Nicolas Cage, a former boyfriend of his wife, who told him he ought to try acting.

After a few glasses of wine, though, Depp will tell you that when he decided to bend to the demands of television, he never thought the show would be as successful as it is, holding the possibility of a long commitment.

BPD ISSUES, SYMPTOMS & JOHNNY DEPP:

I've included parts of the above interview which seemed relevant to Depp's BPD. From the information we can see some BPD symptoms such as:

1) **Self-destructive, impulsive behavior**: Substance abuse (alcohol, mood-altering drugs), petty crime, breaking and entering & vandalism, theft, reckless behavior.

2) **Unstable relationships**: Depp was married at 20 and divorced within a couple years. He's had a long series of intense relationships, fighting, broken engagements, break-ups, hook-ups, make-ups and intense endings.

3) **Insecure, volatile, unbalanced self-identity:** Johnny hung-out with a "bad crowd" in his teen years and has struggled with his identity over the years.

Chapter 20

"You can never, ever understand fully what a woman's life might be like until you step into her shoes. The same thing goes for transvestites."

--Johnny Depp

The Man Who Cried (2000) featured Johnny Depp as Cesar – storyline:

In this historical drama with music, a gifted singer (Oleg Yankovsky) from a Jewish village in Russia travels to the United States in 1927, leaving behind his young daughter Fegele (Claudia Lander-Duke).

Father has promised his family that he'll send for Fegele as soon as he can, but authorities make life hard for the Jewish population, and Fegele is forced to flee with relatives to England. Fegele is adopted by a British family, which renames her Suzie and raises her with little acknowledgement of her ethnic heritage.

As she grows to adulthood, Suzie (Christina Ricci) becomes a gifted vocalist and gets a job singing in a nightclub revue in Paris. Before she leaves England, her adopted family presents Suzie with a picture of her father, still believed to be living in America, and she decides she will go to the United States someday and find him.

In Paris, Suzie makes friends with Lola (Cate Blanchett), a Russian showgirl in the market for a rich husband. Lola becomes involved with opera star Dante Dominio (John Turturro), and soon both Lola and Suzie are extras in Dominio's company, managed by Felix Perlman (Harry Dean Stanton).

As Lola takes up with Dante, Suzie falls for Cesar (Johnny Depp), a poor but handsome gypsy horse trainer. Suzie soon becomes involved with the handsome Cesar, but their happiness proves to be short-lived when the Nazi war machine begins to roll through France. The Man Who Cried was written and directed by Sally Potter, who previously won acclaim for another unusual historical piece (*rottentomatoes*).

JOHNNY DEPP'S LIFE BEHIND THE SCENES:

JOHNNY DEPP DIAGNOSED: UNAUTHORIZED PSYCHOLOGICAL DIAGNOSIS OF HIS SECRET LIFE

I chopped out the star-struck, movie-star worshipping comments made by the writer of the following article. What's left seems to apply to BPD:

Johnny Depp: 'I'm not ready to give up my American citizenship' (D. Aitkenhead, The Guardian, Nov. 6, 2011):

He loathes the media, once threatened the paparazzi with a plank, and at one memorable Cannes film festival cancelled all his interviews and refused to get out of bed.

Smoking is a useful metaphor for **Depp's self-image** – renegade, European, rough around the edges.

"I just said: 'Come on, give me a bang.' Bruce and I were in the plane, and I just said: 'Oh come on.' You know, **we'd had a bit to drink** – and ..."

"The commercial flight thing, it just gets a little weird when you're standing in line and suddenly you're not just a guy standing in line any more, **you become sort of novelty boy**."

Ever since Depp became a teen idol in the 80s TV series 21 Jump Street, the star has been **at war with his own fame**... **Depp spent most of the 80s and 90s getting very drunk**, going out with Kate Moss and Winona Ryder, **brawling with photographers and generating more of the very publicity he found so oppressive**.

"...But I still had paparazzi chasing my tail, so it was the weirdest thing in the world. Everywhere you went you were on display. It was always some kind of strange attack on the senses; I was never able to embrace it. **So self-medication," meaning drink and drugs, "was just to be able to deal with it."**

The couple (Depp & Paradis) retreated behind the walls of homes in Paris, the Bahamas and the south of France...devoted themselves to a private family life...**The only snag is "I just don't go out. I just don't go anywhere. Just don't leave home**."

It's a strange profession where the prize for success is house arrest, isn't it? "But there is a trade-off, as with anything. Somebody's always going to bring you the bill. The invoice comes." And the bill is his liberty.

"...I mean, it's **not like I was ever looking to become franchise boy**, I was never looking to become anything like that. I just latched on to a character I loved."

Depp is a famous enthusiast, with great taste – **he loves hard liquor, good wine** and rock guitar. But then, so do a lot of the men in my local bar in Hackney.

"You know, at my very core **I'm pretty shy**. I just happen to have a weird job."

BPD ISSUES, SYMPTOMS & JOHNNY DEPP:

Consider the parts I put in bold related to BPD:

1) **Volatile, impulsive behavior**: "Johnny be bad" – he abuses alcohol & drugs to "self-medicate" and escape his terrible rich & famous lifestyle; fighting, brawling with photographers for taking his picture.

2) **On-the-edge emotions**: Ego-maniac rages combined with a bit of paranoia. Crazy mood swings.

3) **Insecure, wobbly relationships**: Endless pretty girls jumping on and off Depp's love 'em and leave 'em merry-go-round – "love at first sight," instantly engaged to be married, knock-down drag-out screaming fights, break-ups, make-ups and the final dump…and the cycle continues.

4) **Unhinged, erratic self-image or self-identity**: Who's the "real Johnny"? Novelty boy? Franchise boy? Dark, quirky and arty boy? Shy boy? Raging, insane party monster boy? Angry criminal assaulting photographers? Druggie? Drunk? James Dean juvenile delinquent?

Chapter 21

"I am doing things that are true to me. The only thing I have a problem with is being labeled."

--Johnny Depp

Before Night Falls (2000) featured Depp as Bon Bon/Lieutenant Victor – storyline:

For his sophomore feature film effort, visual artist Julian Schnabel chronicles the life of one of Cuba's most charismatic literary voices, the late Reinaldo Arenas.

Working with Arenas' friends and family, Schnabel recounts the author's impoverished rural upbringing and the intense love and support he receives from his mother (played by the director's wife, Olatz Lopez Garmendia).

As a young man, Arenas (Javier Bardem) is singled out by his teachers and encouraged to further his skills as a writer -- no easy task, considering the Castro regime's censorship of any work considered to be subversive or anti-authoritarian. Still, the author manages to smuggle his work out of the country through friends, who arrange for one of his novels to be published in France.

Not only persecuted for his creative beliefs, the openly gay Arenas is jailed on a bogus sex charge; he escapes internment only to be captured and persecuted later for his contraband dispatches. In 1980, Arenas is finally allowed to leave Cuba for the United States, where he achieves freedom of expression but not prosperity.

Schnabel's first film was another portrait of an artist, 1996's Basquiat; Bardem made his name in several of director Pedro Almodovar's Spanish-language productions.

Before Night Falls premiered at the 2000 Venice Film Festival, where it received the Best Actor and Grand Special Jury prizes, and made its North American premiere at the Toronto International Film Festival.

Bardem would go on to receive a host of accolades, including an eventual Best Actor nomination at the 2001 Academy Awards (*rottentomatoes*).

JOHNNY DEPP'S LIFE BEHIND THE SCENES:

I've deleted parts of the following interview – parts included may give some clues to Depp's BPD symptoms:

Johnny Depp, Tim Burton: Men of the *Shadows* (S. Bowles, *USA Today*, May 11, 2012):

Depp, who has played Willy Wonka, Ichabod Crane and the Mad Hatter for Burton, sees Collins as a continuation of a theme from which the two have yet to stray: **celebrating the rebel.**

"We relate to characters who are a little off," Depp says. "People who don't feel like they fit in anywhere. I think that's why we work well together."

Though he had found stardom as the undercover high school cop in Fox's *21 Jump Street*, **Depp loathed the pinup popularity** and wanted to make the jump to movies.

Even Depp's iconic Jack Sparrow is an **androgynous** swashbuckler that gave Disney second thoughts. (**Depp once teased an exec to relax, that all his characters are gay**.)

"There's an absolute shorthand," Depp says. "Probably because neither of us can string a coherent sentence together."

That **social discomfort** made them simpatico co-workers—and spawned *Shadows*.

"There's reason for that," Depp says. **"I don't think we could finish a coherent thought without help from each other."**

BPD ISSUES, SYMPTOMS & JOHNNY DEPP:

The above interview sort of relates to Depp's unstable self-image, his changeable self-identity. This is a symptom of BPD. He claims to have social discomfort in speaking – Depp identifies with the director, Burton: "Probably because neither of us can string a coherent sentence together."

Johnny played some characters with an androgynous or gay foundation. He identifies with James Dean's style – the stammering, mixed-up adolescent, quirky, androgynous guy stuck in an identity crisis.

I've known actors who consciously or unconsciously get into the shy, mumbling, stammering, confusing way of speaking to mimic Marlon Brando or James Dean which is what Depp seems to do. Except Johnny really has an unstable identity so he doesn't have to fake it.

What are some other BPD behavior patterns seem to fit Depp?

1) **Acting impulsively**: Johnny has either reduced his self-destructive, impulsive and outrageous episodes or maybe his P.R./press agents are better at covering-up his current bad behavior. Depp has had a track record of impulsive, reckless, impetuous behavior from his teenage years and older. From self-mutilation, cutting himself to alcohol-drug abuse, breaking and entering, vandalism, theft, trashing hotel rooms, assaulting people and knock-down-drag-out-screaming fights with his girlfriends. He's recently struggled with alcohol although he's minimized it. Depp continues to have fights, break-ups with his girlfriends.

2) **Feeling rejected and abandoned** – relationship problems: Johnny bounces from feeling abandoned and rejected to withdrawing when he gets close to a woman because he fears engulfment or having his personal boundaries compromised. Depp's see-saw, yo-yo behavior with women stresses them out and sooner or later they fight, break-up, make-up, then finally split in an explosion of disgust.

3) **Misinterpreting threats to his self-esteem**: Because Depp has a rickety, volatile, unbalanced and unstable self-identity or self-concept, he's vulnerable and his self-esteem can easily crash over the most minor bumps and bruises to his ego. A comment or behavior can be distorted in his mind and shatter his self-esteem, throw his self-image for a loop and

unhinge his self-concept. Out of his paranoid perceptions Johnny is motivated to get into verbal abuse, fights, assaulting people, getting intoxicated on booze or loaded on drugs.

Chapter 22

"With every part you act, there must be a little of yourself in it. If there isn't, it's not acting. It's lying."
— Johnny Depp

Chocolat (2000) featured Depp as Roux – storyline:

The most tempting of all sweets becomes the key weapon in a battle of sensual pleasure versus disciplined self-denial in this comedy. In 1959, a mysterious woman named Vianne (Juliette Binoche) moves with her young daughter into a small French village, where much of the community's activities are dominated by the local Catholic Church.

A few days after settling into town, Vianne opens up a confectionery shop across the street from the house of worship

-- shortly after the beginning of Lent. While the townspeople are supposed to be abstaining from worldly pleasures, Vianne tempts them with unusual and delicious chocolate creations, using her expert touch to create just the right candy to break down each customer's resistance.

With every passing day, more and more of Vianne's neighbors are succumbing to her sinfully delicious treats, but the Comte de Reynaud (Alfred Molina), the town's mayor, is not the least bit amused; he is eager to see Vianne run out of town before she leads the town into a deeper level of temptation.

Vianne, however, is not to be swayed, and with the help of another new arrival in town, a handsome Irish Gypsy named Roux (Johnny Depp), she plans a "Grand Festival of Chocolate," to be held on Easter Sunday. Based on the novel by Joanne Harris, Chocolat features a distinguished supporting cast, including Judi Dench, Lena Olin, Carrie-Anne Moss, Peter Stormare, Hugh O'Conor, and Leslie Caron (*rottentomatoes*).

JOHNNY DEPP'S LIFE BEHIND THE SCENES:

Johnny Depp laments fan sites for daughter (R.V. Nepales, *Philippine Daily Inquirer*, May 10, 2012):

LOS ANGELES—In our recent interview with Johnny Depp, he **lamented fan sites or pages devoted to Lily-Rose Melody Depp—his daughter** with singer-actress Vanessa Paradis.

"It's an odd thing when you get to this point where your daughter, who is not even 13, and yet there's a fan page for her," the actor said...**She just happens to be our kid but there's already a fan page and a fan site for her. She certainly finds it weird. I find it bizarre and somewhat ugly**."

He and Vanessa are rumored to have split.

"My son Jack is now 10 and Lily-Rose will be 13 at the end of this month," he said. "It's interesting because for a long time I tried to manage . . . **I practice honesty and openness about my personal life because I'm human and I'm normal.**" Johnny paused, smiled and quipped, "That was questionable but semi-normal."

Then he added: "These days, **my kids have access to the Internet. They are able to read truths, lies, fiction and rumors.** This whole thing has become this mulch of fodder. I've decided to just stay hush-hush about anything and everything. If the rumors spin, let the rumors spin."

Johnny disclosed that he talked to Jack and Lily-Rose about the split rumors: **"I had to sit my kids down. I said, 'Look, this is part of an occupational hazard for me and your mom. It's out of our hands so don't believe a word.** Certainly, don't go looking for it.'"

He recalled: "Stephen Cannell (God rest his soul), Patrick Hasburgh, Steve Beers, Joan Carson, Bill Nuss, **all these** great producers, writers and people at Fox Network put up with me during those early days when I was essentially trying to be fired."

Asked why, Johnny explained: "**Because I felt like I was, on some level, imprisoned creatively. There was no way to deviate when you were stuck in a box** . . . It was a very confusing time for me. **I definitely thought that was the end of the line. I was waiting to be fired.** They wouldn't do it. Then one thing led to another but I was well prepared to go back to pumping gas at that point, for sure."

BPD ISSUES, SYMPTOMS & JOHNNY DEPP:

What Johnny, as a BPD victim, does not get is the impact he has on other people. People have cut him slack because he's a movie superstar making tens of millions of dollars yearly. But let's not humor Depp.

Good parents are concerned about their children. And Borderline Personality Disordered people even more so – unfortunately, because BPDs go to extremes. BPD people will get into lies, rumors, accusations and distortion campaigns. Some will falsely accuse others of harassment and abuse.

Depp has always had a tendency to have zero gratitude for his luck and talent which led to tremendous success as a film actor. A million actors would have killed to get a starring role on *21 Jump Street* – but Depp moans, groans and whines that he wants to be a big movie star instead of a TV star.

Here's a guy who was stealing from grocery stores to get food and starving as a struggling musician. He starts making $45,000 a week in his mid-twenties as a star of *21 Jump Street* and he complains about it like he's in jail.

He ran like hell to be a rock star or a movie/TV star and part of the package is media attention. Depp makes it on TV and in the movies. Then he complains about his success, he claims he doesn't like attention, wants more privacy and more artistic films.

His kids must have been aware that Depp and Paradis, their parents, were constantly bickering, fighting, driving each other crazy and that Johnny was bored out of his mind – which is how Depp described living with Paradis.

So what does Johnny do? He lies to his kids and tells them the media/internet rumors about a split with Paradis is are lies, false rumors and media nonsense. Then Depp and Paradis split up.

Johnny has gotten sort of paranoid about photographers taking shots of him and his family. He distorts their intention and goes on a crazy campaign against photographers – even tracking some down and threatening them with harm. He's threatened legal action without legitimate cause.

Depp over-reacts, catastrophizes when he's threatened with abandonment or rejection when a relationship with a woman breaks up. We all experience feelings of loss, rejection and abandonment when relationships end. But BPDs – borderlines – go to extremes in these threatening situations and resort to distortion campaigns, lying, making up false rumors and accusations.

So when Depp is stressed-out, for example, he may fight losing his identity as a good family man. In breaking-up with Paradis he overplays, exaggerates the consequences – he feels empty, insignificant, helpless and even unable to survive despite having over $350 million in assets.

Over the years when Johnny has broken-up with various women who initially were the "love of his life," he gets into the shame and blame game. His feelings of abandonment and rejection turn into more feelings of inadequacy, failure, shame and humiliation. This leads to intense endings or frequent break-ups with women he's in romantic relationships with.

Chapter 23

"You can close your eyes to the things you don't want to see but how can you close your heart to the things you don't want to feel?"
— Johnny Depp

Blow (2001) starred Depp as George Jung – storyline:

Following the life of cocaine-trafficking pioneer George Jung in a way that recalls Martin Scorsese's Casino, Blow recounts the man's days from his 1950s childhood in Boston to his downfall in the 1980s.

George (played by Johnny Depp) begins his life as the son of Fred (Ray Liotta), an earnest breadwinner, and Ermine (Rachel Griffiths), who frequently walks out on them in pursuit of a more fulfilling life.

When George moves west to California in the late '60s, accompanied by best pal Tuna (Ethan Suplee), he becomes an entrepreneur in the marijuana business, which soon spreads to the East Coast as well, with girlfriend Barbara (Franka Potente) smuggling the product during her stewardess shifts.

George is arrested in 1972 -- at which time Barbara dies of cancer -- but George finds a new ally in Diego (Jordi Molla), who proposes the idea that he become the American conduit for Colombian kingpin Pablo Escobar (Cliff Curtis). George flourishes in the heyday of the disco era, and falls for Mirtha (Penelope Cruz), a self-serving bombshell who eventually has a daughter with him.

Trouble escalates as the FBI threatens to bring George and his crew down, while he desperately tries to be a stable parent to his young offspring. Blow also features Paul Reubens and Max Perlich in featured roles (*rottentomatoes*).

JOHNNY DEPP'S LIFE BEHIND THE SCENES:

Johnny Depp, Vanessa Paradis Split: Actor Was 'Bored Senseless' (The Huffington Post, June 21, 2012):

After months of speculation, **Johnny Depp finally confirmed that he and longtime partner Vanessa Paradis had separated**, and according to *RadarOnline* the reason for their split is absolutely heartbreaking.

The website reports that Depp had become "bored senseless" with his 14-year relationship, which produced two children, and had been **wanting to end the relationship since last year.**

"Johnny didn't want to be with Vanessa anymore. They had **grown so far apart**, and he wanted to be free and **try new things**," a source told *RadarOnline*. "**He was bored senseless with her, being with Vanessa was making him miserable.**"

According to the source, the notoriously quirky and adventurous actor felt the **spark between the two of them was gone**, and Depp just "**wants more from life and believes Vanessa deserves to be happier too.**"

The actor's rep confirmed to *Entertainment Tonight* on Tuesday that the couple had "**amicably separated**," and *Radar*'s source confirms there were no other parties involved in the decision.

"**Depp is not embroiled in some hot and heavy new romance** and **he has no plans to jump straight into something** straight away, but he is keen to have some fun again," admitted the source, who added that Depp is so relieved they've made the separation public, as "it was difficult for him to carry on a farce."

Breakup rumors started making the rounds this spring, and when Depp arrived at the London premiere of "Dark Shadows" solo, the 49-year-old actor was still **denying his relationship was on the rocks.**

"**The rumors are not true. They are absolutely not true**," Depp said in a red carpet interview according to the U.K.'s *The Sun*. "**No matter what I say about this, people believe the opposite ... I can't say enough about it not being over**."

A source close to the couple also revealed in May that Depp and Paradis were **trying to keep their relationship together**, telling *E! Online*, "For the first time in a long time, he is talking about her ... **They both want to make it work**."

The pair met in the late '90s and Paradis told *People* magazine in 2008 that it wasn't exactly love at first sight:

"We were in two different worlds – him in America, me in France – but we had friends in common," the French singer, model and actress explained. "**We saw each other sometimes over the course of four years**. But then, the day **we found each other in Paris**, we were both in the same world and free and **it was just instant**. There was no more time to waste – just no way around it."

BPD ISSUES, SYMPTOMS & JOHNNY DEPP:

What are the predictable stages when one is in a relationship with a BPD person such as Johnny Depp? Some BPD researchers have presented theories of relationship stages (Mason, Kreger). The longer the relationship, the longer the stages which may shift back and forth:

1) **Confusion stage**: Normal or Non-BPDs will be confused at first – not understanding the reason for their BPD romantic partner's strange behavior which brings chaos. Non-BPDs (e.g., Paradis) may blame herself or resign herself to living in anarchy or pandemonium created by her BPD lover (e.g., Depp). She'll finally get it on an intellectual level and then finally on an emotional level which is when they break-up. How many years of Depp's chaos, chronic emptiness and boredom, scrapes or fights in bars and with photographers and drunken bickering would she endure before splitting or kicking Johnny out?

2) **Outer-directed stage**: Non-BPDs (e.g., Kate Moss) focus on the BPD person (e.g., Depp); she/he may urge the BPD victim to get help from a psychotherapist to get him to change. She'll try not to trigger his madness or problematic behavior. The Non-BPD may try to learn more about BPD to empathize with their lover. The Non-BPD or "normal" person may then come to grips with her anger or experience depression, hopelessness and guilt. They may give up the fantasy that the BPD will act normally and let the BPD individual take responsibility for their actions. In the case of Kate Moss – a party-crazed alcoholic-addict – how long and how many incidents of screaming fights did she tolerate before blowing Johnny Depp off?

3) **Inner-directed stage**: Sooner or later the Non-BPD (e.g., Amber Heard), looks inside herself and evaluates her part in the relationship bedlam, turmoil and confusion mainly caused by the BPD (e.g., Depp). She will be seeking insight and self-discovery and not self-recrimination. Does Amber want to simultaneously battle on as a mixed-up bisexual or lipstick lesbian with her lesbian girlfriend on the side while juggling a high-maintenance movie superstar (Depp) who demands to be number one? How many sacrifices to make Johnny happy will Amber tolerate to hopefully help or stimulate her career before they break-up for the 2nd or 3rd or 4th or 5th time?

4) **Decision-making stage**: Once the Non-BPD (e.g., Jennifer Grey) is armed with knowledge and insight about their BPD (e.g., Depp) lover, then she must consider her values and determine if it is worth slogging on with a sick romantic partner or ending it. Is it worth putting up with the disarray, muddle or disaster that living with a BPD involves?

5) **Resolution phase**: In this final stage, Non-BPDs (e.g., Sherilyn Fenn) take action and make decisions about what to do about their BPD (e.g., Depp) partner – either see that he gets help or end it if his unruliness and chaos continues. How many fights, screaming matches or nutty situations can she handle?

Chapter 24

"I don't care. I'm just gonna smoke. I'm just gonna totally smoke. I'll finish these, go to the store and get a brand new pack, smoke the shit out of that one."
— Johnny Depp

From Hell (2001) cast Depp as Inspector Fred Abberline – storyline:

The true-life horror story of *Jack the Ripper* gets a new spin in this screen adaptation of the acclaimed graphic novel by Alan Moore and Eddie Campbell.

In 1888, a ruthless and cold-blooded killer begins hunting prostitutes in East London, and while the murderer's work is savage, the mutilation of his victims suggests the fiend has an extensive medical background.

Amidst a background of political unrest and barely contained scandal among the royal family, the murderer's grisly exploits shock and frighten all of England, and one of Scotland Yard's top inspectors, Fred Abberline (Johnny Depp), is put on the case, along with his partner, Peter Godley (Robbie Coltrane).

Abberline, depending on one's viewpoint, is either blessed or cursed with second sight, and while he blurs his ability to see future events with opium and other drugs, he still has an uncanny ability to ferret out dangerous criminals, which is put to the test as he and Godley search for the Ripper.

As Abberline and Godley investigate the neighborhood where the crimes occur, they become acquainted with the prostitutes and street people who were friends and compatriots of the victims, and Abberline finds himself falling in love with Mary Kelly (Heather Graham), a beautiful Irish streetwalker.

As Abberline tries to identify the killer before Mary Kelly can become the next victim, he and Godley have to contend with Sir Charles Warren (Ian Richardson), their superior who is keen to pin the murders on a culprit who isn't British, and Sir William Gull (Ian Holm), a respected physician who has his own ideas about the murders and the benefits of psychosurgery.

From Hell marked a change of pace for Albert Hughes and Allen Hughes, the sibling directorial team best known for their gritty depictions of America's urban underground in such films as *Menace II Society* and *Dead Presidents* (*rottentomatoes*).

JOHNNY DEPP'S LIFE BEHIND THE SCENES:

I've highlighted and kept parts of the following *Vanity Fair* interview which most applied to BPD:

The Crowded Mind of Johnny Depp (P. Smith, *Vanity Fair*, Jan. 2011)

Captain Jack Sparrow, Willy Wonka, the Mad Hatter, Edward Scissorhands, the Earl of Rochester . . . How many characters can Johnny Depp keep inside himself? ...Friend and rock legend Patti Smith finds him on set, guitar in hand, for a free-floating tour of the inner Depp.

...Johnny himself is in fact very likable, his magnetic energy infused with a **certain shyness**.

Johnny is down to earth, **yet also seems to operate in another universe**. Time is precious—but also worthless. He has a bit of the **Godfather** in him—and also a **bit of the bum**. He is as **rebellious as Rochester**, as loving as the Hatter, and as **ill-behaved as Jack Sparrow**...He is also **intensely loyal**.

Smith: How connected are you with music?

Depp: It's still my first love as much as it ever was, since I was a little kid and first picked up a guitar and tried to figure out how to make the thing go. **Going into acting was an odd deviation from a particular road that I was on in my late teens, early 20s, because I had no desire, no interest, really, in it at all.** I was a musician and I was a guitarist, and that's what I wanted to do.

The weird thing is I think I approach my work the same way I approached guitar playing—**looking at a character like a song.** ….It's the same kind of thing that's required here, with acting: What was the author's intent? What can I add to it that maybe someone else won't add to it?

How do you feel when you enter into the skin of Captain Jack?

Free—free to be irreverent. **I think it's like unlocking a part of yourself and freeing this part of yourself to just be— what do they call it?—the id**, or whatever, just to *be* . . . just to *be*, under whatever circumstances…Captain Jack was kind of like that for me, an opening up of this part of yourself that is somewhat—you know, there is a little Bugs Bunny in all of us.

Angelina…I was so pleased to find that she is incredibly normal, and has a wonderfully kind of dark, perverse sense of humor.

And because here we are working together in this situation where you could really—there are times when you see how ridiculous is this life, **how ludicrous it is, you know, leaving your house every morning and being followed by paparazzi, or having to hide, sometimes not even being able to talk to each other in public because someone will take a photograph** and it will be misconstrued and turned into some other shit.

Something I've always wondered about is: these people that you become for us, or make flesh in a film—do they revisit you ever? Are you able to discard them? What happens to them?

They're all still there, which on some level can't be the healthiest thing in the world. But, no, they're all still there. I always picture it as this chest of drawers in your body—Ed Wood is in one, the Hatter is in another, Scissorhands is in another. They stick with you. Hunter is certainly in there—you know, Raoul Duke. The weirdest thing is that I can access them. They're still very close to the surface.

It must be difficult when you have multiple personalities in one of them, like the Hatter has. What does he say, "It's crowded in here"?

"I don't like it in here. It's terribly crowded." But they all, somehow, have their place. They have come to terms with each other, I suppose.

When you're playing someone—when you're really deep within a character—have you ever had a dream that you felt was not your dream? Do your characters dream within you?

I've certainly had dreams where I was the character. Sweeney was like that. There were a lot of dark Sweeney dreams.

On *The Libertine*...I made an appointment at the hospital where they had his remains. His skeleton is there, a plaster mask is there, and his hat and veil and all this other stuff is there. And right on the wall next to him is this gorgeous poem that he wrote about himself and about his life: **"Dragging this vile body / Round the years / I am not what first appears / A senseless freak / Devoid of hope or tears."** This guy was deep, and so, so gifted.

Is it your grandfather you have tattooed on your arm?

Yeah, Jim. He was a wonderful model. **He drove a bus during the day and ran moonshine at night.** He was a Robert Mitchum type, a man's man. He just said things as they were. He'd call a spade a spade—and piss on you if you don't like it. He was also of a different era—**I always felt like I was meant to have been born in another era, another time.**

BPD ISSUES, SYMPTOMS & JOHNNY DEPP:

Depp has a shallow understanding of photographers who are just trying to make a living taking some photos. He always verbally abuses them as paparazzi trash. Of course, a million unemployed actors would love to have some photographers chasing them.

Part of the BPD syndrome is having no insight into another person's viewpoint. Johnny has absolutely no gratitude or appreciation for being lucky enough to be a movie superstar with over $350 million dollars. The photographers and inconveniences come with the superstar package.

As the interviewer got Depp talking about developing his characters for playing acting roles, it is ironic that the very BPD that includes his unstable self-identity, perhaps enables him to get into strange characters for his films. Certainly some other BPD suffering actors such as Marilyn Monroe and Angelina Jolie have also exploited or made the most of their changeable, volatile, unpredictable and unsteady sense of self or identity.

Chapter 25

"The beauty, the poetry of the fear in their eyes. I didn't mind going to jail for, what, five, six hours? It was absolutely worth it."
— Johnny Depp

Lost in La Mancha (2002) featured Depp as himself – storyline:

For years, one of filmmaker Terry Gilliam's great dreams was to make a screen adaptation of Miguel de Cervantes Saavedra's classic tale *Don Quixote*, and in 2000 it looked as if his dream was to become a reality.

In collaboration with Tony Grisoni, Gilliam had written a script called *The Man Who Killed Don Quixote*, in which a 20th century advertising man accidentally travels back in time and is mistaken by Don Quixote for his faithful companion, Sancho Panza.

After ten years of shopping the project to American studios with no success, Gilliam and his producers had secured financing for the film from a consortium of European sources, and Johnny Depp had been cast as the time-tripping adman, with the venerable French actor Jean Rochefort as Don Quixote.

However, as the production moved closer to its start date, more and more things began to go wrong -- contracts went unsigned, key cast and crew members had not yet arrived, and the carefully prepared budget seemed stressed to the breaking point. Nevertheless, Gilliam soldiered on, but after a mere six days of shooting, during which Spanish Air Force jets ruined several takes, flash floods destroyed several sets, and Gilliam struggled to keep his dream afloat, Rochefort suffered a severe back injury.

The film's financiers decided to cash in their chips and pulled the plug in order to cash in on their insurance, though Gilliam struggled for months afterward to find a way to put the production back on track.

Documentary filmmakers Keith Fulton and Louis Pepe had been invited by Gilliam to make a film about the production of *The Man Who Killed Don Quixote*, and after shooting 80 hours of footage of the chaotic pre-production process as well as the aborted shooting schedule, they instead created Lost In La Mancha, a look at the "un-making" of the film, which along with the story of the project's brief rise and messy collapse, featured a look at several completed scenes from the film, as well as animated versions of the film's storyboards which offered a glimpse of the look and scale of the film Gilliam was attempting to create (*rottentomatoes*).

JOHNNY DEPP'S LIFE BEHIND THE SCENES:

The Hunter in Johnny Depp (N. Tosches, *Vanity Fair*, Nov. 2011):

Our strategy for the day has been for him to get the photo shoot for this story out of the way by midafternoon, then sit down for our interview, so as to leave **us free to go drinking and gambling** into the night, even though he does have to be on the Dark Shadows set very early the next morning.

But the question remains: How can someone who seems to have had his picture on every magazine cover in the world seven times over be so **antagonistic to having his picture taken**? It turns out that "antagonistic" is too mild a word.

"**Well, you just feel like you're being raped somehow**." Strong words from an easygoing, down-to-earth man not given to drama in his everyday life. "**Raped. The whole thing. It feels a kind of weird—just weird, man. Weird**. Like you meet people and they say, 'Can I have a picture with you?' and that's great. That's fine. That's not a problem. But whenever you have a photo shoot or something like that, it's like—you just feel dumb. It's just so stupid."

He says this antipathy is nothing new. He's always hated to have his picture taken. Even a quarter of a century ago and more, back in the days of *A Nightmare on Elm Street*, when he needed all the publicity he could get, photo shoots creeped him out.

"Basically, if they're going to pay me the stupid money right now, I'm going to take it. I have to. I mean, it's not for me. Do you know what I mean? At this point, it's for my kids. It's ridiculous, yeah, yeah. But ultimately is it for me? No. No. It's for the kids."

So I persist. **I know him to be a traditional family man**, in the best, truest sense of that phrase; Vanessa Paradis, his French better half, their two children, Lily-Rose, now 12, and Jack, now 9, are the center of his world. But—

"And, come on, it's for you, too."

"Not really, because I keep working—I'm constantly fucking like—I'm slamming the fucking—you know, every day is like fucking . . ." He takes a breath, takes a drag, takes a sip, and starts again. **"There is a part of me that needs to have this kind of stimulation to the brain. I must have fucking stimulation."**

The wine is going down good.

"Yeah," Johnny says with a smile, "**we have to go gamble.**"

I want to go gambling, too. I have my blue Ritz Club membership card in my wallet and fond memories of our last long night there at the **blackjack tables and the bar**...

Then **he raises his glass of wine**, looks straight at me, and says, "There's also *In the Hand of Dante*."

Who knows? Our **talk drifts, carried along by the tow of the wine** and the night.

It's getting late. Not many hours remain until Johnny has to be back on the set. Even I'm getting slightly drowsy. But **the Ritz Club, the blackjack tables, more wine await us.** Johnny slowly rises, goes to put some cold water on his face and fetch a necktie. I light a smoke, sit with my wine, and rest my eyes. **Eventually it occurs to me that Johnny has been gone for a while**. I push myself up off the couch and call his name. No answer. I look around for him.

He is dead-out asleep in the toilet, the perfect picture of the wages of exhaustion. I don't want to wake him. I just stand for a moment wondering. He has a beautiful château and secluded grounds in France. He has an estate in Los Angeles. He has an idyllic island of his own. But does he have a hammock?

BPD ISSUES, SYMPTOMS & JOHNNY DEPP:

My aim was to dig a little deeper than the surface level of the *Vanity Fair* article/interview with Depp and his old drinking, gambling buddy. I deleted sections that rambled on about Johnny's great movie accomplishments as an actor.

We all know Depp has moved on beyond being a mediocre, unemployed guitar player who got over by crashing on pal's couches, stealing food from grocery stores and selling pens on the phone. His early Hollywood days of drinking, drugging and wild partying now seem romantic and amusing to his fans.

However, a recurrent theme of the subtext in the *Vanity Fair* interview in this chapter relates to going from buzzed to shitfaced smashed drinking alcohol. At the end of the interview, the writer looks for Depp and finds him "**dead-out asleep in the toilet**" – he doesn't wake Johnny because he's just so "exhausted."

For those familiar with alcoholism and drug addiction, this behavior is known as **passing-out**. Passing-out is a sign of an advanced stage of alcoholism. I'd say Johnny is way past time to join A.A. (Alcoholics Anonymous) and perhaps N.A.

(Narcotics Anonymous) because he's admitted to a lot of drug abuse in the past.

Depp appears to have an addictive personality. The discussion in the interview mentions his workaholic tendency – he's addicted to working on movies as an actor which has been profitable for him. Depp claims the hundreds of millions he's making is "for his kids."

That's a kind of people-pleaser, socially-acceptable remark to make. However, I'd point out to Johnny that handing over millions of dollars to his teenage or twenty-something kids would be enabling them in the wrong direction.

I lived in Malibu for over ten years and got to know some adult children of movie superstars and rock stars. Giving young people a fat trust fund usually results in them losing motivation to do anything productive.

Trust fund kids in their 20s and 30s I've met in Hollywood typically waste their lives drinking booze, getting loaded on drugs and partying. They hang-out at the beach surfing, chasing their next romantic conquest or sitting around talking about movies or music they're going to produce – but nothing happens unless their movie or rock star parent helps them. They end up in fancy rehabs, in jail or dead from drug overdoses. Is that what you want "for the kids," Johnny?

What BPD symptoms were revealed by this *Vanity Fair* interview?

1) **Impulsive and self-destructive behaviors such as substance abuse** – Johnny comes off as an alcoholic who ends the interview passed out in the toilet. He seems to be vulnerable to self-destructing as an alcoholic and maybe a gambling addict.

2) **Some paranoia** is indicated by Depp's extreme fear of getting his picture taken. If this is such a problem, why did he rush to be a rock star or a movie star? Apparently, then this is an excuse to assault photographers.

Chapter 26

"Me, I'm dishonest, and you can always trust a dishonest man to be dishonest. Honestly, it's the honest ones you have to watch out for."
— Johnny Depp

Pirates of the Caribbean: Curse of the Black Pearl (2003) starred Depp as Jack Sparrow – storyline:

Following his surprise-hit American remake of *The Ring* in 2002, director Gore Verbinski took on *Pirates of the Caribbean: The Curse of the Black Pearl*, the second of recent films to be based upon Disney theme-park rides (the first being *The Country Bears*).

When Elizabeth Swann (Keira Knightley), the daughter of Governor Swann (Jonathan Pryce) is kidnapped by a group of pirates led by Captain Barbossa (Geoffrey Rush) and taken aboard their ship, *The Black Pearl*, Will Turner (Orlando Bloom), the young man who loves Elizabeth despite the fact that she is promised to another, sets out to rescue her. But he can't do it alone, so he enlists the help of swashbuckling ship captain Jack Sparrow (Johnny Depp).

Together the two chase after The Black Pearl, but they soon discover that the captain and crew aren't your average pirates. Cursed to remain between the living and the dead, Barbossa and his men look like skeletons when basked in the moonlight. When it is revealed that the only thing that can break the curse is Elizabeth's blood, Jack and Will are faced with a race against time and a battle against the undead to save the Governor's daughter (*rottentomatoes*).

JOHNNY DEPP'S LIFE BEHIND THE SCENES:

When Angelina Met Johnny (C. Nashawaty, *Entertainment Weekly*, Nov. 19, 2010):

...Two of the biggest stars on the planet were teaming up for *The Tourist*.

Halfway through the meeting, a bottle of wine was uncorked.

Oh Johnny (L. Daniels, *Smash Hits*, July 1993):

"How do you fancy interviewing Johnny Depp?" After the *Smash Hits* staff had picked me up off the floor and revived me I managed to scream, "Are you mad?! Of *course* I fancy it!"

I'M GOING TO INTERVIEW JOHNNY DEPP!!!! The same Johnny Depp who is a hugely famous American actor, the same Johnny Depp who billions of girls all over the world have posters of on their walls...the same **Johnny Depp who's very good-looking and does everything within his power to disguise it.**

Up in Johnny's suite we are **greeted by a press agent from Johnny's film company**...Depp takes off his battered brown leather jacket and places it neatly on the back of his chair. He's also wearing a tatty dark grey T-shirt with three holes in the right shoulder and a black and white striped waistcoat.

Dark grey jeans cover his legs and to finish the look he's got a pair of slip-on DM boots on his feet. **He looks scruffy but clean and really, *really* lovely**...There's just something about Johnny Depp that makes you want to give him a great big hug and tell him that everything will be OK.

Seeing everybody's confusion he laughs and shrugs, "Oh well." He clicks his blue lighter and asks, "Don't mind if I set my lungs on fire, do you?"

Is it true that you actually scar yourself?

[*Laughing*] **"From time to time! I had this thing, you know, I think that in a way your body is a journal, for me it is anyway. I started scarring myself when I was a kid, it was just a way to remind myself of things that had happened**. I wouldn't advise it though! I haven't done it for a couple of years. Thirty and scarring myself?" [*Shakes his head and laughs.*]

Do you like being mobbed?

"Well I wouldn't say that I go to the mall as much as I used to! I don't think it's something I'll ever be comfortable with but then again **if it were to stop I would probably start worrying**."

Are you scared of being alone?

"I wouldn't say I was scared of it. While filming *Gilbert Grape* **there were times when I was really lonely** but I don't know if that had anything to do with the character I was playing, so I made myself feel that way to prepare for the film."

Did the split with Winona make you feel lonely?

[*He turns in his seat so his whole body is toward me,* **his hand is shaking slightly as he takes a puff of his cigarette**. *His* *voice becomes slower and softer. Up until now, everyone's avoided talking about this subject.*]

"Well, we've been apart for about a month now. You know, when you're with someone and you love someone **it's never easy to cut the connection** between you but I would say that the split was a natural thing, it was something that had to happen. **I wouldn't say that it was devastating to her or me, it was just a natural progression.**"

Are you still friends?

"Oh yeah. The split was very amicable, we'll always be best friends."

How's this for timing? **Just as the conversation is getting intimate, his press officer comes in to tell us the interview must finish now.**

BPD ISSUES, SYMPTOMS & JOHNNY DEPP:

One reason we rarely hear about Depp's BPD symptoms or his negatives is that he's surrounded by moon-struck, love-sick female media interviewers. And the male media people are equally into people pleasing because they want continued access to the celebrities, movie and rock stars.

I've highlighted points in the above interview concerning Depp's press agent whose job it is to protect and sugar-coat Johnny. I've cut most of the fluff, softball questions and superficial material from the two interviews. But I left some of the breathless, star-struck sycophancy, fawning sweet talk and obsequiousness in the latter one.

Fortunately, I found some nuggets that hinted or spelled-out Johnny's BPD symptoms such as:

1) **A pattern of turbulent, volatile, intense and tempestuous relationships.** Depp adroitly ducked when he was asked about breaking-up with Winona Ryder one month prior to the interview. He minimized the break-up as just "natural" and no big deal. Yet there have been many reports of Johnny's traumatic reaction to ending it with Winona. While with Ryder, Depp had many frenzied fights, thundery screaming matches and horrendous scenes with Winona. While violently fighting with Kate Moss he trashed a hotel room and was arrested.

2) **Deliberate self-harm** such as Depp cutting himself. Again, in this interview he dismissed discussion of his self-mutilation – cutting – discounted it with a laugh.

3) **Chronic feelings of emptiness and loneliness.** When the topic of loneliness came up with respect to Winona or anytime, Depp played it down, belittled it. However, Depp appears to have a long-term issue of chronic feelings of emptiness and loneliness he has

punctuated with a series of chaotic romantic escapades, substance abuse (alcohol, mood-altering drugs), self-mutilation such as cutting himself, fights, assaults and arrests.

Chapter 27

"As a teenager I was so insecure. I was the type of guy that never fitted in because he never dared to choose. I was convinced I had absolutely no talent at all. For nothing. And that thought took away all my ambition too."
— Johnny Depp

Once Upon a Time in Mexico (2003) featured Depp as Sands – storyline:

Director Robert Rodriguez returns to the characters of his breakthrough hits El Mariachi and Desperado in this grand scale south-of-the-border action-adventure saga.

Sands (Johnny Depp) is a rogue CIA agent who is working in cahoots with Mexican officials who've caught wind of a plan by corrupt military leader General Marquez (Gerardo Vigil) and ruthless drug kingpin Barillo (Willem Dafoe) to assassinate Mexico's president (Pedro Armendáriz Jr.).

Sands needs to recruit a gunman to take out Barillo's assassins before they can complete their mission, and through barman Belini (Cheech Marin), Sands learns of El Mariachi (Antonio Banderas), a fabled musician turned vigilante with a remarkable talent for violence, and a score to settle with Marquez.

El Mariachi is living quietly in hiding after the death of the woman he loved, Carolina (Salma Hayek), but Sands lures him back into action through the promise of a final showdown with his nemesis Marquez, forcing El Mariachi to retrieve his guitar case (containing a mighty arsenal) and once again do battle against the lawless.

Robert Rodriguez not only directed *Once Upon a Time in Mexico*, but he wrote the screenplay, handled the camera work, edited the film, and composed the musical score (*rottentomatoes*).

JOHNNY DEPP'S LIFE BEHIND THE SCENES:

In *Johnny Depp Starts Here*, Pomerance reported on two fighting/assault incidents:

1) A fight Depp had with photographers outside a London restaurant when he assaulted them with a piece of wood.

2) A second assault against another man in a London pub.

"One night in London, after shooting *Sleepy Hollow*, Johnny was besieged: He and Vanessa were having a quiet dinner in a London restaurant with a couple of friends to celebrate the pregnancy. Before long, photographers started peering in the window, looking for photo ops..."

"'**That angered me**,' explained Depp. 'They were turning something sacred into a product...I asked them nicely, Please, I can't be what you want me to be tonight – **I can't be novelty boy**, a product. Please leave me alone for just this one night.'"

"**When they didn't oblige, he became a drooling beast, taking a three-foot piece of wood and attacking them with it**. Later the young fellow with the pretty looks and leading-man visage reportedly said, '**The beauty, the poetry of fear in their eyes, in their filthy, maggoty little faces was worth it**...'"

In the second fight/assault incident Pomerance wrote: "**The 'real' Johnny Depp behind the multiple screen characterizations, then, is – to put it mildly – confusing**. He is ineffably inconsistent, shifting, migrating, developing, flippy, spontaneous, calculating, literate, punky, handsome and beastly, paternal and pretty, unaimed and destructive, wanton and frivolous, amorous and angry. **In a London pub he pulled both ears – 'very hard' – of a descendant of Sir Robert Walpole**..."

BPD ISSUES, SYMPTOMS & JOHNNY DEPP:

Depp has been arrested a number of times on various charges resulting from fights, vandalism, trashing hotel rooms, assaults and incidents related to substance abuse of alcohol and drugs. In press interviews it is usually discounted as "petty crime" or there is some vague reference to his bad boy days. But now that Johnny is a movie superstar, all seems to be forgiven.

However, if one evaluates Depp as a possible BPD person, some signs and symptoms of Borderline Personality Disorder can be assessed from incidents where Johnny gets into a fight, assaults other people or uses his bodyguards to assault others or threatens to harm people who bother him:

1) **Impulsive and self-destructive behaviors** such as substance abuse (alcohol and drugs); fighting, assaulting others.

2) **Frequent and intense mood swings.**

3) **The intense experience of anger, difficulties controlling anger, or both.** One minute he's people-pleasing and the next minute he explodes into a rage.

4) **Temporary paranoia while under stress.**

5) **Lack of a cohesive identity or a poor or unstable self-image or insecure sense of self.** Johnny could be regressing to his old teenage bad boy self one moment, then transforming into his movie star sense of entitlement the next moment. He flips from zero self-esteem to an ego-maniac Hollywood superstar.

Chapter 28

"People say I make strange choices, but they're not strange for me. My sickness is that I'm fascinated by human behavior, by what's underneath the surface, by the worlds inside people."
— Johnny Depp

Secret Window (2004) starred Depp as Mort Rainey – storyline:

Mort Rainey in *Secret Window* is a writer with a block. His wife has left him for another man, her dog, cozy at his feet as he tries to write, is pleasant but insufficient company, and he is spending far too much time sleeping.

An angry good ol' boy, John Shooter (John Turturro) is convinced Mort has plagiarized from him. Mort tells Shooter he knows nothing about the so-called intellectual theft.

From writer/director David Koepp (Stir of Echoes) comes this filmed adaptation of Stephen King's novella *Secret Window, Secret Garden*, one of four stories in the collection *Four Past Midnight*. Johnny Depp stars as Mort Rainey, a recently divorced author who decides to take some time off at his cottage.

Unfortunately for Rainey, John Shooter (John Turturro), an unbalanced wannabe writer, tracks him down, claiming that Rainey plagiarized his work. Also starring Maria Bello, Charles S. Dutton, and Timothy Hutton, *Secret Window* is the second story from *Four Past Midnight* to be adapted as a film, the first being 1995's made-for-television *The Langoliers* (*rottentomatoes*).

JOHNNY DEPP'S LIFE BEHIND THE SCENES:

Johnny Depp from A to W (C. Kelly, *Sassy*, May 1990):

On the very eve of the release of the John Waters film *Cry-Baby*, Johnny Depp's first movie since *Platoon*, we got the 26-year-old actor to sit still for an interview at his house.

...Winona Ryder, his 18-year-old fiancée. They met last September, were engaged in February, and "Winona Forever" is now tattooed on his right arm above the American Indian.

ACTING. "I don't know why I like acting. Sometimes I like it, sometimes I don't. It's not like it's the greatest, most rewarding thing you can do in life. It's strange when you think about it. Most of the time you're saying somebody else's words as opposed to your own, and that's pretty weird. **It doesn't make for a very stable brain and it doesn't make for a very relaxed person."**

NARCOLEPSY. "I thought I might have had it at one point in my life, but **I found out that I was really just rather bored**."

REBELLION. "When certain things come out about an actor's past or about his life, they immediately put a label on you, something that is marketable for them. The people that wear the suits and sign the checks need something to sell, a product, they need to call it something."

"They say: **'He dropped out of high school—oh, he's a bad boy. He has done drugs at one time in his life, he got in trouble with the law at one time in his life, so he's a bad boy.' The term rebel is what kills me. It's such a played-out thing. It's all so stupid. I would imagine it was a good word about 200 years ago, but now it's such a joke!"**

BPD ISSUES, SYMPTOMS & JOHNNY DEPP:

The above *Sassy* interview brought out some points which revealed some of Depp's BPD symptoms:

1) **Chronic feelings of emptiness, boredom and loneliness**. Depp answers the narcolepsy question and revealed his boredom symptom.

2) **Impulsive and self-destructive behaviors** such as substance abuse (drug and alcohol), breaking and entering, vandalism, theft, trashing hotel rooms, fights, assaults and arrests. Note that Depp is in denial and angry that he has been described as a "rebel" or "bad boy" – impulsive and self-destructive behaviors represent a serious BPD symptom.

Chapter 29

"I was always fascinated by people who are considered completely normal, because I find them the weirdest of all"
— Johnny Depp

Finding Neverland (2004) starred Depp as J.M. Barrie – storyline:

Following up his critically acclaimed *Monster's Ball*, director Marc Forster took on this biography of playwright James Matthew Barrie, the scribe who penned the children's classic *Peter Pan*.

Johnny Depp stars as the turn-of-the-century writer as the film follows Barrie as he struggles to write and have his play produced while he cares for his down-on-their-luck neighbors who inspired the story in the first place. J.M. Barrie's

Neverland also stars Dustin Hoffman, Kate Winslet, and Julie Christie (*rottentomatoes*).

JOHNNY DEPP'S LIFE BEHIND THE SCENES:

Bad Boy to Role Model (E. Warren, *TV Guide*, Jan. 23, 1988):

Once a troublemaker, Johnny Depp of *21 Jump Street* is now admired for his cool and his part in a series about teen problems.

With his angelic punk face and his hair cascading James Dean-style into his eyes, he looks the perfect teen-age rebel.

It comes from years of real-life experience. Depp, 24, grew up in Miramar, Fla., where he wasn't exactly on the road to becoming a National Merit scholar. "**I hung around with bad crowds**," he admits.

"**We used to break and enter places. We'd break into the school and destroy a room or something. I used to steal things from stores**." And, like some of the kids Officer Tom Hanson has busted on *21 Jump Street*, **Depp was into drugs**. "**Pretty much any drug you can name," he says, "I've done it.**" At 13 he lost his virginity, and at 16 he dropped out of high school.

Fast-forward eight years to Vancouver, where *Jump Street* is shot. **Depp has acquired a taste for $80-a-shot cognac** and is a fan-magazine star, routinely mobbed by adoring teen-age girls.

How cool is Johnny Depp? He's so cool that **he orders a $75 bottle of wine** without blinking...he moved out of his house to live in a car with his best friend...It was a '67 Impala that they filled with empty beer cans...

Back in blue-collar Miramar, where Depp's father was director of public works and his mother was a waitress, **Johnny and pals were into drugs, girls, petty crime** and, most of all, music. Music was how they kept the faith within their isolated teen-age world of **angry parents and threatening teachers**.

At the same time, he took a seedy apartment in Hollywood...He also got **married, got divorced** and met actor Nicolas Cage, a former boyfriend of his wife, who told him he ought to try acting.

After a few glasses of wine, though, Depp will tell you...

BPD ISSUES, SYMPTOMS & JOHNNY DEPP:

The *TV Guide* interview confirms the BPD symptoms including:

1) **Volatile emotions.**

2) **Turbulent relationships.**

3) **Impulsive, self-destructive and anti-social behavior.**

4) **Unstable, variable identity or wobbly, unhinged self-concept or rickety erratic self-image.** In some interviews Depp hates the label "bad boy" or "rebel" – in other interviews he either laughs off the wild times or omits serious incidents when he was arrested or discounts his self-destructive and impulsive behavior. He's in denial about the significance.

Chapter 30

"On buying a private island... Money doesn't buy you happiness, but it buys you a big enough yacht to sail right up to it."
— Johnny Depp

The Libertine (2004) starred Depp as John Wilmot, aka the Earl of Rochester – storyline:

A man who lives for pleasure finds his hedonism betrays him in time in this film adaptation of the play by Stephen Jeffreys. The second Earl of Rochester, John Wilmot (Johnny Depp), was a notorious figure in 17th century Europe; well-respected as a poet and author, Wilmot also earned no small degree of gossip for his freewheeling sex life and appetite for decadence.

Wilmot was close friends with Charles II (John Malkovich), the powerful and Machiavellian ruler of England, and enjoyed a passionate romance with Elizabeth Barry (Samantha Morton), an actress of note. But Wilmot's seemingly charmed life took a turn for the worse when he wrote a satirical play lampooning his friend Charles II; the monarch failed to see the humor, and exiled the author from Britain.

Wilmot found little solace in his relationship with Barry, especially after he contracted syphilis and began drinking heavily as the disease tore away at his body and his mind. The Libertine was produced in part by John Malkovich, who played the role of John Wilmot in a production of Stephen Jeffreys' original play (*rottentomatoes*).

JOHNNY DEPP'S LIFE BEHIND THE SCENES:

Amber Heard Reportedly Freaked Out By Attention Over Johnny Depp (*The Huffington Post*, July 19, 2012):

Last month it was reported that actress **Amber Heard broke up with her girlfriend**, artist-photographer Tasya van Ree, only to hook up with her recently single *The Rum Diary* co-star Johnny Depp. Though they do make a beautiful couple, *RadarOnline* reports that **things have cooled down between the former co-stars.**

"Johnny and Amber were definitely involved," a source told the website, of the couple who met on set while Depp was still involved with his partner of 14 years, Vanessa Paradis, and Heard was still with Ree.

The source didn't suggest that either cheated on their former partner, but said that the two actors "definitely had chemistry that carried over from the set," and they just happened to find themselves single at the right time.

The source tells *RadarOnline* that Depp and Heard were hooking up for months -- way before he ever made his split with Paradis public.

"They did a really good job of keeping their relationship on the down low for a while, especially since many people assumed that Amber was only into girls."

But there's a reason that so many celebrity couples try to keep their relationships private, as Heard allegedly freaked out when it was reported she was seeing Depp.

"She prides herself on being free-thinking and independent -- not some home-wrecker trying to sleep her way to the top. As soon as the media started publicizing the romance, she told Johnny that she needed some space," explained the source.

Depp and Paradis' relationship was rumored to be on the rocks for months, and after the actor finally announced their breakup, there were reports about how much of it was due to the fact that **Depp had become "bored senseless."**

Depp's alleged boredom makes his reported relationship with the gorgeous 26-year-old make all the more sense. But even if Depp was looking for something a little more exciting, sources say Heard wants things to be more low-key.

"She really likes Johnny, but she doesn't like the drama. She isn't really sure what is going to happen with them, but just wants the attention to cool down before anything progresses," the source told the website.

BPD ISSUES, SYMPTOMS & JOHNNY DEPP:

Johnny's BPD symptoms, based on some information in the above *Huffington Post* article include:

1) **Erratic, volatile relationships**. Depp jumped into a movie-set romance with Amber Heard and split with Vanessa Paradis. As of 2013, Johnny and Amber has already broken-up at least once, made-up and now are struggling with a second-round in their relationship. To add further stress and tension to the Johnny and Amber love affair, openly bisexual Amber keeps a simultaneous lipstick lesbian affair going with her current girlfriend.

2) **Chronic feelings of emptiness and boredom.** Contributing to Johnny's volatile choices, he's chronically feeling empty, bored and lonely.

Chapter 31

"Throughout my lifetime I've left pieces of my heart here and there. And now, there's almost barely enough to stay alive. But I force a smile, knowing that my ambition far exceeded my talent."
— Johnny Depp

The Rum Diary (2005) cast Depp as Paul Kemp – storyline:

Based on the debut novel by Hunter S. Thompson. Tiring of the noise and madness of New York and the crushing conventions of late Eisenhower-era America, Paul Kemp (Johnny Depp) travels to the pristine island of Puerto Rico to write for a local newspaper, run by downtrodden editor Lotterman (Richard Jenkins).

Adopting the rum-soaked life of the island, Paul soon becomes obsessed with Chenault (Amber Heard), the wildly attractive Connecticut-born fiancée of Sanderson (Aaron Eckhart).

Sanderson is one of a growing number of American entrepreneurs who are determined to convert Puerto Rico into a capitalist paradise in service of the wealthy.

When Kemp is recruited by Sanderson to write favorably about his latest unsavory scheme, the journalist is presented with a choice: to use his words for the corrupt businessmen's financial benefit, or use them to take the bastards down (*rottentomatoes*).

JOHNNY DEPP'S LIFE BEHIND THE SCENES:

From Baby Face to *Cry-Baby* (C. Willman, *Los Angeles Times*, April 4, 1990):

Johnny Depp of Fox's *21 Jump Street* plays a juvenile delinquent in his first starring film role. The teen idol insists he'll never do another TV series again.

"Never. I'd rather pump gas. I would never do it again, ever. There's not enough money in Los Angeles."

"...Whenever a young actor comes out, they have to pin him with some sort of **label so they call him a bad boy or that horrible word *rebel*,** which is so played out and stupid. This made fun of people's perceptions. It was really the only way I wanted to go."

Waters came upon the idea of casting Depp...And then there's the typecasting factor. Waters enthuses: "Johnny *was* a juvenile delinquent!" Depp himself doesn't go quite that far.

"I wasn't, really. I was just a curious kid. **I was bored with high school so I dropped out**; I wanted to play music so I kept doing that. I wouldn't say that I was one of the cool kids in high school at all, but I also wasn't square. **I probably was perceived as a burnout because I had long hair**..."

Depp seems an unlikely candidate for idolization among the preteen fan magazine set: **Stories in the adult press have made ample note of his admitted drug use at 11**, **petty theft** and sexual experiences at 13, exit from school at 16, **marriage at 20 and divorce at 22**.

BPD ISSUES, SYMPTOMS & JOHNNY DEPP:

The parts of the L.A. Times article that I've included document Depp's BPD symptoms – despite his denial and discounting of his self-destructive, impulsive behavior. His BPD symptoms include:

1) Impulsive, self-destructive behavior.

2) Chronic feelings of emptiness, boredom and loneliness.

3) Volatile, unstable relationships.

Chapter 32

"I don't think of myself as being a celebrity, it's too mortifying. I have a hard time watching myself on screen and it's getting worse. I can't tell whether my work is good or not."
— Johnny Depp

The Corpse Bride (2005) used Depp as a voice – storyline:

Tim Burton returns to the dark but fanciful animated style of *The Nightmare Before Christmas* with this stop-motion black comedy. Victor (voice of Johnny Depp) lives in a small European village in the 19th century, where he is pledged to marry Victoria (voice of Emily Watson), a partnership arranged by their parents.

The two only meet the day before their scheduled nuptials, and Victor performs disastrously in the wedding rehearsal. Later that evening, while he is walking through the woods and hopelessly practicing his vows, he puts Victoria's wedding band on what looks like a branch.

Victor quickly discovers this was a big mistake; as it happens, he has put the ring on the skeletal finger of the enchanted *Corpse Bride* (voice of Helena Bonham Carter), who then whisks him off to a dark and mysterious netherworld where they are now married.

Victor is frightened in the land of the dead, and even realizes that he has fallen in love with his true fiancée, Victoria, so he searches for a way back to his own world. Directed by Tim Burton in collaboration with animator Mike Johnson, *Corpse Bride* features a stellar voice cast, including Albert Finney, Christopher Lee, Richard E. Grant, Joanna Lumley, and Danny Elfman (*rottentomatoes*).

JOHNNY DEPP'S LIFE BEHIND THE SCENES:

Baby Face (T. Fletcher, *Sky Magazine*, June 1990):

Rock star good looks aside, Depp also boasts an intriguing bad-boy past—perfect credentials for another ready-made movie hero.

In torn jeans and T-shirt, his disheveled hair partly hidden by a bandanna, his face unshaven and his lips curled around a cigarette, **Depp's casual appearance only emphasizes his desirable street-tough image**.

"I thought, 'This guy looks great,'" recalls Waters, who was even more delighted to see Depp described in the teen press as a **"juvenile delinquent."**

"He came in dressed completely in rags," said Waters, "with Levi's ripped to his underpants, boxer shorts hanging out through the holes, hair completely askew . . . and he looked really like a movie star."

Depp says he relished the opportunity to **send up "the labels and the image** . . . that manufactured thing," but admits that much of his younger audience might not appreciate the parody. The advertising campaign in particular seems to polish, rather than demolish, Depp's image.

Without knowing it, Depp has been in training for the part of Cry-Baby all his life.

Johnny met and married Lori Anne Allison in Florida, the marriage collapsed within two years.

Now, as Depp waits to hear about a fifth season—he is contractually obliged to appear in two more seasons if asked to—he seems determined to bad mouth the show into dropping him.

"...I don't really agree with the idea of cops in high schools. Morally I don't agree with it. I think it's slightly unjust, I think it's borderline fascism."

Cry-Baby...**bringing Depp a million dollars up front** for the chance to work with his heroes. "**I don't think any of us would have gotten into this business if we weren't in one way or another starved of attention**," he admits.

Discussion of Winona, who in the brilliant *Heathers* also starred in a send-up of the teen movie genre, gets Johnny Depp positively glassy-eyed. "**I love her more than anything else in the whole world**," he says, quite unashamedly. Which is just as well; **with the new tattoo that he proudly shows off to all who ask, he will be living with Winona forever whether he likes it or not.**

BPD ISSUES, SYMPTOMS & JOHNNY DEPP:

Contrary to Depp's frequent denials, he certainly was a juvenile delinquent as a teenager. Besides substance abuse of drugs and alcohol, he has admitted hanging-out with a bad crowd of criminal addicts who committed burglaries, breaking and entering, vandalized property, stole food out of grocery stores, got into fights, assaulted people, engaged in self-mutilation or cutting himself, chronically felt bored and empty and had unstable relationships.

The interview in this chapter documented the following BPD symptoms:

1) **Depp's impulsive and self-destructive behavior** – substance abuse, petty crime, self-mutilation, etc.

2) **His unstable relationships**. He leaps into marriage at 20, dumps her two years later and continues his serial relationship merry-go-round with Winona and other women – a number who will instantly get engaged to Johnny then break-up with him after chaotic fights.

3) **Johnny's volatile self-identity or self-image** – he denies this obvious bad-boy past yet builds on it to advance his movie career. He purposely selects sort of ragged clothes and messes up his hair to carefully cultivate his image – at first glance he appears to be a homeless bum or a punk rocker while in reality he's a rich movie star who lives a very spoiled life.

Chapter 33

"It's all kinds of these profound things crashing on you when your child arrives into the world. It's like you've met your reason to live."
--Johnny Depp

Charlie and the Chocolate Factory (2005) starred Depp as Willy Wonka – storyline:

Director Tim Burton brings his unique vision and sensibility to Roald Dahl's classic children's story in this lavish screen interpretation.

Willy Wonka (Johnny Depp) is the secretive and wildly imaginative man behind the world's most celebrated candy company, and while the Wonka factory is famously closed to visitors, the reclusive candy man decides to give five lucky children a chance to see the inside of his operation by placing "golden tickets" in five randomly selected chocolate bars.

Charlie Bucket (Freddie Highmore), whose poor but loving family lives literally in the shadow of the Wonka factory, is lucky enough to obtain one of the tickets, and Charlie, escorted by his Grandpa Joe (David Kelly), is in for the ride of a lifetime as he tours the strange and remarkable world of Wonka with fellow winners, media-obsessed Mike Teavee (Jordan Fry), harsh and greedy Veruca Salt (Julia Winter), gluttonous Augustus Gloop (Philip Wiegratz), and ultra-competitive Violet Beauregarde (AnnaSophia Robb).

Over the course of the day, some of the children will learn difficult lessons about themselves, and one will go on to become Wonka's new right hand. Charlie and the Chocolate Factory also stars Christopher Lee, James Fox, and Noah Taylor; the book was famously adapted to the screen before in 1971 under the title Willy Wonka and the Chocolate Factory, with Gene Wilder as the eccentric candy tycoon (*rottentomatoes*).

JOHNNY DEPP'S LIFE BEHIND THE SCENES:

Depp Charge (J. McClellan, *The Face*, July 1991):

The other half of Hollywood's hippest couple, Johnny Depp is better known here as Winona Ryder's boyfriend.

On Edward Scissorhands... "I connected with it really well. I sort of already knew the character and what he represented. Edward seemed more of a feeling than a person. The metaphor of the scissors is about wanting to touch, but if you touch, you destroy. **Nothing you do seems right. It's the feeling you get when you're growing up, very adolescent. I felt that way.** I think everyone did."

The Hollywood publicity machine has always thrived on star romance, but it seems in the post-AIDS age, with Warren Beatty-style bedhopping publicly frowned on, big-name couples are a real item. Yet amid all the usual sleaze about Bruce and Demi and Julia and Kiefer, **the youthful Depp and Ryder have been treated with kid gloves so far, cast as hip, romantic innocents. A recent fashion shoot in *Vogue*, which showed the couple embracing, packaged them as a "fairytale couple"—a symbol of "Hollywood Romance"**—

Not surprisingly, it irritates Depp to see his love-life diagnosed like a cultural symptom. Still, isn't he scared that once their press honeymoon is over, the scandal rags will go all out to break them up? **"We've already had rumors we're splitting up. Such bullshit. Things like *People Magazine* don't really bother me—it's like the flies buzzing around this trailer. I can deal with their presence if I have to, but I'd much rather squash them like a pea."**

Depp was so embarrassed by the show (*21 Jump Street*), he couldn't watch it. What irked most was being a teen heart-throb.

"I got angry because it wasn't me and I couldn't control it, all these publicity fuckers from Fox TV trying to market me like I was a box of cereal… **Or you fight it. I was lucky in that at least I had half a brain cell, so I fought it**."

Hence his reputation for being "difficult." …So he won't be doing any more TV? "I'd rather dig a hole through the center of the earth with my tongue."

Depp's first post-TV break came with John Waters' *Cry-Baby*. …Aside from the pastiche of teen pics, Waters slyly reworks **Depp's heart-throb image, presenting his baby-faced tough guy moves as an object of gay as well as straight desire.**

On Depp marrying Winona Ryder: "We'll do it when we have a chunk of time and we can do it quietly with a three-month honeymoon. I've heard about places in Australia, islands where you can be dropped off and there's nothing there at all. I guess you just run around eating coconuts and foliage and bugs."

Now that the subject has come up again, it's perhaps time to broach the **touchy matter of proposing**. There have been suggestions that the holes in Depp's jeans could have come from the number of times he's been down on his knees to the various women in his life. Apart from Winona and his first wife (he's now divorced), **he's been engaged to *Dirty Dancing's* Jennifer Grey and *Twin Peaks'* Sherilyn Fenn.**

"**That's not quite true. I was sort of engaged.** But if you haven't made some mistakes by 28, it's abnormal. People do whatever they do for whatever reasons, and it's not for anyone else to understand. And basically, it's none of their business..."

"...**If some guy came up to me on the street and said, 'I understand this and this about you,' I would fucking club him—in a second. But because people know you and you have a past, the attitude is, 'Let's dissect this fucker.'** " As in all the pseudo-psychological suggestions that Depp is trying to make up for his parents (divorced when he was 16).

So does he believe in **marriage** as an institution? "**I believe in marriage if that's what feels right. If you feel something, do it**. Why regret later? But it's true you never really know until you hit that one. Believe me, **when I met Winona and we fell in love, it was absolutely like nothing ever before, ever.**"

Did his tattoos hurt? **"Yeah, but I liked the pain. It was electric, kind of nice."**

Does fame turn people into assholes? "I think it reveals what people are rather than changes them. I'm pretty sure I'm not an asshole, although I could be wrong. But fame does fuck with you. **I've become more paranoid**."

What did you do with the pubic hair that one fan sent you? "I threw it away. I didn't touch it. I thought about burning it, but I didn't want to inhale the air. **You never know, it may have been poisoned, cyanide pubic hair**."

BPD ISSUES, SYMPTOMS & JOHNNY DEPP:

The Face interview reveals evidence of some BPD symptoms such as:

1) **Unstable relationships.** He's been engaged a number of times but it means nothing in the long run. Depp's ashamed of being caught proposing marriage to every woman he meets – so he's in denial. His relationships are on an insane rollercoaster.

2) **Unstable identity**. Depp's self-concept, identity, personality, self-esteem is precarious and unpredictable.

3) **Unstable emotions**. Under stress Depp starts getting quite paranoid. If things don't go Johnny's way in TV, films or relationships, for instance, he can get furious, fearful and depressed.

Chapter 34

"France and the whole of Europe have a great culture and an amazing history. Most important thing, though, is that people there know how to live! In America they've forgotten all about it. I'm afraid that the American culture is a disaster."
— Johnny Depp

Ils se marièrent et eurent beaucoup d'enfants (*...And They Lived Happily Ever After*) (2004) – Depp was featured in it - storyline:

Writer, director, and actor Yvan Attal takes another look at the ups and downs of love and monogamy in this biting romantic comedy.

Vincent (Yvan Attal), Fred (Alain Cohen), and Georges (Alain Chabat) are three Parisian men in their early forties who are coming to the unfortunate realization that their love lives are not what they dreamed of in their youth.

Vincent is married to Gabrielle (Charlotte Gainsbourg), and while there's still some spark left in their marriage, it usually appears only after an argument. Vincent is having a furtive affair with a beautiful woman (Angie David), while Gabrielle is tempted to do the same when a handsome man in a record shop (Johnny Depp) begins silently flirting with her.

Fred is the bachelor of the group, and seems to have an endless parade of women passing through his bedroom, but no one misses the fact that he longs for the sort of long-term relationship that has so far evaded him.

And Georges is reaching the end of his rope with his wife, Nathalie (Emmanuelle Seigner), an abrasive feminist who insists on making every aspect of their lives a political matter, but lacking the courage to break up with her, Georges deals with his feelings in the traditional manner -- he buys a new car. *Happily Ever After* was Attal's first project as writer and director after his international hit *Ma Femme Est une Actrice* (*rottentomatoes*).

JOHNNY DEPP'S LIFE BEHIND THE SCENES:

JOHNNY DEPP DIAGNOSED: UNAUTHORIZED PSYCHOLOGICAL DIAGNOSIS OF HIS SECRET LIFE

Johnny Depp (J. Waters, *Interview Magazine*, April 1990):

What made you quit school?

"I had no credits. I mean, basically, I had, like, eight credits, and I was in my third year of high school, and I didn't want to be there, and **I was bored out of my mind, and I hated it."**

"Shit. They all thought I was going to end up in jail**, a drug addict."**

On playing in a band: **"Well, after we did two shows I got really drunk, *really* drunk. I was at the bar after the club had closed. I was, I don't know, getting ready to puke or something.** And I saw Iggy in skimpy little pants, wandering around the club with a dog."

"...And for some reason, and I don't know why—I think I just wanted to get a response out of him—I started screaming at him. I started calling him names and shit. I started screaming and yelling at him, 'Fuck you!' I don't know why, because I always idolized him. And he walked over to me and just looked at me, and I thought he was gonna hit me. And he said, 'You little turd.' And he walked away."

BPD ISSUES, SYMPTOMS & JOHNNY DEPP:

The Waters interview was cut down to a couple points related to Depp's BPD symptoms:

1) **Volatile, impulsive, self-destructive behavior** including substance abuse of alcohol and drugs. Once Johnny starts drinking and drugging he never knows what's going to happen – the example in the interview had Depp screaming curses and insulting a famous rock star which could have got him fired from his gig.

2) **Chronic feelings of emptiness, boredom and loneliness** led Depp to quit high school and has led to his other excessive behavior including self-mutilation, cutting himself and other self-destructive activity.

Chapter 35

"Better to not know which moment may be your last. Every morsel of your entire being alive to the infinite mystery of it all."
— Johnny Depp

Pirates of the Caribbean: Dead Man's Chest (2006) starred Depp as Captain Jack Sparrow – storyline:

Captain Jack Sparrow (Johnny Depp) returns to the screen for another round of supernatural adventures on the high seas in this spirited sequel to the 2003 Disney hit, which re-teams original director Gore Verbinski with original screenwriters Ted Elliott and Terry Rossio.

As Will (Orlando Bloom) and Elizabeth (Keira Knightley) prepare to exchange vows at the altar, their wedding plans hit rough waters with the arrival of sea-bound scallywag Jack Sparrow.

It seems that Sparrow owes a substantial blood debt to half-octopus sea captain Davy Jones (Bill Nighy), and that the only way for the flamboyant sea rover to elude the wrath of his otherworldly pursuer is to seek the aid of mysterious and powerful voodoo priestess Tia Dalma (Naomie Harris), whose ability to resurrect the dead and gaze into the future may provide just the advantage needed to avoid a waterlogged fate in the locker of his legendary nemesis (*rottentomatoes*).

JOHNNY DEPP'S LIFE BEHIND THE SCENES:

Sweet Sensation (B. Zehme, *Rolling Stone*, Jan. 10, 1991):

On the cutting edge with Johnny Depp, the offbeat hero of *Edward Scissorhands*

He was born Depp. He has always been Depp. As a boy, he was ridiculed for it. In the schoolyard, he was called Dipp. Or Deppity Dawg.

"Coupla tequila worms flying out here and there," Depp said, but he was joking about that. **He hadn't touched the**

hard stuff for a solid month, maybe longer. Depp was as dry as he'd been in all of his twenty-seven years.

"Johnny could play a wonderfully sexy mass murderer. I mean, it is a part *made* for him." Which is to say, there is a **shadiness to Depp**. He looks unattractively unwashed. ("Nobody looks better in rags," said Waters of the basic Depp sartorial statement.)

But you look at him and you get a feeling. There is a lot of pain and humor and darkness and light. I think for him [the role] is probably very personal. **It's just a very strong internal feeling of loneliness.** It's not something he talks about or even can talk about, because it's sad, ya know. What are ya gonna do?"

Rebellious in school, he was once suspended for mooning a gym teacher. He learned to smoke by age twelve and then **drink and finally take drugs**. Two years later, his parents divorced, and soon after, Depp quit high school to join a rock band...

At twenty, he married Lori Anne Allison, a twenty-five-year-old makeup artist and they left Florida for Hollywood, where they broke up.

He was undercover high-school cop Tom Hanson on Fox's *21 Jump Street*...Beautiful actresses flocked to his side. Before it was over, **there were two failed engagements:** to Sherilyn

Fenn (*Twin Peaks*) and to Jennifer Grey (*Dirty Dancing*)... he met Winona Ryder, the girl who would change his life forever.

They then traced the history of their romance for me: Ryder said. "**It was a classic glance**," he said, "like the zoom lenses in *West Side Story*, and **everything else gets foggy**." She said, "It wasn't a long moment, but it was suspended." **They knew it was love...**

Tabloid photographers terrorize them at airports, and tabloid reporters regularly report imaginary squalls and breakups. So he gets angry, and she gets incredulous. Winona: "They try to *trip* me at airports!" Depp: **"What's shitty about them is they feel like you *owe* them! That you should stop dead in your tracks and let them piss on you!"** Winona: "I will say that there *are* some really nice ones." Depp: "A couple of them are real nice." Winona: "But aren't we allowed to be in a bad mood sometimes? Everybody else is."

Spooning up corn chowder in a tiny restaurant, he was openly penitent about his **"younger, hellion, hitting-the-sauce-hard kind of days."** He owned up to his short fuse: **"I've got a bit of a temper."** He spoke of a tussle or two and of the circumstances surrounding **his arrest in Vancouver** during his *21 Jump Street* tenure.

Apparently, he tried to visit some friends late one night in their hotel, where Depp himself had once lived, and a security guard would have none of it. "The guy had a boner for me," Depp said. **"He had a wild hair up his ass, and he got real mouthy with me, saying 'I know who you are, but you** can't come up unless you're a guest here.' The mistake he eventually made was to put his hands on me. I pushed him back, and then we sort of wrestled around a bit, and I ended up spittin' in his face."**

The police didn't want to hear Depp's story. He was jailed for a night, fingerprinted, posed for mug shots ("I wish I could have them."), and in the morning he walked.

But the most beloved legends of Depp are not violent legends. Hardly. For Depp is a name synonymous with great romance. **In his young life, he has asked for the troth of four separate women. Whereas other actors are elusive Lotharios, Depp is the marrying kind, unintimidated by the notion of connubial permanence.**

"I've never been one of those guys who goes out and screws everything that's in front of him . . . When you're growing up, you go through a series of misjudgments. Not bad choices, but wrong choices . . . You know, people make mistakes. We all fuck up . . . I was really young for the longest time. We were young. **My relationships weren't as heavy as people think they were.** I don't know what it is, possibly I was trying to rectify my family's situation or I was just madly in love . . ."

"You're the first person that I've talked to about this kind of stuff. And I'm being really honest with you when I say that **there's been nothing ever throughout my twenty-seven years that's comparable to the feeling I have with Winona** . . . It's like this weird, bounding atom or something.

He then said this about his engagement to Winona: "People don't realize this, but we've been together almost a year and a half. Out of any, whatever, *thing* I've been through before, it hasn't been this long. **It wasn't like, 'Hi, nice to meet you, here's a ring.' It was about five months [before we got engaged]**. They thought we ran away to Las Vegas and got married."

When will their nuptials actually transpire? "The wedding thing?" he said. "We're just gonna do it when we both have time, because we both know we're gonna end up working in the next couple of months. And **we want to be able to do it when we can get hitched and then go away for a few months. Leave the country, just go wandering around, and be on a beach somewhere with tropical drinks**."

BPD ISSUES, SYMPTOMS & JOHNNY DEPP:

Depp exposes some Borderline Personality Disorder symptoms unintentionally in the above 1991 *Rolling Stone* interview:

1) **Unstable, precarious relationships** – by Depp's mid-twenties he'd been married and engaged at least four times. Depp jumps into relationships, gets engaged or married, then gets into knock-down-drag-out-screaming fights with "the love of his life" until they break-up, make-up, break-up and continue the rollercoaster until it ends.

2) **Hot-tempered, explosive emotions** – his anger is out of control and he's admitted his bad temper which has led to hot-blooded fights and arrests.

3) **Volatile, zany, capricious behavior** – self-destructive, impulsive substance abuse of alcohol and drugs; assaulting and fights with people he's angry with when things don't go his way.

Chapter 36

"Just keep moving forward and don't give a shit about what anybody thinks. Do what you have to do, for you."
― Johnny Depp

Sweeney Todd: The Demon Barber of Fleet Street (2007) starred Depp as Sweeney Todd – storyline:

In the Victorian London, the barber Benjamin Barker is married to the gorgeous Lucy and they have a lovely child, Johanna. The beauty of Lucy attracts the attention of the corrupt Judge Turpin, who falsely accuses the barber of a crime that he did not commit and abuses Lucy later after gaining custody of her.

After fifteen years in exile, Benjamin returns to London under the new identity of Sweeney Todd, seeking revenge against Turpin. He meets the widow Mrs. Lovett who is the owner of a meat pie shop who tells him that Lucy swallowed arsenic many years ago, and Turpin assigned himself tutor of Johanna. He opens a barber shop above her store, initiating a crime rampage against those who made him suffer and lose his beloved family (*IMDb*).

JOHNNY DEPP'S LIFE BEHIND THE SCENES:

Johnny Depp: Hollywood's Tough, Rough New Romeo (T. Burke, *Cosmopolitan*, Jan. 1991):

He dropped out of school, had tried "every kind of drug there was" by age eleven, and his tattoo reads Winona Forever. Your typical leading man this raunchy maverick is not!

The girl at the bar who has been gazing at Johnny Depp...this twenty-seven-year-old whom television's *21 Jump Street* turned into what a British tabloid called **"the 1990s' woman's ultimate wet dream."**

"One day, a friend brought Winona to lunch, and it was an instant connection between us. Skyrocket!" He thrusts his cigarette toward McSorley's moldy ceiling, causing those in the bar not already aware of him to turn. "A BLT and love. Winona and I hung out the whole day—and night. We've been together ever since."

He stayed in high school three years, "I was bored to death, hated it...Though I got it out of my system, **by age eleven I'd tried every kind of drug there was."**

"God, I looked way too old to be in high school, but at the show, they said, 'We want you to do interviews for all these magazines.' I said, 'What magazines?' They said, 'Sixteen! Teen Beat! Teen Dream!' That's how TV's sold." Of the ten thousand letters a week Johnny got, he says sadly, "**Really, things are very bad when kids have to write to an actor for advice. I can't tell anybody what to do. I'm just as screwed up as the next guy**."

"I'm old-fashioned," he murmurs. "I believe that Winona is forever."

"Brando says, 'Everybody acts, every day, every second,' and that's so true. Most of the movie business is such bull. TV ratings and Oscars are taken as seriously as if life depended on them. **All I am is a guy who pretends he's someone else and gets paid for it**."

If movies are sexier than ever, Hollywood life, at least what Johnny's seen of it, is far more reserved. "**Those who did drugs, a lot of them are cleaned up, and Alcoholics Anonymous has become really huge out there, almost like a club." No, he hasn't been to an AA meeting**

himself. And as for sex, the luckiest thing, he feels, is to have a girl who makes promiscuity unnecessary, unthinkable.

Ask what keeps him grounded in the face of stardom; why a wild kid is now a quiet man; why, instead of popping pills, he's popping corn, and **every answer begins with the name Winona**. The countless ladies who'd love to love him for a night? Since Winona, they just don't apply, and the inevitable day when he'll no longer look young, or even good, doesn't matter a whit.

Now he asks the time—Johnny doesn't wear a watch—and steps to a phone booth nearby. **"Winona's kind of expecting me about now..."** he says apologetically.

BPD ISSUES, SYMPTOMS & JOHNNY DEPP:

The *Cosmopolitan* interview touches on some of Johnny's BPD symptoms:

1) **Unstable identity**: His acting enables Depp to use his eccentric self-identity which is volatile. Part of his intense attachment to women is making them his higher power – Winona was his solution to everything.

2) **Unstable behavior**: Depp has substance abuse problems with alcohol and possibly drugs which he's in denial about – he admits avoiding A.A. or treatment.

3) **His chronic feelings of emptiness** have led him to hop from one woman to the next, from one drink or drug to the next, from one self-mutilation, cutting himself to tattoos – he says he enjoys the pain from getting tattooed.

Chapter 37

"There's a drive in me that won't allow me to do certain things that are easy."
— Johnny Depp

Pirates of the Caribbean: At World's End (2007) starred Depp as Captain Jack Sparrow – storyline:

After Elizabeth, Will, and Captain Barbossa rescue Captain Jack Sparrow from the land of the dead, they must face their foes, Davy Jones and Lord Cutler Beckett. Beckett, now with control of Jones' heart, forms a dark alliance with him in order to rule the seas and wipe out the last of the Pirates.

Now, Jack, Barbossa, Will, Elizabeth, Tia Dalma, and crew must call the Pirate Lords from the four corners of the globe, including the infamous Sao Feng, to gathering. The Pirate Lords want to release the goddess Calypso, Davy Jones's damned lover, from the trap they sent her to out of fear, in which the Pirate Lords must combine the 9 pieces that bound her by ritual to undo it and release her in hopes that she will help them fight.

With this, all pirates will stand together and will make their final stand for freedom against Beckett, Jones, Norrington, the Flying Dutchman, and the entire East India Trading Company (*IMDb*).

JOHNNY DEPP'S LIFE BEHIND THE SCENES:

Depp Charge—Johnny Depp Catches Fire (J. Schneller, *GQ Magazine*, Oct. 1993):

JOHNNY ANGEL—Behind *Johnny Depp's* teen-idol facade lies the soul of a philosopher-king and the heart of a juvenile delinquent.

He is a stoner—he is the philosopher-king of the stoners...One good thing about being a teen idol: You get all the babes. One bad thing: You're hounded for it. All together now, let's recite the story of **Depp's love life—lost his virginity at 13, married at 20, divorced two years later, then proposed and proposed and proposed, to Sherilyn Fenn, Jennifer Grey and, especially, Winona Ryder.**

Depp *tattooed her name on his body*, a banner reading "WINONA FOREVER" all over his upper right arm. **It was more than romantic, it was reckless.**

Depp's alter ego, the way-cool burned-out bad boy, grinds his truck through the traffic on Wilshire Boulevard, banging a new pack of Marlboros on his knee for several long blocks. The Corvette engine he stuck under the hood revs and revs. He stops for five seconds in a tow-away zone to light a smoke. A security guard materializes at his window. "Sir, you can't park here," the guard says.

"Yeah, yeah Officer, we're just looking at the angle of light across the dashboard here. It's important to see it from just this angle," Depp says in the exaggeratedly polite, deliberately stupid voice of the die-hard delinquent.

The guard is baffled. "Sir, you can't park here for *any length* of time."

"Yeah, right, okay, hmm, right," Depp says. He waits another two minutes to prove his point, then drives away.

The angel, you see, has a devil inside. The birdies chirping in the park and the engine revving in his truck are the twin sound tracks of Depp's life; the little girl on her Hot Wheels and the obtuse security guard, his dual muses.

Johnny Reb dropped out of high school at 16, **experimented freely with chemical substances** and came to California to play guitar. **"I'm sure my brain stopped at 17**," he says. "I was really happy then. I was playing in a band, reading books I hadn't wanted to read in school. There were girls around. In a way, **I'm sort of stuck there**."

Depp has been arrested, twice, though nothing came of either charge. Once for getting into a fight in Vancouver, where *Jump Street* was shot, and **once in Beverly Hills, for jaywalking**.

"**The cop was one of those guys who puts on a uniform and suddenly he feels his penis begin to grow**," Depp says. "He's all bent out of shape and hard as nails, a real idiot." As he was writing out the jaywalking ticket, the cop ordered Depp to put out his cigarette. Depp refused, so the cop twisted his wrist until the cigarette fell from his hand. He lit another. "**Next thing I knew, him and his partner handcuffed me and put me in a cell for a few hours. I'm not scared by those people, they just make me angry. You get the feeling there's nothing you can do, but there is something you can do. Don't take shit from them.**"

That's the Depp philosophy in a nutshell: **Live, give, and don't take shit.** One night **he was dangerously drunk**, hanging by his digits from the top of the five-story parking garage at the Beverly Center Mall with Nicolas Cage. Another night, **he and Gibby Haynes, lead singer of the Butthole Surfers, spotted some guy's motorcycle in Sherilyn Fenn's driveway, kidnapped the helmet, painted it garish colors (including the visor), and returned it with a love note.**

JOHNNY DEPP DIAGNOSED: UNAUTHORIZED PSYCHOLOGICAL DIAGNOSIS OF HIS SECRET LIFE

Entering the Depp Zone...But once you're there, **you still have to learn to tune in to his frequency, where deep thoughts are communicated though sentences are never finished.**

Depp went to the Reagan White House? "I had this publicist, he wanted me to, I just had to check it out," he says.

Check what out? He sighs. "It was about the 'Just Say No' thing."

Wait a second. Johnny Depp, self-proclaimed taker of every drug known to man, went to a "Just Say No" event?

Depp's ability to see way beyond the other side of the coin inspires deep Depp-love in people as diverse as Roddy McDowall, Vincent Price, Timothy Leary and Douglas, a homeless man who frequents Highland Avenue.

One long, dull afternoon in Miramar, in southeastern Florida, where Depp and Sal grew up, **Depp actually set himself aflame while trying to breathe fire.** His friend Bones, a skinny guy with chipped teeth and lank red hair, put the fire out with his hands. The scars are visible on Depp's right cheek.

"And sometimes you play roles that are close to you, you identify with the guy. Not that you become the person, because I don't buy into that shit at all. But this movie was a rough time for me. I poisoned myself constantly: **drinking**, didn't eat right, no sleep, lots of cigarettes.

It was really a lonely, really fucking lonely, time."

Gilbert's life could easily have been Depp's. During Depp's "**weird upbringing**," his family moved all over Kentucky before he was 7. When they finally landed in Miramar, they lived in "probably thirty different houses" before he left, at 20. Thirty houses, in a town of 33,000 people.

BPD ISSUES, SYMPTOMS & JOHNNY DEPP:

The *GQ Magazine* interview exposes some of Depp's BPD symptoms such as:

1) **Unstable, zany behavior**: As an example, Depp gulped a mouthful of gasoline, blew it out and lit it on fire. He burned part of his face. His self-destructive and impulsive behavior such as substance abuse (alcohol and drugs) has included fighting with police and security guards – which led to several arrests. Johnny gets antagonistic – the devil under his angel exterior. An alcoholic-addict like Depp can't afford to act-out his self-righteous anger.

2) **Unstable, volatile relationships**: Depp's "weird upbringing" contributed to his relationship volatility – his parents broke up and he moved around dozens of times. He had little experience of stable relationships as a child and teenager. His relationships with women bounce from passionate, over-romanticized and

intensely loving – when Johnny idealizes her – to angry and abusive when he demonizes her.

3) **Unstable identity:** Johnny shifts from one bizarre self-image to another – he's an angel to pretty girls who chase him, a devil to cops he antagonizes. He tends to identify with rebel, alcoholic-addict writers such as the Beat types.

Chapter 38

"If there's any message to my work, it is ultimately that it's OK to be different, that it's good to be different, that we should question ourselves before we pass judgment on someone who looks different, behaves different, talks different..."

--Johnny Depp

Public Enemies (2009) starred Depp as John Dillinger – storyline:

This is the story of the last few years of the notorious bank robber John Dillinger. He loved what he did and could imagine little else that would make him happier. Living openly in 1930s Chicago, he had the run of the city with little fear of reprisals from the authorities.

It's there that he meets Billie Frechette with whom he falls deeply in love. In parallel we meet Melvin Purvis, the FBI agent who would eventually track Dillinger down. The FBI was is in its early days and Director J. Edgar Hoover was keen to promote the clean cut image that so dominated the organization through his lifetime.

Purvis realizes that if he is going to get Dillinger, he will have to use street tactics and imports appropriate men with police training. Dillinger is eventually betrayed by an acquaintance who tells the authorities just where to find him on a given night (*IMDb*).

JOHNNY DEPP'S LIFE BEHIND THE SCENES:

Johnny Depp gets serious: Actor talks about life (J. Gerstel, *Knight Ridder/Tribune News Service*, Dec. 8, 1993):

Now he is ready to confess. **Now that he hasn't touched "a drop of liquor or anything in quite a while."** That would be about four months.

Now that he's trying to clear the air about **his nightclub, the Viper Room, where River Phoenix spent the last half-hour of his young life before dying from drugs on the sidewalk outside.**

Now that there's nobody special, Winona Ryder being ex-special, though her name is still tattooed into his flesh. ("Just because we broke up doesn't mean that when I put it on my body it wasn't an honest moment," he said.)

Circumspect Johnny Depp engaged in heavy-duty damage control, trying to distance himself in the media from the **young Hollywood drug scene that did in Phoenix.**

"As far as drugs and the unfortunate, untimely death of River Phoenix—and that nightclub—they're not connected at all," he insisted.

"Let's put things in perspective. **River was in the club for all of 27 minutes.** And do people think I'm insane? Do they think I'm ignorant? To open a nightclub and allow people to do drugs, even in the bathroom? **That I'm going to throw everything away so that some people can get high in a nightclub?"**

"If you're talking about drugs, you're talking about America. People die from drug overdoses every single day. You can't say specifically Hollywood or Sunset Boulevard. The problem is everywhere, and it's been going on for 30 years at least."

"And the people benefiting from the drugs are very rich, and it's a huge business. So let's not pretend. **The problem is not necessarily on the streets with the kids.** Though there's a lot of curious kids who will try this and try that. The real problem is way up there—with the higher-ups. The upper, upper echelon."

"And you can't own a nightclub where you shake down every single person who walks in the room. You cannot do a body search and check their pockets."

He said Phoenix was not a close friend, and besides, "What's done is done. We all make mistakes, and I've made 'em just as much as anybody else—done things that I shouldn't have. **Spent a lot of time getting drunk or gettin' high or whatever.** Spent too much time being very indulgent and pained."

So how come he's still alive at 30 while Phoenix will never see 24? **"I saw it was enough,"** he said. **"And luckily, I had friends and family who saw a different side of me that wanted to be saved."**

"My mom and dad are very smart," he said. "I'm actually very lucky. Very lucky. I've escaped some of the traps that actors of my generation can easily fall into. The tortured artist thing. '**Oh, it's so painful to be famous**.'"

Depp said, "**The late 20s were not the greatest period...I felt suspended. I don't like middles; <u>I like extremes</u>. I like very hot and very cold, you know? And the late 20s were sort of unextreme. <u>Kind of just gray</u>.**"

He never did see himself as a voice of twenty-somethings because he doesn't think his generation has a specific voice.

"It's a dangerous, very confusing world out there for my generation and the generation beneath mine just coming up—it's not a great time to grow up.

"There doesn't seem to be any hope. There doesn't seem to be anything on the horizon. Everything's been said. Everything's been done."

But now that he's 30, Depp does feel more focused. "I can feel things changing, and I like it," he said. "I'm paying more attention to things. I like different things. **I'm growing up**."

He feels no sense of loss. "It feels like all gain," he said. "**Because I do still feel 17 in a lot of ways. It's 17 but better, a clearer 17, a more adult 17...**"

"**Part of me still needs the freedom to wander**, you know? To go anywhere, everywhere and do anything. That's a strong part."

"**But another part of me wants the stability** of normal family life, or what we think of as normal family life. I want kids, and I want a wife who is beautiful and brilliant and . . . fun. I want all those things."

Others have noted **Depp's charismatic winsomeness darkened with a hint of something sinister**.

Children respond to what's childlike in him, and young adults identify with his alienation. And nobody can take their eyes off that beautiful face.

"I'm not sure what first attracted me," she said, and then recites his attributes precisely. **"His voice, his looks, his attitude, and something mysterious . . . he seemed so innocent but he had to be tough."**

His escapes, now that **drugs and booze are history**, are cars and music.

BPD ISSUES, SYMPTOMS & JOHNNY DEPP:

It is interesting that Depp admits he likes extremes – not the middle or gray areas:

"The late 20s were not the greatest period...I felt suspended. I don't like middles; <u>I like extremes</u>. I like very hot and very cold, you know? And the late 20s were sort of unextreme. <u>Kind of just gray</u>."

In BPD theory, flipping from one extreme to the other is known as "splitting" – this explains some of the Depp unstable, wild, outrageous relationship rollercoaster pattern. Johnny jumps into relationships with women claiming to be wildly in love – he **idealizes** her, puts her on a pedestal, views her through rose-tinted glasses, romanticizes her, gets a "Winona Forever" tattoo, proposes marriage to Winona Ryder, Jennifer Grey, Sherilyn Fenn and God only knows how many other women including possibly Amber Heard.

Except with openly bisexual lipstick-lesbian Amber, who has a lesbian lover, I'd expect that Depp might keep it a secret engagement. Because with Amber he might have to commit to a three-way wedding with Amber, himself and her latest lesbian lover.

Then Johnny gets "bored senseless" with the "love of his life," gets into knock-down screaming fights and comes to blows with his former dream-girl who now is **demonized**. He unrealistically discounts and degrades her to the devil when prior to this she was his angel. No middle-ground, no grays.

The *Knight Ridder/Tribune News Service* interview revealed several of Depp's BPD symptoms and an underlying dynamic ("splitting"):

1) **Unstable, shaky relationships**: Depp's "splitting" results in his romantic partner flipping from an angel, idealized to a devil, evil spirit or monster when he unrealistically labels her a demon. As she is tossed from one extreme category – idealized or demonized – to the other the relationship is smashed, shattered and ends.

2) **Unstable, impulsive behavior**: Johnny is in denial about substance abuse – abusing alcohol and drugs. He makes up alibis about why people OD at the club he once owned. When River Phoenix died of an OD, it was hard for Depp to deny drug abuse which he enabled. Of course you'll never hear of Depp going to A.A. or a rehab because he can "just say no."

Chapter 39

"I pretty much try to stay in a constant state of confusion just because of the expression it leaves on my face."
--Johnny Depp

Alice in Wonderland (2010) starred Depp as the Mad Hatter – storyline:

Alice, an unpretentious and individual 19-year-old, is betrothed to a dunce of an English nobleman. At her engagement party, she escapes the crowd to consider whether to go through with the marriage and falls down a hole in the garden after spotting an unusual rabbit.

Arriving in a strange and surreal place called "Underland," she finds herself in a world that resembles the nightmares she had as a child, filled with talking animals, villainous queens and knights, and frumious bandersnatches. Alice realizes that she is there for a reason--to conquer the horrific Jabberwocky and restore the rightful queen to her throne (*IMDb*).

JOHNNY DEPP'S LIFE BEHIND THE SCENES:

Depp Perception (S. Morgan, *Harper's Bazaar*, May 1993):

Once a TV heartthrob, now an avatar of the outré and the outcast, Johnny Depp is bringing otherworldly insight to upcoming films...

"**The most intriguing thing to me about tattoos is that your body is your journal**," he remarks, rolling down his sleeves and covering up everything that has been recorded on his upper arms. "I've been tempted to get more, but I guess these were the ones I needed. But maybe in my line of work, it's not too smart to get any more."

Famous People Get Anxious, Too...*If you have an anxiety disorder, take comfort in knowing that celebrities do, too.* (J. A. Scott, *everydayhealth*)

Anxiety disorders such as phobias and obsessive-compulsive disorder (OCD) affect 40 million American adults every year, and celebrities aren't immune from them. In fact, they're fairly commonplace in Hollywood. Check out our list of anxiety-afflicted stars, and the next time you feel overwhelmed by your anxiety disorder, let the successes of these celebrities inspire you.

Johnny Depp

Never mind the oldies classic — not everyone loves a clown. Despite the clownish makeup he wore in *Edward Scissorhands* and *Alice in Wonderland*, **Depp has a fear of clowns**, a condition known as **coulrophobia**. He even had nightmares about them as a child. "It's impossible to distinguish if clowns are happy or if they're about to bite your face off," Depp says.

BPD people = good at acting? *(Psychforums* reports, Jan. 3, 2010):

Actors, who are rumoured to have Borderline Personality Disorder (BPD) don't have a strong sense of self and take on many different personas throughout their life.

So this means that it would make them good at acting as they would be able to mould easily into the character they would be playing...

Some actors/celebrities who may have BPD include: Johnny Depp, Angelina Jolie, Courtney Love, Marilyn Monroe, Britney Spears, Amy Winehouse, Kurt Cobain and Princess Diana.

Anxiety can strike anyone even Johnny Depp (*examiner*, Feb. 17, 2010):

With the upcoming release of one of his most fantastical films and his years of stage and screen experience one might think he would be immune to such a common place disorder, yet even Johnny Depp has been noted as suffering from this mental malady. In fact an estimated six million Americans over the age of 18 struggle with panic disorder in a given year. Surprisingly, panic disorder is 'all in your head'.

Panic disorder is characterized by the sudden and repeated intrusion of fearful and in the most severe cases, terrorizing feelings experienced by a person when presented with known or unknown stressors. It is a legitimate mental health condition that is diagnosable and treatable.

What people do not necessarily understand about this disorder however is that the brain is what impacts the physical body symptoms as much as the emotional being. The basal ganglia, located under the cortex of the brain is the initial area of impact.

Underneath this area is the limbic system, considered the oldest portion of the brain, which is divided into even more complex systems that regulate emotional reaction, memory, mood, logic, decision making, temperature systems, voluntary body functions, and the ability to regulate dangerous situations.

There is functionality in the "fight or flight" response induced during anxiety as it allows a person to immediately be removed from a questionable situation however when the anxiety overwhelms the brain systems neurotransmission what occurs is reduced regulation of morality, reality, and logic leading to irrational responses.

The good news is this disorder can be treated with Cognitive Behavioral Therapy which is rated as one successful approach to healing. There are also numerous medications available to treat anxiety however, without addressing potential sources underlying the loss of control often at the root of anxiety, medication tends to mask symptoms rather than treat so a collaborative approach of therapy and medication is recommended versus singular treatment. And remember, if you struggle with anxiety, you are not alone, just ask Johnny Depp!

BPD ISSUES, SYMPTOMS & JOHNNY DEPP:

From the articles and interviews in this chapter there is evidence of Depp's BPD:

1) **Unstable, impulsive and self-destructive behavior**: Depp has transitioned from self-mutilation, cutting himself – he has seven or eight scars on his arm – to enjoying the pain of getting tattoos; both cutting scars and tattoos are considered part of his "journal."

2) **Volatile, erratic emotions**: Johnny suffers from panic disorder. Add to this his track record of uncontrolled anger and chronic feelings of emptiness or boredom.

To review some of those BPD people mentioned, see my books ANGELINA JOLIE PSYCHOANALYZED; PRINCESS DIANA DIAGNOSED; ROCK STARS DIAGNOSED; MARILYN MONROE DIAGNOSED.

Chapter 40

"When kids hit one year old, it's like hanging out with a miniature drunk. You have to hold onto them. They bump into things. They laugh and cry. They urinate. They vomit."
--Johnny Depp

The Tourist (2010) starred Depp as Frank - storyline:

Elise (Angelina Jolie) sits next to an American tourist, Frank (Johnny Depp), on a train going to Venice. She has chosen him as a decoy, making believe that he is her lover who is wanted by police.

Not only will they need to evade the police, but also the mobster whose money her lover stole. A woman sitting in a Parisian café reads a letter telling her to take the train to

Venice, pick a man of the sender's height and build, and chat him up.

She's being watched: Scotland Yard and a mobster with a crew of Russian thugs are looking for a man she knows. On the train, she talks to an American, Frank, suggests they have dinner, and, once in Venice, invites him to her hotel.

The bait is set: the Russians think Frank is the man they want: Alexander Pearce, who stole billions from the mobster. Scotland Yard realizes Frank is a just a tourist, but by now he's in danger, smitten by the mystery woman, and in their way. Can the Yard keep Frank from death and still catch Pearce? (*IMDb*)

JOHNNY DEPP'S LIFE BEHIND THE SCENES:

The 'US' Profile: Johnny Depp (B. Israel, *US Magazine*, May 1993):

He emerged an **alienated teenager**—but a musical one. He snuck into bars, gigged with local bands, launched a precocious (and much-chronicled) run of sex, **drugs**, "yeah and sloppy rock & roll." At age 16 he dropped out of high school and within a year formed his own band, the Kids. The Kids became popular: they opened for the B-52's and Talking Heads and, in 1983, they left Florida for Los Angeles and the L.A. club scene.

Depp recalls this time in his life as "hard. Loud. **A lot of drinks**."

The Career Within You (E. Wagele, *psychologytoday* blog, Nov. 1, 2011):

Finding the perfect job for your personality

Johnny Depp - "Romantic" Type: Unusual roles and twists to roles typify this introverted actor.

Johnny Depp is questioning, sensitive, and guided by his feelings. He sounds to me like a Romantic type influenced by his Observer "wing" (the personality next to his): Gabrielle Donnelly of the *Daily Mail* describes him as "softly spoken and, endearingly, still retaining about him something of the questioning air of the student."

Depp's family moved over 30 times. Donnelly quotes him, "**I recall hearing my parents argue and thinking, 'Come on, this is torture. Just split!**' They stuck it out until I was 15, but I'd seen it coming for years. When they finally did divorce, I thought: 'OK, this is the right thing.' **My mum got ill after my father left, so my attention was taken up in making sure she was OK. I didn't have the time until later to mourn that loss of a sense of family, however unhappy**." The next few years he turned inward and isolated with his guitar, headed toward becoming a musician.

Donnelly's description of him as an offbeat art house maverick also fits the Romantic. Before he met Vanessa Paradis, he had been married once and engaged at least three times. He was

rebellious, as some Romantics are. Romantic types are known for their compassion, their interest in the arts (though not all have this interest), and doing things in unusual or special ways. Depp in his career has done the **unexpected.**

In the TV crime series *21 Jump Street*, 1987, he played a baby-faced police officer posing as a teenager investigating crimes in high schools and colleges. This made him a teen idol at 24, which didn't match his values or his introversion. **"If the choice is to be gawked at constantly or to sit in a dark room, I'd choose the dark room. I felt as if I had been turned into a novelty, and it was mortifying. When I was in a social situation, I was nervous and uncomfortable. The only way I could get through it was to drink my guts out! I wasted a lot of years."**

One more thing: **Depp's talents are special and rare, but who knows what his unusually beautiful face contributed to his personality, fame, and confidence?**

BPD ISSUES, SYMPTOMS & JOHNNY DEPP:

The articles in this chapter touch on several Depp BPD symptoms:

1) **Impulsive, self-destructive behavior**: Depp admits to a lot of substance abuse of alcohol and drugs.

2) **Unhinged, unstable identity**: Johnny's self-concept or self-identity is volatile and unbalanced. Depp chased after a rock star or movie star career. Then when he got acting work on TV, his erratic sense of self resulted in an angry, self-destructive reaction abusing alcohol and drugs: **"If the choice is to be gawked at constantly or to sit in a dark room, I'd choose the dark room. I felt as if I had been turned into a novelty, and it was mortifying. When I was in a social situation, I was nervous and uncomfortable. The only way I could get through it was to drink my guts out! I wasted a lot of years."**

Chapter 41

"I like the challenge of trying different things and wondering whether it's going to work or whether I'm going to fall flat on my face."
--Johnny Depp

Pirates of the Caribbean: On Stranger Tides (2011) starred Depp as Captain Jack Sparrow – storyline:

Captain Jack Sparrow (Depp) crosses paths with a woman from his past (Cruz), and he's not sure if it's love -- or if she's a ruthless con artist who's using him to find the fabled Fountain of Youth.

When she forces him aboard the Queen Anne's Revenge, the ship of the formidable pirate Blackbeard (McShane), Jack finds himself on an unexpected adventure in which he doesn't know who to fear more: Blackbeard or the woman from his past.

In London, Captain Jack Sparrow escapes from the soldiers that are chasing him and learns that an impostor is recruiting a crew and a vessel using his name. He meets the impersonator and finds that she actually is Angelica, a woman that he had seduced in a convent in Seville.

Jack is abducted and when he awakes aboard, the ship is sailing, Angelica tells him that her father, the pirate Blackbeard, is cursed and he needs to find the legendary Ponce de Leon's Fountain of Youth to save his life. They force Jack, who knows the location of the fountain, to guide them.

Meanwhile, Barbossa is hired by King George to lead the British crew and dispute against the Spaniards and Blackbeard who arrives first in the fountain. But along their dangerous quest, they need to find first two chalices that belonged to Ponce de Leon and a tear of mermaid (*IMDb*).

JOHNNY DEPP'S LIFE BEHIND THE SCENES:

Health, Feb. 1, 2006 reported:

JOHNNY DEPP DIAGNOSED: UNAUTHORIZED PSYCHOLOGICAL DIAGNOSIS OF HIS SECRET LIFE

Johnny Depp, a young actor well known for his past "bad boy" behavior, was born in Owensboro, Kentucky in 1963. In a 1999 Avantgarde interview Johnny said, "**As a teenager I was so insecure. I was the type of guy that never fitted in because he never dared to choose. I was convinced I had absolutely no talent at all. For nothing. And that thought took away all my ambition too.**"

Even today he still has feelings of insecurity about himself. In 1999 he said, "**My self-image it still isn't that alright. No matter how famous I am, no matter how many people go to see my movies, I still have the idea that I'm that pale no-hoper that I used to be. A pale no-hoper that happens to be a little lucky now. Tomorrow it'll be all over, then I'll have to go back to selling pens again.**"

During his teens he was drinking, smoking and doing drugs. There were episodes of petty theft and vandalism. He dropped out of high school at the age of sixteen so that he could concentrate on being a musician. **He continued to have problems with drugs and drinking into his twenties.**

Johnny has a series of seven or eight scars on his left forearm where he has cut himself with a knife on different occasions to commemorate various moments or rites of passage in his life.

In a *Talk* magazine interview he said, "**It was really just whatever [times when he hurt himself]--good times, bad times, it didn't matter. It wasn't like 'Okay, this just happened, I have to go hack a piece of my flesh off.'**" In a 1993 *Details* magazine interview Johnny explained his self-injury, "**My body is a journal in a way. It's like what sailors used to do, where every tattoo meant something, a specific time in your life when you make a mark on yourself, whether you do it yourself with a knife or with a professional tattoo artist**." Johnny has several tattoos, such as the one that says 'Wino Forever' (used to be 'Winona Forever" when he was dating the famous actress, Winona Ryder). Johnny Depp claims he has quit doing drugs and no longer drinks heavily.

In a 2001 *Movie Star Magazine* interview he talked about how he is currently the happiest he has ever been, "**There were many years I was feeling at a loss about my life or how I grew up. I couldn't understand what is right or what is precious. At that time, I was so miserable and self-defeating... I was feeling angry with various things. My anger came up to the surface then. I don't say such tendency has disappeared. Even now there are anger and the dark side in myself. But it's the first time I've been so close to the light**."

BPD ISSUES, SYMPTOMS & JOHNNY DEPP:

The above article documents some of Depp's BPD symptoms including:

Disturbance in self-concept: Depp, like other BPD people, has a highly variable self-image. **"There were many years I was feeling at a loss about my life or how I grew up. I couldn't understand what is right or what is precious. At that time, I was so miserable and self-defeating..."**

"My self-image it still isn't that alright. No matter how famous I am, no matter how many people go to see my movies, I still have the idea that I'm that pale no-hoper that I used to be. A pale no-hoper that happens to be a little lucky now. Tomorrow it'll be all over, then I'll have to go back to selling pens again."

Impulsive behaviors: Substance abuse of alcohol and drugs. **During his teens he was drinking, smoking and doing drugs. There were episodes of petty theft and vandalism**. He dropped out of high school at the age of sixteen so that he could concentrate on being a musician. **He continued to have problems with drugs and drinking into his twenties.**

Self-destructive activity: Self-mutilation or cutting of Depp's body. **"It was really just whatever [times when he hurt himself]--good times, bad times, it didn't matter. It wasn't like 'Okay, this just happened, I have to go hack a piece of my flesh off.'"**

"My body is a journal in a way. It's like what sailors used to do, where every tattoo meant something, a specific time in your life when you make a mark on yourself, whether you do it yourself with a knife or with a professional tattoo artist."

Labile affect (marked and rapid mood shifts): Sudden, frequent and intense changes in affect or emotions. "**I was feeling angry with various things. My anger came up to the surface then. I don't say such tendency has disappeared. Even now there are anger and the dark side in myself. But it's the first time I've been so close to the light.**"

Chapter 42

"I am doing things that are true to me. The only thing I have a problem with is being labeled."
--**Johnny Depp**

The Rum Diary (2011) stars Depp as Paul Kemp – storyline:

Hard-drinking journalist Paul Kemp takes a job at a besieged newspaper in San Juan, Puerto Rico. His volatile editor, Lotterman, assigns him to tourist pieces and horoscopes, but promises more.

Paul rooms with Sala, an aging and equally alcoholic reporter, in a rundown flat. Sanderson, a wealthy entrepreneur, hires Paul to flack for a group of investors who plan to buy an island near the capital and build a resort. Sanderson's girl-friend, the beguiling Chenault, bats her eyes at Paul.

His loyalties face challenges when he and Sala get in trouble with locals, when a Carnival dance enrages Sanderson, and when the paper hits the skids. Is the solution always alcohol?

Paul Kemp is a freelance journalist who finds himself at a critical turning point in his life while writing for a run-down newspaper in the Caribbean. Paul is challenged on many levels as he tries to carve out a more secure niche for himself amidst a group of lost souls all bent on self-destruction (*IMDb*).

JOHNNY DEPP'S LIFE BEHIND THE SCENES:

Johnny Handsome (S. Rebello, *Movieline*, May 1990):

By the time his parents divorced (each has remarried since), Depp, 15, was **Johnny Too Bad**. A striking, rangy kid, he had **dabbled in "every kind of drug there was" by age 11. Between bouts of swiping six-packs, breaking and**

entering, and classroom-trashing, Depp lost his cherry at age 13, and ditched school for good at 16.

"It was fairly normal," Depp says. "When you're 13, 14, and you hang out with a bunch of guys and the junior high prom just doesn't do it for you, you go out and *do* something. **Experiment. You live in Miami as a kid and [drugs are] everywhere. You try it for the usual reasons: peer pressure, curiosity, boredom.**" Depp left home to live in a '67 Impala with a buddy who had nowhere else to go.

In 1983, at 20, Depp and the band members moved to Los Angeles for their shot at stardom. The same year, **he married Lori Allison**, a younger sister of a musician pal, whom a friend at the time describes as "tiny, dark, pale, beautiful, and quiet. Johnny was the more outgoing of the two." Money got so tight that Depp sold ballpoint pens by phone. Although he and **Allison divorced two years later**, Allison's one-time boyfriend, actor Nicolas Cage, hooked up Depp with his agent.

"If you're honest with people, without splitting yourself open, sometimes you can help somebody in trouble," says Depp, who told the press early on about his former **drug and alcohol use**. He's no one's idea of a role model, which suits him fine.

"Things are pretty bad if kids have to write to an actor for advice. I couldn't tell anyone what to do. I don't want to be the Messiah or some spokesman for 'Just Say No' to drugs. I'm just as fucked up as the next guy. If I can help people by saying, 'I've done this and it really feels bad after a while. I wouldn't do it if I were you,'

that's great. But also, the [producers] were trying to make me out to be this, like, perfectly baked cake. I don't want to be what these people *created*."

Some observers say that what "these people" created is, in fact, an ego monster who keeps cast and crew members of *21 Jump Street,* which is filmed in Vancouver, B.C., in an uproar. **According to reports, Depp has set fire to his underwear, been deliberately belligerent to his producers, and even thrown them a punch or two.**

And just before Depp left to begin filming *Cry-Baby*, **he was arrested for assaulting a hotel security guard.** (And, later, he was completely cleared of those charges.) "**Guys have gotten a little cocky with me sometimes**," Depp says, in defense of his alleged behavior.

"**They either see that they can make themselves look good in front of their friends by being a man—something about their penis size, I guess—or they see free lunches in their future. So, they figure if they fuck with you, you'll hit then and they can take you to court.**"

Jabbing his umpteenth Marlboro into an overflowing ashtray, Depp says, "**I'm a little long in the tooth to be in high school. Clay won't help the bags under my eyes anymore...**"

For his part, Depp, who would "sooner fry burgers or pump gas than do Fabian movies," says, "**On my movies, I make my** own decisions based on what I feel, not on [what] someone says the public wants to swallow. I try to fight the everyday, normal leading man stuff as much as I can..."

"Winona and I are engaged. It's official. She has a lot of talent and, aside from that, I also happen to love her..." **Depp declines to discuss the fact that he also became officially engaged to his two previous girlfriends**, actress Sherilyn (*Two-Moon Junction*) Fenn and, more recently, actress Jennifer (*Dirty Dancing*) Grey, except to say, **"I'm pretty old-fashioned."**

Depp adds, cautiously, that for the first time, "I have beds tables, chairs, a TV set. And they're *mine*." And as for friends? "I've got a couple who are very important to me and **I have Winona who is very, very important to me. That's all I need."**

BPD ISSUES, SYMPTOMS & JOHNNY DEPP:

Johnny revealed BPD symptoms in the *Movieline* article:

<u>*Unpredictable, erratic relationships*</u>:   **"Winona and I are engaged.** It's official. She has a lot of talent and, aside from that, I also happen to love her..." **Depp declines to discuss the fact that he also became officially engaged to his two previous girlfriends**, actress Sherilyn (*Two-Moon Junction*) Fenn and, more recently, actress Jennifer (*Dirty Dancing*) Grey, except to say, **"I'm pretty old-fashioned."**

Unstable, volatile emotions: Johnny's emotions are a rollercoaster bouncing on a track consisting of anger to emptiness, loneliness, and fears of abandonment which is expressed as rage, bitterness and despondency:

Some observers say that what "these people" created is, in fact, an ego monster who keeps cast and crew members of *21 Jump Street,* which is filmed in Vancouver, B.C., in an **uproar. According to reports, Depp has set fire to his underwear, been deliberately belligerent to his producers, and even thrown them a punch or two.**

And just before Depp left to begin filming *Cry-Baby*, **he was arrested for assaulting a hotel security guard.** (And, later, he was completely cleared of those charges.) "**Guys have gotten a little cocky with me sometimes**," Depp says, in defense of his alleged behavior.

"**They either see that they can make themselves look good in front of their friends by being a man—something about their penis size, I guess—or they see free lunches in their future. So, they figure if they fuck with you, you'll hit then and they can take you to court.**"

Chapter 43

"For a long time I tried to manage an honesty and openness about my personal life because I'm human and I'm normal - well, semi-normal."
--Johnny Depp

Dark Shadows (2012) stars Depp as Barnabas Collins - storyline:

In the year 1752, Joshua and Naomi Collins, with young son Barnabas, set sail from Liverpool, England to start a new life in America. But even an ocean was not enough to escape the mysterious curse that has plagued their family.

Two decades pass and Barnabas (Johnny Depp) has the world at his feet-or at least the town of Collinsport, Maine. The master of Collinwood Manor, Barnabas is rich, powerful and an inveterate playboy...until he makes the grave mistake of breaking the heart of Angelique Bouchard (Eva Green).

A witch, in every sense of the word, Angelique dooms him to a fate worse than death: turning him into a vampire, and then burying him alive. Two centuries later, Barnabas is inadvertently freed from his tomb and emerges into the very changed world of 1972.

He returns to Collinwood Manor to find that his once-grand estate has fallen into ruin. The dysfunctional remnants of the Collins family have fared little better, each harboring their own dark secrets (*IMDb*).

JOHNNY DEPP'S LIFE BEHIND THE SCENES:

Depp Gets Deeper (J. Ryan, *Vogue,* Sept. 1994):

Johnny Depp escaped an unhappy childhood to become a teen idol, then fled that image by playing a bunch of quirky, alienated youths, and has now graduated to adult roles. But as James Ryan learns, the actor hasn't forgotten his roots—or his taste for the bizarre.

Depp in high school..."**I was not the most popular kid in school. I always felt like an absolute and total freak.**

Edward Scissorhands. That feeling of wanting to be accepted but not knowing how to be accepted as you are, honestly. Wanting to hold a girl but thinking I'll screw it up."

On *Don Juan DeMarco...* "It's really strange," he will say after filming the scene. "The first thing I felt was uncomfortable. When you walk into a room full of 250 naked women, you can't . . . you almost can't, it's impossible to focus on it. It's almost, in a way, wallpaper."

These days getting neo-adult Depp to talk about his **stints in jail, his chemical abuse, his tattoos, his scars,** paying people to smell rancid sausages, is like squeezing tears from a rock. Depp reinvented himself once before, shrewdly spoofing his image in John Waters' *Cry-Baby* to escape the bubble-gum strait-jacket of *21 Jump Street*. **Now he's determined to graduate from boy-man to, well, at least man-boy.**

His own parents split when he was fifteen, and he did more than his share of filial hand-holding, as well as picking up the support checks from his dad. "It's always taxing to play something that's closer to reality," he says. "Those four months were a very difficult time in my life. I just felt awful." (Asked what he inherited from his parents, he replies, "**Insanity** and chain-smoking.")

"He's one of those guys from the forties who were real gentlemen, very charming, loyal to his people," says Depp. **"Don Juan was also very chivalrous. Those guys don't**

exist anymore. Everybody is trying too hard to be hip or be accepted."

"...With acting, you're forming images with emotions. If you're satisfied, you're dead in the water because you stop. **I can just make this face, and make it look like I'm sad or like I'm angry. If I ever look at something I did and say, 'That was great,' I'll immediately dive in the river."**

"I feel closer to that character than any I've ever played. Like me, he was an outsider. That's the string, the mono-filament, that ties all my characters together. I can't escape that."

As a kid, Depp loved to dig tunnels in a vacant lot near his home, getting off on the fear of a cave-in. A few years back, he **hung by his fingers five stories above the ground from the edge of the Beverly Center. Now he looks for that same pure adrenaline rush** in his roles; the possibility that he might mess up keeps it exciting.

An informal poll of the *Don Juan* makeup trailer comes close to qualifying Depp for sainthood: sweet, kind, and above all, generous. Patty York, Depp's makeup artist on four of his last five films, says, **"He'll give you the shirt off his back."** (Literally: The other day she said she liked the shirt he had on. He took it off and gave it to her.) **He also regularly treats the crew to champagne at the end of the day.**

JOHNNY DEPP DIAGNOSED: UNAUTHORIZED PSYCHOLOGICAL DIAGNOSIS OF HIS SECRET LIFE

"Johnny is so totally different from most actors," says Smiley. **"He really likes who he is, and he's really secure in that. He treats other people the way he wants to be treated.** That's why we stay with him."

Saint Johnny is not without his demons. Between takes, he reveals these: **insomnia, a fear of crowds, chain-smoking, an antagonism toward authority figures that has landed him in jail on at least three occasions (after jaywalking in Los Angeles, assaulting a hotel security guard in Vancouver, and speeding in Arizona)**...

Depp has an "erratic" personality that makes him a little tough to live with. "I'm 30 different people sometimes," he says. **"One day you wake up and you're somebody else, nowhere near who you were when you went to sleep."**

There was a time not too long ago when Depp would readily volunteer to interviewers that his only real goal in life was to **"get married and have kids**." These days the actor is more circumspect. **"I believe in loyalty and commitment, but the idea of marriage is not the end-all. I don't think that's the ultimate answer to true love, if there is such a thing as true love**."

He was married once at 20, but divorced two years later. Depp legend has him again popping the question to Sherilyn Fenn, Jennifer Grey, and, of course, Ryder. **He insists that reports of his engagements have been "complete**

fabrications" but refuses to elaborate "because I don't want to hurt anybody's feelings."

He's also mute on what exactly happened to the famous WINONA FOREVER tattoo inked on his right shoulder. "It transformed itself," he says, then adds to further cloud the issue, **"But it was never WINONA FOREVER. They got it wrong." (Photos would seem to contradict this.)**

Cultivating an aura of mystery has always been a major component of Depp style. And now more than ever, he seems compelled to keep secrets.

"There's a huge part of him that's not within your reach," says Mary Steenburgen, who played his lover in *Gilbert Grape* and is now a close friend. **"He doesn't casually let himself over to people and let you know who he is.** If you're his oldest friend or his lover, perhaps that's not true, but for most people, I think he's both accessible and inaccessible."

When pressed for details, he closes the door, gently but firmly. **"My relationship with my girl isn't something I'm going to discuss with anybody, especially a guy with a tape recorder,"** he explains. "No matter how much I like them."

"Initially, I tried to be open," he says of his Hollywood Camelot days. "[I thought,] I'll just say what I'm feeling right now, let them swallow that, and then they'd leave

me alone. But that creates even more of a monster. You're walking around, you eat a piece of pizza, go visit the Coliseum, next thing you know there's a guy with a lens as long as your leg taking pictures.

Whether Kate and I are together or not is not going to save anybody's life. It's nobody's business but mine or hers. **I'd rather come out in the press and say I'm screwing dogs, or goats, or rats than attempt to rely on them to write anything real about my relationship."**

There is venom in his choice of words, but they are spoken matter-of-factly, with an almost eerie absence of malice. Depp is uncomfortable in the role of the angry man; he'd much rather play the clown.

He derives fiendish pleasure, for example, from checking into hotels under naughty pseudonyms, forcing friend and stranger alike to participate in the joke. "It's funny to get a wake-up call at some ludicrous hour, like 5:30 in the morning, and the guy has to say, **'Good morning, Mr. Donkey Penis. Good Morning, Mr. Drip Noodle. You have to get up now.'"**

Most nights after work he can be found at his Sunset Boulevard club, the Viper Room, modeled after a speakeasy from the 1930s. Despite the media frenzy that ensued to look for a scapegoat following River Phoenix's overdose there last Halloween, it remains one of the few safe places he can retreat to.

"It's horrible when anybody dies, especially when somebody's made a fatal mistake," he says. "But the tabloid press grabbed ahold of that thing and made a circus out of it. Drugs are the number one business in this country, yet they have to come down on one club on the Sunset Strip. River was trying to escape something. He could have been at a supermarket, in a hotel room, driving in a car. Either way it's really sad."

For the time being he'll have to be satisfied with the protected world of the movie set. "**Unfortunately, I feel more comfortable in front of the camera now than I do in life**," he admits. "**On the set, you feel close to the people, you're working together. When you're in a restaurant in real life, you're having dinner with the girl, drinking wine, you're looking around and there are all these people looking at you. It's a little weird.**"

BPD ISSUES, SYMPTOMS & JOHNNY DEPP:

The above *Vogue* interview points to some of Depp's BPD symptoms. While I'm stretching it a bit to categorize some of his behavior or quotes in the temporary paranoid/dissociation box but Depp sometimes talks and acts like people are out to get him – he's a Hollywood superstar!

What does he expect when he's in a restaurant or when River Phoenix dies of an OD after leaving Depp's Viper Room? "Dissociation" is an abnormal psychological state in which one's perception of oneself and/or one's environment is altered significantly.

Some of my points are somewhat counter-intuitive such as noticing Depp's people-pleaser activity as a symptom of an unstable identity or variable self-concept. Johnny varies from being an ego maniac making outrageous demands one moment and then bends over backwards with people-pleasing behavior to manipulate people to like him or perfume his low self-esteem and guilt.

Unstable, volatile emotions: **Saint Johnny is not without his demons**. Between takes, he reveals these: **insomnia, a fear of crowds, chain-smoking, an antagonism toward authority figures that has landed him in jail on at least three occasions (after jaywalking in Los Angeles, assaulting a hotel security guard in Vancouver, and speeding in Arizona)**...

Unstable, erratic relationships: **He was married once at 20, but divorced two years later**. Depp legend has him again popping the question to Sherilyn Fenn, Jennifer Grey, and, of course, Ryder. **He insists that reports of his engagements have been "complete fabrications" but refuses to elaborate "because I don't want to hurt anybody's feelings."**

Unstable, impulsive, self-destructive behavior: "These days getting neo-adult Depp to talk about his **stints in jail, his chemical abuse, his tattoos, his scars (self-mutilation, cutting himself)**..."

Unstable, insecure, variable identity: **Depp has an "erratic" personality that makes him a little tough to live with. "I'm 30 different people sometimes," he says. "One day you wake up and you're somebody else, nowhere near who you were when you went to sleep."**

People-pleaser activity (insecure identity): "An informal poll of the *Don Juan* makeup trailer comes close to qualifying Depp for sainthood: sweet, kind, and above all, generous. Patty York, Depp's makeup artist on four of his last five films, says, **"He'll give you the shirt off his back."** (Literally: The other day she said she liked the shirt he had on. He took it off and gave it to her.) **He also regularly treats the crew to champagne at the end of the day.**"

Depp in high school... (Insecure self-concept): "I was not the most popular kid in school. I always felt like an absolute and total freak. Edward Scissorhands. That feeling of wanting to be accepted but not knowing how to be accepted as you are, honestly. Wanting to hold a girl but thinking I'll screw it up."

"Johnny Depp **escaped an unhappy childhood** to become a teen idol, then fled that image by playing a bunch of quirky, alienated youths..."

Temporary psychotic – paranoid ideation or dissociation: **"On the set, you feel close to the people, you're working together. When you're in a restaurant in real life, you're having dinner with the girl, drinking wine, you're looking** around and there are all these people looking at you. It's a little weird."

"It's horrible when anybody dies, especially when somebody's made a fatal mistake," he says. "But the tabloid press grabbed ahold of that thing and made a circus out of it. Drugs are the number one business in this country, yet they have to come down on one club on the Sunset Strip. River was trying to escape something.

Whether Kate and I are together or not is not going to save anybody's life. It's nobody's business but mine or hers. **I'd rather come out in the press and say I'm screwing dogs, or goats, or rats than attempt to rely on them to write anything real about my relationship."**

Cultivating an aura of mystery has always been a major component of Depp style. And now more than ever, he seems compelled to keep secrets. "There's a huge part of him that's not within your reach," says Mary Steenburgen, who played his lover in *Gilbert Grape* and is now a close friend. "**He doesn't casually let himself over to people and let you know who he is.**

Chapter 44

"Everything here is edible; even I'm edible. But that, dear children, is cannibalism, and is in fact frowned upon in most societies."
— Johnny Depp

The Lone Ranger (2013) starred Depp as Tonto – storyline:

In the 1930s, an elderly Tonto tells a young boy the tale of John Reid, the Lone Ranger. An idealistic lawyer, he rides with his brother and fellow Texas Rangers in pursuit of the notorious Butch Cavendish.

Ambushed by the outlaw and left for dead, John Reid is rescued by the renegade Comanche, Tonto, at the insistence of a mysterious white horse and offers to help him to bring Cavendish to justice.

Becoming a reluctant masked rider with a seemingly incomprehensible partner, Reid pursues the criminal against all obstacles. However, John and Tonto learn that Cavendish is only part of a far greater injustice and the pair must fight it in an adventure that would make them a legend (*rottentomatoes*).

JOHNNY DEPP'S LIFE BEHIND THE SCENES:

Dear Johnny (J. Calkin, *Elle Magazine (UK)*, April 1994):

Sweet teen idol Johnny Depp, now 30, has matured into a seductive screen star. He talks to Jessamy Calkin about drugs, demons and dressing up . . . in women's clothes.

It's as if his roles are all connected by an invisible thread: the outsider, the misfit, the gentle melancholic oddball. Depp says he is neither sad nor lonely, but finds these qualities easy to tap into. He has a great understanding of the vulnerability of people; an empathy with solitude and the daily heartbreak of ordinary life.

"When I met him," laughs *Cry-Baby* director John Waters, "his face was in every magazine and he couldn't go outside. Girls would cry when they saw him—cry! **He hated being a teen idol, *hated* it**. I said, 'Stick with us, Johnny—we'll take care of you . . .'"

In person, Johnny Depp is both accessible and enigmatic. He looks tougher than he does on screen, and his hair, shorter now, is stuffed into a woolen hat. ("Believe me," says Waters, "Johnny invented grunge 10 years before everyone else was into it.") **He has a natural perversity about him which is very appealing.**

Depp's demons occasionally creep into his angelic face. But his charm is so mercurial, his manner so seductive, his humor so intriguing, that you really want to be his best friend. "There is something cool about him, cooler than he realizes," says Vincent Gallo, who starred with him in *Arizona Dream*. "**He thinks he's cool because of the hair and the clothes and the junked up cars, but it's what he really is that's cool. He's a very complicated kid and he pays the price—he feels the feelings and it's not easy for him.**"

He rarely goes out in LA, except to The Viper Room, where he feels safe. "For me the club has a protective atmosphere—all the people who work there are like family." **But the club took on a new significance last Halloween, when River Phoenix died on the pavement outside. This is a painful subject for Depp, who was playing on stage when it happened.** He was deeply upset by Phoenix's death and closed the club for 10 days as a mark of respect for his family and friends.

But he was also annoyed with the hysterical, moralizing attitude of the media—with the fact that, by association, he was deemed in some way responsible and his club condemned as a drug hangout.

Depp knew Phoenix—not well, but enough to have respect for him. "He was a really good guy and a fine actor, but he made a mistake and that should be a lesson to people: be careful. It doesn't make him a bad person, he just made a mistake, and we all make mistakes. No one is exempt."

Depp himself is no stranger to drugs; they used to be, he says, his way of dealing with things "until I discovered that it didn't work—that sooner or later I would have to face the inevitable. But I feel focused now, and much calmer." He seems quite self-contained, and hesitantly attributes this to growing older, to a reconciliation of conflicting desires.

And Johnny Depp likes girls. **He has been married (when he was 20, to Lori Anne Allison; it lasted two years) and engaged three times—to actresses Sherilyn Fenn, Jennifer Grey and Winona Ryder, who he split with a year ago.** When asked about his private life, he will usually evade the issue or tell a convoluted but amusing tale which has little to do with the question.

He is much more interested in discussing other things. He has a definite sense of *schadenfreude*. **He likes to see people choke. That cracks him up. And he is riveted by Tourette's syndrome, the peculiar affliction whereby the** sufferer cannot contain himself and goes round spitting and using abusive language in a sort of verbal convulsion. "I'm fascinated by that," says Depp. "It's so honest, somehow."

Depp plays Wood, and admits that he loved the ritual of dressing up in women's clothes. The role needed a lot of preparation, and Depp started wearing exotic underwear all the time. When he was staying at the Ritz in Paris, a room service waiter was surprised to find him answering the door in a slip and high heels. **"I totally forgot what I was wearing, until I saw the shocked look on his face.** "It's interesting—as a man I'm not a big guy, but as a woman I'm enormous. I'm an enormous woman."

BPD ISSUES, SYMPTOMS & JOHNNY DEPP:

The *Elle Magazine* interview in this chapter reveals Depp's BPD symptoms including:

<u>Unstable, unpredictable, volatile relationships</u>: "**He has been married (when he was 20, to Lori Anne Allison; it lasted two years) and engaged three times—to actresses Sherilyn Fenn, Jennifer Grey and Winona Ryder, who he split with a year ago.**"

<u>Erratic identity or variable self-concept</u>: "**Depp plays Wood, and admits that he loved the ritual of dressing up in women's clothes.** The role needed a lot of preparation, and Depp started wearing exotic underwear all the time. When he was staying at the Ritz in Paris, a room service waiter was surprised to find him answering the door in a slip and high

heels. **'I totally forgot what I was wearing, until I saw the shocked look on his face. It's interesting—as a man I'm not a big guy, but as a woman I'm enormous. I'm an enormous woman.'"**

"When I met him," laughs *Cry-Baby* director John Waters, "his face was in every magazine and he couldn't go outside. Girls would cry when they saw him—cry! **He hated being a teen idol, *hated* it**. I said, 'Stick with us, Johnny—we'll take care of you . . .'"

"It's as if his roles are all connected by an invisible thread: the outsider, the misfit, the gentle melancholic oddball."

<u>Unstable, impulsive behavior</u>: "...**But the club took on a new significance last Halloween, when River Phoenix died on the pavement outside. This is a painful subject for Depp, who was playing on stage when it happened.** He was deeply upset by Phoenix's death and closed the club for 10 days as a mark of respect for his family and friends."

"But he was also annoyed with the hysterical, moralizing attitude of the media—with the fact that, by association, he was deemed in some way responsible and his club condemned as a drug hangout."

While the River Phoenix incident seems indirect, Depp was there and has had a history of alcohol and drug abuse – and has never gotten treatment for it.

Chapter 45

"I think everybody's nuts."
--Johnny Depp

Cannes Man (1996) – Depp plays himself – storyline:

While at the Cannes Film Festival, producer Sy Learner (Seymour Cassel) makes a bet that he can turn any nobody into a star. A cabbie from New York named Frank (Francesco Quinn) becomes his test case as Sy tries to get Frank noticed amidst the stars and glitter of Cannes (*rottentomatoes*).

JOHNNY DEPP'S LIFE BEHIND THE SCENES:

Johnny Be Good (K. Sessums, *Vanity Fair*, Feb. 1997):

For all his offbeat roles, such as the leads in *What's Eating Gilbert Grape* and the upcoming Mafia movie *Donnie Brasco*, Johnny Depp has the elegance of the silent-screen star and a decidedly European cut that includes his choice of companion, British model Kate Moss. Kevin Sessums finds the nomadic founder of Hollywood-style grunge making his directorial debut, *The Brave*, and settling into a $3-million 1930s mansion

Johnny Depp is homesick for his own bed back in Hollywood, as well as for the company of his girlfriend, model Kate Moss, who is working the runways of Europe's fall fashion shows.

Red Crow from *The Brave* said, "Depp goes beyond getting angry. He likes off-center, artsy roles as an actor, and he's that way in his personality, too."

"Johnny invented grunge," claims director John Waters, whom Depp once proudly described as his personal guru. "I don't remember a movie star with that look before him."

There is, indeed, a dirty sweetness about the actor; his unkempt, soulful slouch has combined with his dry disregard for the rougher shoals of machismo to deconstruct the very notion of male glamour.

"I've never consciously played into any image," insists Depp, a high-school dropout who dreamed of being a rock guitarist but who, in transplanting himself to Los Angeles more than a decade ago, accidentally became a teen heartthrob with his role on the 1980s Fox Network hit *21 Jump Street,* in which he also played an undercover cop. "I never wanted to emulate anybody else. Every young actor who comes out of the blocks, they say, 'James Dean,' because it's easy."

"Jimmy Dean was my best friend," says Martin Landau, who won an Oscar for best supporting actor for his portrayal of Bela Lugosi opposite Depp in *Ed Wood.* **"The point is that it is not easy to compare young actors to James Dean. Yet I don't know anybody who's closer to Jimmy than Johnny . . . They share a similar subtlety in their work. But Jim's was a fragile talent—not as developed as Johnny's is."**

"I'm not 'Blockbuster Boy.' I never wanted to be. I wasn't looking for that," "I mean, it would be nice to get a whole shitpile of money so you can throw it at your family and friends . . . I just don't know if movies can ever be considered art, because there's so much money involved," he continues, perhaps protesting a tad too much, since he himself recently crossed the $4 million-per-picture threshold.

". . . **We're all a mishmash of extremes. I know that I have demons,"** Depp confesses, firing up one of his ever-present cigarettes. **"I don't know if I want to get rid of them altogether, but I would like to experience them in a different way. Maybe go face-to-face with them. I've never really had the time to go into therapy. Well, here and there. But not enough to help."**

At seven, Depp left Kentucky with his family and headed for Florida. **By the time he was a teenager, he, along with his brother and two sisters, had called more than 30 houses home**.

Depp's early nomadic existence may have played havoc with his sense of security, but it only strengthened his bond with his mother, Betty Sue, a waitress who was divorced from his father when Depp was 15; he's even got her name tattooed inside a heart on his left biceps.

"Somehow it all leads back to family," Depp insists. "I mean, in a town like this, you become on some level a commodity. But when you get back to your family, that all goes away. You're Johnny again. At a certain point I wasn't Johnny Depp anymore. I'd become 'Johnny Depp.' "

"Are you surprised that you and Kate are still a couple?" I ask, taking this as a warped cue to ask him some woman questions. **"I am amazed," he admits. "I am doubly amazed at how great it still is. It's still new. It's still fun**. It's still very naïve—even though we have all this history together now and all this luggage. But it's still a good time. She makes me laugh. And man, you can't beat that South London accent."

Depp and Moss met in February 1994 at Café Tabac, the trendy downtown Manhattan spot. **Though they've had their public ups and downs, both have claimed that it was love at first sight.**

Back at the Viper Room...One of the quadrants offers a perfect view of the part of the sidewalk in front of the club where, in 1993, River Phoenix collapsed and died from a drug overdose. "It was a fucking wake-up call for everybody for sure," Depp says.

"They tried to drag the club through the mud. They tried to drag me through the mud. But I don't give a fuck what the tabloid press writes. Forget about me. Forget about the club. This club is going to go away at some point. It's just a piece of real estate. But to drag River's name through the mud and turn the incident into a fucking circus was just a horrible thing. It was unforgivable."

"Did you go through your own drug phase?" I ask.

"Yeah. I experimented—especially when I was a kid. I remember when weed was $25 an ounce! And they don't have nickel bags anymore! Remember nickel bags?"

"Did River's death make you question your own temptations? You've been arrested a few times for rowdy behavior. You've admitted in the past you've had a few drinks in your life."

"No, a few drinks have had me. It's just kind of pointless. I mean, some people can drink—you know, a few whiskeys or vodkas. But I just keep going."

"Oh, sure, yeah, Johnny was unhappy then . . . **It was a pretty dark time for me. I don't know what was going** on. Well, I was poisoning myself beyond belief." He points to his soda. "I'd eat that glass, man. There was a lot of liquor. A lot of liquor. I was pretty unhealthy."

"Were you doing heroin?"

Depp takes a deep breath. "Oh, let's not talk about that . . . It was a very sad time for me…"

"We chase our tails for so long," Depp softly says. "Getting high is about fucking trying to numb something. Getting loaded and trying to destroy yourself . . . Well, you just get to a point and you go, Fuck! What am I doing? What the fuck am I trying to do to myself?"

Depp climbs into the back of the Ford Bronco parked in front of his trailer and **opens a cooler stocked with Coronas. He sticks a slice of lime down a Corona's neck and quickly chugs half the bottle.** Wiping his mouth, he grins and grabs a box hidden behind the cooler. "The animal wranglers—they've never worked on a movie before—gave me these as a present," he says as he pulls from the box salt and pepper shakers in the shape of white and black penises.

BPD ISSUES, SYMPTOMS & JOHNNY DEPP:

The above Vanity Fair interview revealed some of Depp's BPD symptoms such as:

<u>Unstable, volatile emotions</u>: ". . . **We're all a mishmash of extremes. I know that I have demons,"** Depp confesses, firing up one of his ever-present cigarettes. **"I don't know if I want to get rid of them altogether, but I would**

like to experience them in a different way. Maybe go face-to-face with them. I've never really had the time to go into therapy. Well, here and there. But not enough to help."

<u>Unstable relationships</u>: Depp and Moss met in February 1994 at Café Tabac, the trendy downtown Manhattan spot. **Though they've had their public ups and downs, both have claimed that it was love at first sight.**

<u>Unstable, impulsive behavior</u>: **"We chase our tails for so long," Depp softly says. "Getting high is about fucking trying to numb something. Getting loaded and trying to destroy yourself . . . Well, you just get to a point and you go, Fuck! What am I doing? What the fuck am I trying to do to myself?"**

Depp climbs into the back of the Ford Bronco parked in front of his trailer and **opens a cooler stocked with Coronas. He sticks a slice of lime down a Corona's neck and quickly chugs half the bottle.**

"Did you go through your own drug phase?" I ask.

"Yeah. I experimented—especially when I was a kid. I remember when weed was $25 an ounce! And they don't have nickel bags anymore! Remember nickel bags?"

"Did River's death make you question your own temptations? You've been arrested a few times for rowdy behavior. You've admitted in the past you've had a few drinks in your life."

"No, a few drinks have had me. It's just kind of pointless. I mean, some people can drink—you know, a few whiskeys or vodkas. But I just keep going."

"Oh, sure, yeah, Johnny was unhappy then . . . **It was a pretty dark time for me. I don't know what was going on. Well, I was poisoning myself beyond belief.**" He points to his soda. "**I'd eat that glass, man. There was a lot of liquor. A lot of liquor. I was pretty unhealthy.**"

<u>Unstable identity</u>: **By the time he was a teenager, he, along with his brother and two sisters, had called more than 30 houses home…Depp's early nomadic existence may have played havoc with his sense of security**

Chapter 46

"One of the greatest pieces of advice I've ever gotten in my life was from my mom. When I was a little kid there was a kid who was bugging me at school and she said "Okay, I'm gonna tell you what to do. If the kid's bugging you and puts his hands on you; you pick up the nearest rock..."
— Johnny Depp

Into the Woods (2014) stars Depp as The Wolf – storyline:

A witch conspires to teach important lessons to various characters of popular children's stories including *Little Red Riding Hood*, *Cinderella*, *Jack and the Beanstalk* and *Rapunzel*.

Stephen Sondheim's *Into the Woods* is adapted in this musical from director Rob Marshall and Walt Disney Studios. Johnny Depp and Meryl Streep star (*rottentomatoes*).

JOHNNY DEPP'S LIFE BEHIND THE SCENES:

Ghost in the Machine: Now You See Johnny Depp, Now You Don't (H. Millea, *Premiere*, Feb. 1995):

"When I was a kid I used to have these dreams," says Depp. "But they *weren't* dreams. I was awake, but I couldn't move. I couldn't speak. And a face would come to me. Someone told me it was the spirit of someone who died that was very close and never got to say something that they wanted to say. And I believe it."

In the Mark Hotel incident, Depp deconstructed the furniture in his room at a cost of more than $9,000 and several hours in jail. "I thought it was funny—I have to go to jail for assaulting a picture frame or a lamp! The rags said, 'Well, he was drunk and he was having a huge fight with his girlfriend.'

Complete bullshit! But, you know, let's say the guy over here in the bar, he's having a hard day, man, and eventually—one more stubbing of the toe—the guy's gotta hit something. So you punch a wall or do this and that. Fuck it, I'm normal and I want to be normal. But somehow I'm not allowed to be. Why can't I be human?"

JOHNNY DEPP DIAGNOSED: UNAUTHORIZED PSYCHOLOGICAL DIAGNOSIS OF HIS SECRET LIFE

"...I have a lot of love inside me and a lot of anger inside as well. If I love somebody, then I'm gonna love 'em. If I'm angry and I've got to lash out or hit somebody, I'm going to do it and I don't care what the repercussions are. Anger doesn't pay rent, it's gotta go. It's gotta be evicted."

After taking just so much of being "scrutinized, judged, even stalked at times," Depp escapes to Europe, where he moves undetected. "It's a different thing in Paris. It's more about the work than about anything that's called celebrity. It's not as sensationalized."

 "If someone were to harm my family or a friend or someone I love—I would eat them," he says quite seriously. **"I might end up in jail for 500 years—but I would eat them."**

Just about the only unknown is the extent of his dental work. Running a finger along his zigzagging bottom front row, he says, "I'm proud of these. When I see people with perfect teeth, it drives me up the wall. I'd rather swallow a tick than have that!"

"You know," he continues, lighting another cigarette, **"I was married when I was twenty. It was a strong bond with someone but I can't necessarily say I was *in love*. That's something that comes around once, man, maybe twice if you're lucky. And I don't know that I experienced that, let's say, before I turned 30."**

If he really hasn't been *in love* before 30, that would make model Kate Moss the only woman eligible for *in love* status. The two met a year ago in a restaurant, introduced by a mutual friend. "And we've been together ever since," says Depp, eager to fade from the topic. "We're just having fun. A lot of fun."

The peanut gallery roars, and Depp recovers when the **bartender delivers another round on the house.**

Sipping his merlot, Depp is anticipating. "I hope I don't get a wink of sleep tonight!"

"There is something haunting about him," says Parker. "But it's not like Johnny is this troubled young actor and he's poetic and brooding. It's just that he's real and complicated. He's not like a showman. He doesn't belong in show business. He belongs somewhere better."

BPD ISSUES, SYMPTOMS & JOHNNY DEPP:

The *Premiere* interview provided evidence of some of Depp's BPD symptoms including:

<u>Unstable emotions</u>: **"If someone were to harm my family or a friend or someone I love—I would eat them," he says quite seriously. "I might end up in jail for 500 years—but I would eat them."**

"...I have a lot of love inside me and a lot of anger inside as well. If I love somebody, then I'm gonna love 'em. If I'm angry and I've got to lash out or hit somebody, I'm going to do it and I don't care what the repercussions are. Anger doesn't pay rent, it's gotta go. It's gotta be evicted."

Unstable, impulsive behavior: The peanut gallery roars, and Depp recovers when the **bartender delivers another round on the house...Sipping his merlot, Depp is anticipating.** "I hope I don't get a wink of sleep tonight!"

Unstable identity: **Just about the only unknown is the extent of his dental work. Running a finger along his zigzagging bottom front row, he says, "I'm proud of these. When I see people with perfect teeth, it drives me up the wall. I'd rather swallow a tick than have that!"**

"There is something haunting about him," says Parker. "But it's not like Johnny is this troubled young actor and he's poetic and brooding. It's just that he's real and complicated. He's not like a showman. He doesn't belong in show business. He belongs somewhere better."

Unstable relationships: **In the Mark Hotel incident, Depp deconstructed the furniture in his room at a cost of more than $9,000 and several hours in jail.** "I thought it was funny—I have to go to jail for assaulting a picture frame or a lamp! The rags said, '_**Well, he was drunk and he was having a huge fight with his girlfriend**_.'

Temporary dissociation: "When I was a kid I used to have these dreams," says Depp. "But they _weren't_ dreams. I was awake, but I couldn't move. I couldn't speak. And a face would come to me. Someone told me it was the spirit of someone who died that was very close and never got to say something that they wanted to say. And I believe it."

Chapter 47

"They stick you with those names, those labels -- 'rebel' or whatever; whatever they like to use. Because they need a label; they need a name. They need something to put the price tag on the back of."
— Johnny Depp

Mortdecai (pre-production 2013) stars Depp as Charles Mortdecai – storyline:

Art dealer, Charles Mortdecai, searches for a stolen painting rumored to contain a secret code that gains access to hidden Nazi gold (*IMDb*).

JOHNNY DEPP'S LIFE BEHIND THE SCENES:

***Playboy* Interview: Johnny Depp** (K. Cook, *Playboy*, Jan. 1996):

A candid conversation with America's quirkiest actor about Kate Moss, River Phoenix, his offbeat films and why he likes to stick strange things in his pants.

Johnny Depp looks rotten. Or so he says…Along the way he has fallen for some of America's most desirable women. **He has had offscreen relationships with Jennifer Grey (*Dirty Dancing*) and Sherilyn Fenn (*Twin Peaks*). A rumored liaison—public, if not pubic—with Madonna was followed by a notorious engagement to Winona Ryder and the requisite tattoo, WINONA FOREVER…**Today he and his latest love, ubermodel Kate Moss, are the prom king and queen of young Hollywood—beautiful, thin chain-smokers with an air of sex and tragedy.

Depp is all about his past. In 1970, when he was seven years old, his family left Kentucky for Miramar, Florida, where the Depps moved from house to house and sometimes lived in motels. Depp's father took off when Johnny was 15. His mother, Betty Sue, worked as a waitress, and Johnny counted her tips after work. He also developed a fierce devotion to society's outcasts.

In high school he was suspended for mooning a teacher. Shortly after that he dropped out and worked pumping gas. **Once, trying to learn to breathe fire like circus performers, he blew a mouthful of gasoline at a flame. His eyes lit up as the blaze raced toward him—then his eyebrows and hair lit up, too. He barely escaped.**

As with his work, there is a twitchy humor to his collectibles, his conversation, even his arrests. They're all funny if you view them as he does—as brief excursions on our common march to the graveyard. **In 1994 he was jailed for trashing a $1200-a-night suite in New York City's Mark Hotel. Handcuffed and led by police to a sidewalk jammed with reporters demanding his reaction, he nodded toward the cops and said, "I've met some really nice people."**

If you wanted big money you could have also made *Mobsters*, a potential hit. You've turned down other mainstream films for movies such as *Dead Man*. How much did that one pay?

Less than my expenses during the shoot. But it's a poetic film. I did *Dead Man* so I could work with Jim Jarmusch. I trust Jim as a director and a friend and a genius.

How do you see your career? Is it something you're sculpting as you go along, a body of work?

It's more primitive. I look at the story and the character and say, "Can I add any ingredients to make a nice soup?" In some sense there is a monofilament running through the guys I've played. They are outsiders. They're people society says aren't normal, and I think you have to stand up for people like that.

Do you remember the first time you saw yourself-on-screen?

I got sick. I went to see dailies on *Nightmare on Elm Street*. I was 21, and didn't know what was going on. It was like looking in a huge mirror. It wasn't how I looked that bothered me, though I did look like a geek in that movie. It was seeing myself up there pretending.

And you heaved?

I didn't actually vomit, but I felt like vomiting.

These days when Hollywood makes you sick, you and Kate Moss run off to London or Paris. What are you escaping from?

Fame, celebrity—it's not such a big deal in Europe. People seem to understand that you just have a weird job. They're not running after you trying to carve chunks out of you. It's strange in the States. Most fans here are great, but there's a handful who have seen the movies and feel they know you. They think it's all right to touch you and ask personal questions.

So there's an island on your Christmas list?

If there's anything I really want, it's privacy. It's the island idea. You do get to where your money can help your family, and that's a great thing. You can buy that wristwatch you want, too. But mostly you now have to pay for simplicity. You use your money to buy privacy because during most of your life you aren't allowed to be normal. You're on display, always looked at, which puts you at a disadvantage for the people looking at you know that it's you. They say, "It's you!" But you don't know them. That's bad for an actor because the most important thing you can do is observe people. And now you can't because you're the one being observed.

Some of it must be enjoyable.

It's very nice when people come up and say, "I really liked *Don Juan DeMarco*, please sign my napkin." What gets to me is being watched, whispered about. Would you ever walk up to someone on the street and say, "Can I kiss you?" No, you'd get smacked. "Can I look inside your wallet?" "What size is your shoe?" "Can I have your hat?" Some requests are too fucking surreal. On *Dead Man* I was hanging out with Jarmusch and the crew, smoking cigarettes, and there was a guy lurking, checking me out. He looked normal enough, but his eyes were a little too open. So I knew he'd come up to me, which he did. "Hi, Johnny! Wanna go have a drink?" I said, "Thanks, I'm OK." He said, "Listen, you could really help me out. My wife and I are separating, but I want to get back with her. She's a big fan of yours." He wanted me to go home with him and mediate his divorce. I wouldn't, so he said he'd call her on the phone and we could talk it out. Now, that stuff goes too far. You want to say, "Can't we just kiss? Could you just shove your tongue down my gullet and be done with it?"

You once said you feel more comfortable dining in a movie than in a restaurant.

Calmer, anyway. In a real restaurant you may notice people talking under their breath, staring. It builds up in your head and you want to run.

Do you and Kate have techniques for avoiding bad scenes?

If we run into a gaggle of paparazzi I'll avoid eye contact. I'll also put on my sunglasses. That way they don't get paid as much for the picture.

Are you and Kate going to get married?

I love Kate more than anything. Certainly enough to marry her. But as far as putting our names on paper, making weird public vows that signify ownership—it's not in the cards.

Are you monogamous?

I'm very true. I wouldn't hurt her and I expect she wouldn't hurt me. Fidelity is important as long as it's pure. But the moment it goes against your insides—if you want to be somewhere else, if she wants to dabble—then you need to make a change. I'm not sure any human being is made to be with one person forever and ever, amen. My own parents didn't do it; my dad left when I was 15. And maybe in some of my public relationships . . . maybe I was trying to right the wrongs of my parents by creating a classic fairy-tale love. **Trying to solve the fear of abandonment we all have. Anyway, it didn't work. That's not to say I didn't love those people. I have been with some great girls and I certainly thought I loved them, though now I have my doubts. I felt something intense, but was it love? I don't know. So now I can't say I can love someone forever, or if anybody can.**

According to a recent story, you and Kate had set a wedding date. She wanted engraved invitations, but you wanted to send out a riddle so your friends would have to guess where to show up.

It's fiction. I can guarantee you that if I woke up one day with a wild hair up my ass to get hitched, there wouldn't be invitations. We'd run out and do it.

Does all the gossip bother you?

It's part of the game. You know that the tabloids—from the obvious ones to the subtler ones such as Time and Newsweek—will print anything to sell those fuckers. But you hear it and it can be stressful. Suppose you and I are at a bar, and you say hello to a girl. That's innocent. For me the same thing becomes: *They were dangling from the St. James Hotel with hairbrushes sticking out of their asses.* That can cause a strain.

What happened on September 13, 1994, when you smashed up a room at New York's Mark Hotel?

Another instance of not being allowed to be normal. I was having a bad day. I think we all have those, but if somebody else does what I did it's not usually in the news. A security guy came to my door, and I said, basically, "I'm sorry, I broke some things. I'll repay you." But that's not good enough. I go to jail. And the next day this gets equal billing with the invasion of Haiti, me beating up a hotel room. Imagine if I had hit somebody.

You've said journalistic "fictions" bother you. What has been the worst?

When something heavy happens and nine out of ten magazines turn it into a fucking vulture fest. They turn *you* into something sick.

You're talking about River Phoenix.

When River passed away, it happened to be at my club. Now that's very tragic, very sad, but they made it a fiasco of lies to sell fucking magazines. **They said he was doing drugs in my club, that I allow people to do drugs in my club.** What a ridiculous fucking thought! "Hey, I'm going to spend a lot of money on this nightclub so everyone can come here and do drugs. I think that's a good idea, don't you? We'll never get found out. It's not like this place is *high profile* or anything, right?"

That lie was ridiculous and disrespectful to River. But aside from River, and his family trying to deal with their loss, what about people who work in the club? They have moms and dads in, like, Oklahoma, reading about the place where their daughter tends bar and thinking, Jesus, she's out in Hollywood swimming around with these awful creatures!

How did you cope?

I closed the club for a few nights. To get out of the way so River's fans could bring messages, bring flowers. And I got angry. **I made a statement to the press: "Fuck you. I will not be disrespectful to River's memory. I will not participate in your fucking circus."**

Were you geeky as a kid?

I'm geeky now. I sure don't look around and say, "Hey, isn't this great?" I've never felt that and probably never will.

You were a kid when the family moved from Kentucky to Miramar, Florida.

We moved like gypsies. From the time I was five until my teens we lived in 30 or 40 different houses. That probably has a lot to do with my transient life now. But it's how I was raised so I thought there was nothing abnormal about it. Wherever the family is, that's home. We lived in apartments, on a farm, in a motel. Then we rented a house, and one night we moved from there to the house next door. I remember carrying my clothes across the yard and thinking, this is weird, but it's an easy move.

Were you a bully? Ever beat up anyone?

The guys I hung out with in my early teens were bullies, kind of, so I did a little of that. Picking on someone, pushing people around. I didn't like it. It got me so angry that I'd be on the poor guy's side.

You were 15 when your parents split up. Were you crushed?

There wasn't time. It was too traumatic for my mom.

Betty Sue—her name is on the heart tattoo on your left arm.

She got very ill. Her life as she had known it for 20 years was over. Her partner, her husband, her best friend, her lover, had just left her. I felt crushed that he had left, but when you're faced with something like that, it's amazing how much abuse the human mind and heart can take. You just get past what you need to get past. Sure, on some level I was thinking, wait a minute, what happened to my family? What about stability, the safety of the home? But my feelings were secondary to thinking about my mom. All the focus was on her getting through that time, which she finally did, and now everyone is pretty OK. I'm even on good terms with my dad.

You were sensitive.

A total paranoid.

You dropped out of high school about that time. Did the other Depps try to talk you out of it?

No, they were supportive. It was other people, family friends, who thought I was a shithead. They figured I was proving them right by dropping out of school to play guitar in nightclubs. And I thought maybe they were right. My main feeling when I left school was one of insecurity. It was, what the fuck am I gonna do? I'm nobody. I'm a fuckup, just like those outside voices say. I seriously considered joining the Marines because I didn't want to be a fuckup. I thought that if I joined the Marines and learned to deal with authority, maybe I could be a normal guy.

You were 17. Your band, the Kids, rubbed shoulders with major acts when they toured Florida. There's a famous tale about you and Iggy Pop.

We opened for the Ramones, the Pretenders, and the Talking Heads. One night we opened for Iggy. It went great. After the show I was pretty drunk, and in the Iggy tradition I wanted more, **so I started screaming at him. Just sophomoric insults: "Iggy Poop! Who the fuck are you? Iggy Slop!" He got in my face and said, "You little turd."** And walked away. So of course I was delighted. I looked over at the bass player and said, "Yeah, that was Iggy. He's a god."

At the parking garage of a local mall?

That's the story. **We were messing around one night at the Beverly Center, having a giggle. We may have been drinking. We were goofing around, and the story is that we wound up hanging by our fingers five stories up on the parking structure.** I don't remember, but I'm thinking we did.

It seems that there's something particularly postmodern about daredevil acts at a mall.

It was the ultimate death-defying white-trash act.

After *Elm Street* you moved to *21 Jump Street*. You reportedly detested the show that made you famous. Did you really think *21 Jump Street* was "fascist"?

Sure it was. Cops in school? I mean, bad things happen in schools, but this was even worse than cops in school. It was preachy, pointing the finger. And it was hypocritical because the people running that show, the very highest of the higher-ups, were getting high. They were getting loaded. And then to say, **"Now kiddies, don't do this" was horseshit. I was miserable living that lie for three years. Mortified. I was getting loaded, too. Am I really the one to say, "Don't get high"?**

You must have enjoyed being America's dreamboat at least a little.

Not for one day. To enjoy lying? Enjoy being a piece of a machine, the product of a huge assembly line? No. And fighting the label of heartthrob is hard, too. By then I wanted to be an actor, and that was impossible on TV.

Family things. Childhood things. Fear and abandonment. Rage. You just feel stupid having this be a part of your job, and it fucks with you in bad ways. When you're really flopping around in there [*bitter laugh*], you feel like an idiot for doing it. For going through it. It can make you miserable for three or four months. But you do it. You feel like an idiot, but you do it because it's your fucking job.

According to the tabloids you were hurting because of your breakup with Winona Ryder.

That wasn't really it. That's what was written, but we hadn't broken up yet, we were still up and down. It had more to do with me, with the difficulty of being inside my skin. I was doing what I could to numb that feeling, doing some in-depth poisoning.

What were your poisons?

Pretty much anything I could ingest. And I was soused, drinking heavily, really doing myself in. When it gets constant, when you're going to sleep drunk, waking up and starting to drink again, that stuff will try to kill you.

Did you swear off drugs and alcohol?

Well, I'm a little thick so it took a while. I eventually curbed my drinking. A few beers or a couple glasses of wine, that's not abuse.

Is drug use always harmful?

It depends on the drug and the person. Some kids escape into sports. Some people go to the movies. **Some escape with drugs. There's one school of thought that drugs are recreational; there's another school of thought that they can be therapeutic, a way to deal with problems. I think they're usually a crutch, a way to avoid problems. I have never known a junkie who got away, never seen one that heroin didn't get. But it always depends on the drug, doesn't it? Reefer, obviously, is fine. I have never seen a guy smoke a joint and get so stoned he had to beat the shit out of someone.

BPD ISSUES, SYMPTOMS & JOHNNY DEPP:

The *Playboy* interview revealed some of Depp's BPD symptoms including:

Unstable relationships: Depp always has socially-acceptable excuses for his series of love-sex affairs and rollercoaster relationships such as his comment, "…**Trying to solve the fear of abandonment we all have. Anyway, it didn't work. That's not to say I didn't love those people. I have been with some great girls and I certainly thought I loved them, though now I have my doubts. I felt something intense, but was it love? I don't know. So now I can't say I can love someone forever, or if anybody can.**"

"…**We moved like gypsies. From the time I was five until my teens we lived in 30 or 40 different houses. That probably has a lot to do with my transient life now**."

Unstable emotions: **What happened on September 13, 1994, when you smashed up a room at New York's Mark Hotel?**

"**Another instance of not being allowed to be normal. I was having a bad day. I think we all have those, but if** somebody else does what I did it's not usually in the news. A security guy came to my door, and I said, basically, 'I'm sorry, I broke some things. I'll repay you.' But that's not good enough. I go to jail. And the next day this gets equal billing with the invasion of Haiti, me beating up a hotel room. Imagine if I had hit somebody."

<u>Unstable identity</u>: After the show I was pretty drunk, and in the Iggy tradition I wanted more, **so I started screaming at him. Just sophomoric insults: "Iggy Poop! Who the fuck are you? Iggy Slop!" He got in my face and said, "You little turd."**

Johnny chased after fame and fortune as a rock star or a movie star. Then when he got it – as of 2013 he's worth over $350 million – he complains that fans or photographers bother him. His variable, volatile self-concept or identity seems to zip from lowlife-loser Depp like he was in his teen years to this ego-maniac-superstar-party-monster Depp with a sense of entitlement. One moment he's poor picked-on Johnny, the next moment he's trashing hotel rooms because Kate Moss won't do things Depp's way.

<u>Unstable, impulsive behavior (substance abuse of drugs, alcohol)</u>: "**Reefer, obviously, is fine. I have never seen a guy smoke a joint and get so stoned he had to beat the shit out of someone...**"

"**Now kiddies, don't do this**" was horseshit. I was miserable living that lie for three years. Mortified. I was

getting loaded, too. Am I really the one to say, "Don't get high"?

"It had more to do with me, with the difficulty of being inside my skin. I was doing what I could to numb that feeling, doing some in-depth poisoning."

What were your poisons?

"Pretty much anything I could ingest. And I was soused, drinking heavily, really doing myself in. When it gets constant, when you're going to sleep drunk, waking up and starting to drink again, that stuff will try to kill you."

Did you swear off drugs and alcohol?

"Well, I'm a little thick so it took a while. I eventually curbed my drinking. A few beers or a couple glasses of wine, that's not abuse."

    I should point out to Johnny that: A) It's not how much alcohol you drink but what it does to you; B) Depp's endorsing "reefer" or pot or marijuana is typical of alcoholics-addicts who minimize addiction. I'd expect that Johnny will also tell you that it is okay to get loaded on prescription mood-altering drugs.

    He makes a point of saying he's quit "hard drugs" like heroin. But I wonder how many exceptions he makes. The only safe approach is to quit alcohol and mood-altering drugs totally to be sober – if you are an alcoholic-addict as I suspect Depp is. But he's in denial. He should attend A.A. or N.A. meetings for 90 days and if he still wants to drink alcohol and use "a little reefer" or whatever mood-altering drug on the side, he's welcome back to his misery.

"...We were messing around one night at the Beverly Center, having a giggle. <u>We may have been drinking</u>. We were goofing around, and the story is that we wound up hanging by our fingers five stories up on the parking structure...It seems that there's something particularly postmodern about daredevil acts at a mall."

What people in denial, like Depp, don't want to face is that self-destructive substance abuse of alcohol and drugs can lead to his death or jail. Well, Johnny's been arrested and put in jail a few times. What's next?

Chapter 48

"If someone were to harm my family or a friend or somebody I love, I would eat them. I might end up in jail for 500 years, but I would eat them."
― Johnny Depp

Alice in Wonderland 2 (2015) stars Depp as the Mad Hatter.

JOHNNY DEPP'S LIFE BEHIND THE SCENES:

Johnny Depp's Savage Journey (C. Heath, Rolling Stone, June 11, 1998):

The star of *Fear and Loathing in Las Vegas* goes Gonzo into the psyche of Hunter S. Thompson and lives to tell about it

JOHNNY DEPP DIAGNOSED: UNAUTHORIZED PSYCHOLOGICAL DIAGNOSIS OF HIS SECRET LIFE

Johnny Depp sighs. Hell. Maybe none of this can be explained. **He puts down his pool cue and reaches for his drink**.

Thompson knew little about Depp. He had seen only one of Depp's movies, *Cry-Baby*. "I never saw the end, of course," Thompson apologizes, "because I had a little acid. It seemed like watching *Oklahoma* go on for three years."

It was now two in the morning. "Hunter says, 'Tape these on the propane canister.' I was, 'What are these things?' and he says, 'Oh, that's nitroglycerin:' the cigarette immediately went in the sink."

They took the completed bomb into the back yard. "He knew what he was going to do," Depp says. "And, fuck, I trusted him. You know he was not going to get you killed, somehow. He's survived all these years."

Depp hit the target first time. "I shoot this fucker," he says. "A seventy-five-foot explosion, an enormous, huge burst of fire." Though Depp was having fun, this violent late-night behavior made others in his party a little edgy.

In December, Depp went to Louisville, Kentucky, to read at a Hunter S. Thompson tribute. **Scared, Depp loaded up on red wine.**

Depp would stay in Hunter Thompson's basement. "In the dungeon," Depp says. "It's a little room with makeshift bookshelves and a lot of spiders, and a small, little sofa thing that folds out into a bed, and this enormous keg of gunpowder, which they let me know about when I'd probably been there, smoking in bed, about five days."

"I did it straight," Depp says. "Well, I remember Hunter telling me that ether was the equivalent of twenty-three bottles of wine in a quick sitting, so I might have had some wine."

This is a book, of course, whose **central characters start out with a stash of grass, mescaline, acid, cocaine, tequila, Budweiser, ether, amyls and assorted other uppers and downers, then start searching for kinds of chemical strangeness that will really get them going.**

"OoooOOOOWARRRGGGGHHHH!!!!!!" Hunter S. Thompson lets out a scream that is truly primal. He must, I assume, be undergoing some unimaginable torment. Whatever it is that could quell such anguish, I'm sure it is beyond the knowledge of ordinary humans.

I meet Depp in a Hollywood bar two days after shooting finishes... The next month, Depp and I meet in San Francisco. The Rolling Stones are also in town, so tonight we go to their concert and spend the rest of the evening at Depp's favorite San Francisco drinking haunt, where we play pool.

BPD ISSUES, SYMPTOMS & JOHNNY DEPP:

<u>Unstable, impulsive behavior</u>: The BPD symptom Depp reveals in hanging-out with Hunter Thompson is Johnny's impulsive, self-destructive behavior connected with substance abuse of alcohol and drugs.

"I did it straight," Depp says. "Well, I remember Hunter telling me that ether was the equivalent of twenty-three bottles of wine in a quick sitting, so I might have had some wine."

In December, Depp went to Louisville, Kentucky, to read at a Hunter S. Thompson tribute. **Scared, Depp loaded up on red wine.**

Johnny Depp sighs. Hell. Maybe none of this can be explained. **He puts down his pool cue and reaches for his drink**.

Chapter 49

"We're all damaged in our own way. Nobody's perfect. I think we're all somewhat screwy. Every single one of us."
― Johnny Depp

Pirates of the Caribbean: Dead Men Tell No Tales (2016) will star Depp as Captain Jack Sparrow in the fifth installment of the blockbuster franchise that follows the adventures of Captain Jack Sparrow.

JOHNNY DEPP'S LIFE BEHIND THE SCENES:

Playboy **Interview: Johnny Depp** (B. Weinraub, *Playboy Magazine*, May 2004):

Johnny Depp Cleans Up - Has the anti-star gone Hollywood?

JOHNNY DEPP DIAGNOSED: UNAUTHORIZED PSYCHOLOGICAL DIAGNOSIS OF HIS SECRET LIFE

In *Fear and Loathing in Las Vegas, Ed Wood* and *What's Eating Gilbert Grape*, Depp specialized in playing misfits. In real life **Depp specialized in getting liquored up, arrested and involved with the likes of Winona Ryder and Kate Moss.** Now with an Oscar nomination and a $300 million hit under his belt, Depp has emerged at 40 as the hottest actor in Hollywood. Is he a changed man? In his most revealing interview to date the rebel actor talks frankly about his life as an exile, a dad and a **former boozehound**.

PLAYBOY INTERVIEW: JOHNNY DEPP

A candid conversation with the brooding actor about growing up, getting sober, being a middle-aged sex symbol and **smacking the hell out of the paparazzi**.

Depp's run-ins with the paparazzi are tabloid fodder, as are his bad-boy exploits involving drink, drugs, and a long list of beautiful women, including Sherilyn Fenn, Jennifer Grey and Winona Ryder. He and Ryder were serious enough that he emblazoned himself with a WINONA FOREVER tattoo. (When they broke up he had it laser-altered to WINO FOREVER.) **He was dating model Kate Moss when he famously trashed a New York Hotel room and was arrested.** Depp co-owned a popular Hollywood club called The Viper Room. It was there on Halloween night in 1993 that rising star River Phoenix died of a drug overdose. The tragedy contributed to Depp's image as an actor teetering on the edge.

Depp has since settled down with his girlfriend of six years, Vanessa Paradis, the French actress and pop singer. They have two children, Lily-Rose, four, and Jack, two. The couple divide their time between Los Angeles and St. Tropez, France.

Are you often in that position?

Yeah, and this was nice. I could sit there in France and drink wine. Ultimately, though, what I love about being over there is the culture, which is very old.

Now that you're back in the public eye in a big way, do you feel more exposed?

We've always had our run-ins with the paparazzi. That hasn't changed. They are very ambitious. They're looking for God knows what. You think, why that kind of intense invasion?

Did it cause you to question making *Pirates of the Caribbean* in the first place?

No, I'm not going to complain. When we're in a public place, like at some opening or premiere, I don't mind the press. My girl took my kids to the park the other day, and the paparazzi surrounded the perimeter just to photograph her playing with our children. It's ugly. I don't mind so much when they do it to me, but when it's my kids, that's another story. It's evil.

Is there less harassment in France?

Not necessarily. They fly helicopters over our property, in front of the kitchen window. They have these long lenses.

You once said that everyone thinks of you as a drug-addicted, brooding, angry and rebellious mental case. How apt was that description?

Well, for many years they said I was a wild man. Now they say I'm a former wild man, former bad boy, and former rebel. I guess "former" because now I'm a dad. The media tries to stuff you in a mold. It happens to everybody. He's the new bad boy, the new James Dean, the new whatever. It's both amusing and annoying. My mom reads that stuff. So do my nieces and nephews and all my family. At times it was flat out fiction.

At one point your life did seem out of control. Was it drugs?

Mostly alcohol. There were drugs, too—pills—and there was a danger that I would go over the edge. I could have. I thank God I didn't. It was darkest during the filming of *Gilbert Grape*.

What were your drugs of choice?

I was never a cokehead or anything like that. I always despised that drug. I thought it was a waste of time, pointless. But I was poisoning myself with alcohol and medicating myself. I was trying to numb things.

What things?

I was trying not to feel things, and that's ridiculous. It's one of the dumbest things you can do, because all you're doing is postponing the inevitable. Someday you'll have to look all those things in the eye rather than try and numb the pain.

How far did it go? Were you ever an addict?

No, thank God I was never hooked on anything. I never had a monkey on my back. I just wanted to self-medicate, to numb myself through liquor. It's how I dealt with life, reality, stress, change, sadness, and

memories. The list goes on. I was really trying to feel nothing.

What led you to stop?

Family and friends sat me down and said, **"Listen, we love you. You're important to us, and you're fucking up. You're killing yourself. You're killing us in the process."**

Did you listen to them?

Not right away. You don't listen right away because you're too dumb. You're ignorant. You're human. Finally it seeps in. Finally the body and mind and heart and psyche just go, "Yeah, you're doing the wrong thing."

Did your family and friends actually do an intervention?

At a certain point they intervened. At the time I said I appreciated it. I went through the motions. I said I was okay, and I went for a couple of months being a dumb ass. But I could see things turning into a nasty tailspin. And then I thought, Maybe I'm slow, but this is ridiculous. Fuck it, just stop! So I stopped everything for the better part of a year. **I guess I just reached a point where I said, "Jesus Christ, what am I doing? Life is fucking good. What am I doing to myself?" Now I drink a glass or two of red wine and that's it.**

River Phoenix died of a drug overdose outside your club. What impact did that have on you?

It was devastating. I can't imagine the depth of pain that his family and close friends felt. It was rough for me, but for them it must have been unbearable.

Did it affect your drinking and drug use?

That was 1993, when I was doing *Ed Wood*. **I was completely sober—no hard liquor, no wine, no nothing.** Even so, all the tabloids started saying we were having drug parties. The whole thing was weird, awful, ugly and sad. The incident is seared onto my brain, onto my heart.

Are that and the other darker times in your life reflected in your work? Tim Burton once said you had an affinity for damaged people. Do you?

I do have an affinity for damaged people, in life, in roles. I don't know why. **We're all damaged in our own way. Nobody's perfect. I think we are all somewhat screwy, every single one of us.**

Did you feel damaged as a child, or was yours a relatively normal childhood?

It was strange, though then again, it was normal to us. It wasn't until I started going to other kids' houses and hanging out, having dinner, seeing what a family is supposed to do that I saw that we weren't so normal.

How was it different?

Even down to sitting around a dinner table together—it wasn't an everyday occurrence in my house. At my house dinner easily could have consisted of a bologna sandwich, and then you'd split. You might come back later and grab a few peanuts, and then you'd split again. That was it. I would go to my buddy Sal's house for dinner. I couldn't understand what was going on with everyone sitting down together. I'll never forget seeing romaine lettuce for the first time. I thought it was weird—I was afraid of it. There was salad and appetizers and soup. I had no idea about that. I grew up on hillbilly food.

Apparently you were no more at ease in school. Were you a problem student?

There was this vicious woman, a teacher. If you weren't in her little handpicked clique, you were ridiculed and picked on. She was brutal and unjust. One day she told me to do something, I can't remember what. Her tone was nasty. She got very loud in my face in front of the rest of the class and tried to embarrass me. I saw what she was doing, that she was trying to ridicule me. I turned around and walked away. As I did, **I dropped my pants and mooned her...** She went out of her mind. Then of course I was brought before the dean and suspended for a couple of weeks. At that time it was coming anyway. I knew my days were numbered.

What effect did your parents' divorce have on you?

I was 15, I think. It had been coming for quite a long time. I'm surprised they lasted that long, bless their hearts. I think they tried to keep it together for the kids, and then they couldn't anymore.

How were they as parents?

They were good parents. They raised four kids. I was the youngest. They stuck it out for us all those years. But we lived in a small house, and nobody argued in a whisper. **We were exposed to their violent outbursts against each other. That stuff sticks.**

Then you landed a starring role on *21 Jump Street*. How do you look back on that experience?

It did great things for me, and I'm thankful for the experience. It was a great education, but it was very frustrating. I felt like I was filling up space between commercials.

Yet it was very successful and launched your career.

Yeah, I'd been evicted from an apartment and had moved into a friend's place. I was scrambling to pay the rent, waiting for residual checks from other things that I'd done to pay the bills. I went from that to making a bunch of money. I went from anonymity to going to a restaurant and having people point at me. **It was a shock. But what really bothered me was that I could see the machine. I could see the wheels turning. I could see where it was all going, and it scared the shit out of me.**

Where was it going?

Fox was creating the Fox network, using *21 Jump Street* to build it. **They were shoving my face out there, selling me as this product. It made me crazy. I thought, after this you'll be in a sitcom. You'll be on a lunch box and then a thermos and a notebook. And in two years you'll be ridiculous.** It paid good money and was a good gig, but I wanted something else.

You've had other public troubles, including the time you trashed the hotel room with Kate Moss. What happened?

Very simply, I had a bad day. I'd been chased by paparazzi and was feeling a little bit like Novelty Boy.

Obviously something wasn't working in my life. For a few years I wasn't angry but just sort of frustrated and upset because I didn't know what it was all about.

What do you mean?

I didn't know what it was all for. When they said, "Come on, do this movie. You can make tons of money," it just pissed me off. Fuck that. What does that mean? That's not what it's about. So it built up, and I lost it. It was the culmination of many things, a bad spark, and I went off. I did what I felt was necessary. **Thank God it wasn't a human being but a hotel room that I took it out on. It was a weird incident. There was a hotel security guard who was really kind of pissy and arrogant. I wanted to pop him. But I knew that if I did, it would obviously be a horse of a different color—lawsuits and God knows what else.**

What happened exactly?

I did my business, and they came up to the room. By that point I had cooled down. **I said, "I'll of course pay for any damages. I apologize." That wasn't enough. The guy got snooty and shitty. The next thing you know, the police were at the door. As dumb as the incident was, I don't have any regrets about it.** I don't think it merited the amount of press it got, and **I certainly don't think that I needed to go to the Tombs in New York City in handcuffs. I was in three different jails that night.** But it was all part of my education, you know?

You had another run-in with the police, in London, this time directly related to a clash with paparazzi.

We were at a restaurant, and Vanessa was extremely pregnant. All they wanted were photographs of me and Vanessa and the belly. At that point I thought, Man, I'm not one of those whiny actors who says, **"Oh, the paparazzi, they won't leave me alone." I could give a fuck about it. However, on this particular night I just decided, "Look, this is my girl. This is our first baby. I'm not going to let you fucking people turn this into a circus. You ain't turning this deeply, profoundly beautiful, spiritual, life-changing experience into a novelty. Not without a fight."** I went out and talked to them. I said, "Look, guys, I know what you're after. I understand that you have a job to do. But you're not going to turn this into a circus. Just give us a break. You're not going to get what you want tonight. I'll see you another time."

To which they of course said, "We're sorry. We'll leave."

Right. They were very aggressive: "Fuck you, Johnny." That kind of shit. I swung around and told Vanessa, "Go out the front door, get in the car so they don't get us together or get your belly." She did. She was in the car, so everything was going to be cool, but they were so shitty. **One guy was trying to hold the door open. He had his hand wedged in there. I looked down at the ground, and there was a 17-inch wooden plank, a two-by-two or something. Instinct took over. I picked it up and whacked the guy's hand. I went outside and said, "Now I want you to take my picture, because the first fucking guy who hits a flash, I'm going to kick his skull in. Let's go. Take my picture."** They didn't take my picture. I was livid. They walked backward down the street. I walked them away from Vanessa in the car and down this other street. It was beautiful. It was well worth it. **It was kind of poetic. The next thing I knew, I saw flashing lights on the buildings around me. And a paddy wagon.**

How long were you in jail?

It was brief. It was around 11:30 or midnight, and I was out by five or six the next morning. No one filed charges against me, because they didn't want their names exposed. Had they filed charges they would have had to give their names and would have lost their anonymity. The cops were actually terrific, real sweet. As I said, I didn't mind as much before I had kids. Everything changes when it comes to my children.

Like what?

Everything. The way you sleep changes. Your whole life is changed. Every inch of it is different.

How are you different?

I think it just wakes you up and kind of gives you the opportunity to be who you really are. Before my kids came along I was freaked out to hold a kid. When I was a teenager and my brother had babies, I was always freaked out to hold them. They just seemed so fragile. I'd hold them for a minute and then, "Okay, here. Take the kid." So I was surprised how quickly almost instantly, I was okay with my own baby. Within 24 hours I was fine with it all—the diapers, everything. One of the most amazing moments in my life was holding my brand-new baby, Lily-Rose, just after she was born. She wasn't three hours old, and I was holding her. Her little eyes were kind of half open. She was drifting into sleep. Looking into those little eyes, I thought, My God, I'll never be closer to another human being in my life. And you're not, until your second one comes. Before the second one came, there was this strange thing, a snippet of worry. I thought, how can I love the second as much as the first? Is it possible? And when little Jack arrived it was instant. Instant. They just seem so fragile.

Who gave you parenting tips?

One of the greatest pieces of advice I got was from my brother. When I told him Vanessa was pregnant, he said, "Congratulations. You'll never sleep the same way again. You'll never have another calm day as long as you live, but it's worth it." He said it just off-the-cuff, but it was right on the money.

Have you considered marriage?

Sure, but it would be a shame to ruin her last name. It's so perfect—Vanessa Paradis. So beautiful. It would be such a drag to stick her with Paradis-Depp. It's like a flat note. But for all intents and purposes, we are married. We have two kids together, and she's the woman of my life. If she ever said, "Hey, let's get hitched," I would do it in a second. We'll do it if the kids want us to, or maybe when the kids are old enough to enjoy it with us.

How many tattoos do you have in all?

Let's see. [*counts*] There are 10, I think.

The WINONA FOREVER tattoo is somewhat famous.

Yeah, it's here on my arm. It was the kind of thing you do on the spur of the moment—"Fuck it, let's do it." Then you break up, but it's still there: a girl's name on my arm.

Did it put a damper on new relationships following your split with Ryder?

Yeah, it can turn a situation a little sticky. I changed it to WINO FOREVER, which is actually a bit more accurate.

How painful is it to have a tattoo removed?

Painful. The guy said, "I should give you a local anesthetic, but I said no, "I'm fine." He hit me with a laser and it seemed as though someone had stretched an electric rubber band all the way to Mars and snapped it on the end. Your skin burns and bubbles up.

Do you find it ironic that after your public relationships with people like Winona Ryder, it's only now—when you're married and have children—that *People* magazine pronounces you the sexiest man alive?

My sister called me and said, "Hey, guess what." It's so odd. I was glad I was in Paris at the time, because I thought nobody would know. Then, at the bar at the Ritz Hotel, a guy goes, "Hey, man, congratulations." A friend of mine ran into Gerard Depardieu. **When I saw my friend, he said, "Oh by the way, Gerard says to tell the sexiest man alive . . ."** I mean, if somebody actually believes it, I'm deeply flattered, but I don't get it myself. It's mortifying. You think, where does that come from? Why did they choose me? Why now? I guess it's just my time.

BPD ISSUES, SYMPTOMS & JOHNNY DEPP:

Depp has a kind of antagonistic, self-righteous anger he acts-out at times – revealing a BPD symptom:

<u>Unstable, volatile emotions</u>: Depp was kicked-out of high school for mooning a teacher…. She got very loud in my face in front of the rest of the class and tried to embarrass me. I saw what she was doing, that she was trying to ridicule me. I turned around and walked away. As I did, **I dropped my pants and mooned her…** She went out of her mind. Then of course I was brought before the dean and suspended for a couple of weeks.

"Oh, the paparazzi, they won't leave me alone." I could give a fuck about it. However, on this particular night I just decided, "Look, this is my girl. This is our first baby. I'm not going to let you fucking people turn this into a circus. You ain't turning this deeply, profoundly beautiful, spiritual, life-changing experience into a novelty. Not without a fight."

One guy was trying to hold the door open. He had his hand wedged in there. I looked down at the ground, and there was a 17-inch wooden plank, a two-by-two or something. Instinct took over. I picked it up and whacked the guy's hand. I went outside and said, "Now I want you to take my picture, because the first fucking guy who hits a flash, I'm going to kick his skull in. Let's go. Take my picture." They didn't take my picture. I was livid. They walked backward down the street. I walked them away from Vanessa in the car and down this other street. It was beautiful. It was well worth it. **It was kind of poetic. The**

next thing I knew, I saw flashing lights on the buildings around me. And a paddy wagon.

Unstable, impulsive behavior – substance abuse of alcohol and drugs: "...**I guess I just reached a point where I said, "Jesus Christ, what am I doing? Life is fucking good. What am I doing to myself?" Now I drink a glass or two of red wine and that's it."**

Unstable, variable identity: Depp has an insecure self-concept. One moment he was down-and-out in his teens and early twenties. The next moment he was making $45,000 per episode of *21 Jump Street* with absolutely no gratitude or stable sense of self. "...**They were shoving my face out there, selling me as this product. It made me crazy. I thought, after this you'll be in a sitcom. You'll be on a lunch box and then a thermos and a notebook. And in two years you'll be ridiculous."**

"…When I saw my friend, he said, 'Oh by the way, Gerard says to tell the sexiest man alive . . .' I mean, if somebody actually believes it, I'm deeply flattered, but I don't get it myself. It's mortifying. You think, where does that come from? Why did they choose me? Why now? I guess it's just my time…"

Chapter 50

"I think everybody's weird. We should all celebrate our individuality and not be embarrassed or ashamed of it."
— Johnny Depp

Depp participated in the documentary: Brando: The Documentary (2007) – storyline:

As originally screened at the Tribeca Film Festival, at the Cannes Film Festival, and on Turner Classic Movies, the mammoth, epic-length documentary Brando chronicles in encyclopedic detail (and with a consistently reverent overtone) the life and career of the man widely regarded as the most formidable American actor of the 20th century - famous for not only reshaping, but reinventing the craft of film acting and teaching audiences how to view a motion picture performance.

Divided into chronological, thematically-unified segments, the film first treats Marlon Brando's dysfunctional upbringing -

his alcoholic mother, his abusive father, his stint at a military academy - before charting his acting tutelage at the behest of Stella Adler and his early cinematic and theatrical roles, including work for Elia Kazan, who famously made many aggressive (and unsuccessful) attempts to discipline the headstrong actor onscreen.

Throughout this segment, many Hollywood A-list actors appear - among them, Al Pacino, Johnny Depp and Robert Duvall - expostulating at length on Brando's influence over their approaches to performance, and attempting with great effort to define the elusive style known as "method acting" that Brando helped to create.

The second half of the documentary moves into Brando's career during the '70s, '80s and '90s, covering the production of *The Godfather*, the actor's noteworthy political activism, and his tumultuous personal life. Francis Ford Coppola, who of course teamed with Brando for the first Godfather installment and for Apocalypse Now, is noticeably absent from the proceedings (*rottentomatoes*).

JOHNNY DEPP'S LIFE BEHIND THE SCENES:

The Continuing Adventures of Tim & Johnny (C. Fussman, Esquire Magazine, January 2008):

Burton and Depp are known as two of the strangest, quietest geniuses ever to work in movies. Turns out they're not that strange. Or quiet.

What I've Learned: Johnny Depp
Actor, 44, Los Angeles
Interviewed on October 25, 2007

My mother taught me a lot of things. The first thing that comes to mind is: **Don't take any shit off anyone, ever. When I was a little kid, we moved constantly. Bully picks on you in the new place? Don't ever take any shit off anyone, ever.** Eloquent and right.

I'm in a very privileged position. And I'm certainly not going to bite the hand that feeds me. I like doing the work. But I'm not a great fan of all the stuff that goes along with it. I don't want to be a product. Of course you want the movies to do well. But I don't want to have to think about that stuff. I don't want to know who's hot now and who's not and who's making this much dough and who's boffing this woman or that one. I want to remain ignorant of all this. I want to be totally outside and far away from all of it.

There's no limit to the possibilities of what I could do to the paparazzi if I catch them photographing my children.

You don't go through the front door of hotels anymore, you go through the garage. Or you go through the kitchen of a restaurant. Some people want to think that's cool, that's exciting. **But it'll definitely make you a little weird if you're constantly being stared at.** Part of the process that I've always enjoyed is being the observer. You know, just watching people and learning. **At a certain point, the reversal took place. I was no longer the observer—I was being observed. That's obviously very dangerous because part of an actor's job is to observe.**

My definition of freedom is simplicity, really. Anonymity. I'm sure it will be a possibility someday again. Maybe when I get old. They get tired of you.

"Didn't you use to be Johnny Depp?" That will be the clincher.

BPD ISSUES, SYMPTOMS & JOHNNY DEPP:

Unstable identity: "…**At a certain point, the reversal took place. I was no longer the observer—I was being observed. That's obviously very dangerous because part of an actor's job is to observe."**

"**…But it'll definitely make you a little weird if you're constantly being stared at."**

"**…I'm in a very privileged position. And I'm certainly not going to bite the hand that feeds me. I like doing the work. But I'm not a great fan of all the stuff that goes along with it. I don't want to be a product."**

Unstable, impulsive, self-destructive behavior: Depp seems to have taken his mother's advice to extremes since he's been arrested several times for throwing temper tantrums and antagonizing people including the police.

"**…Don't take any shit off anyone, ever. When I was a little kid, we moved constantly. Bully picks on you in the new place? Don't ever take any shit off anyone, ever."**

Diagnostic conclusion:

1) Johnny Depp suffers primarily from Borderline Personality Disorder.

2) Depp's secondary diagnosis: Substance abuse – alcoholic-addict.

APPENDIX – PHOTOS

Depp 2010

Depp 2013

Moss & Depp

Depp 2004

Depp at age 50

Depp & Moss

Depp & Moss

Johnny & Vanessa

Paradis & Depp

Amber & Johnny

Johnny & Amber

Depp & Moss

Depp

JOHNNY DEPP DIAGNOSED: UNAUTHORIZED PSYCHOLOGICAL DIAGNOSIS OF HIS SECRET LIFE

Depp & Paradis

Paradis & Depp split-up.

Depp with "trademark" hat.

Depp at film event.

Depp & date.

Depp close-up.

Amber Heard & Depp

Amber Heard as a teenager.

Keith Richards, Johnny Depp, Amber Heard

Bisexual Amber Heard & girlfriend, Tasya Van Ree.

Depp & Steve Jones of the Sex Pistols

Winona Ryder & Depp

Ryder & Depp

Depp in 2012

Kate Moss & Johnny Depp 1995

Johnny Depp 2013

Depp and Paradis's last red carpet appearance together in 2010.

Depp under arrest in 1994.

Hunter S. Thompson & Depp

Depp in 2013

Depp in *Platoon*.

Depp in 1988.

Depp & Ryder, 1991

Depp 1990s

Depp 1995

Depp 1991

Depp – early 1990s

Depp 1993

Depp – early 1990s

Depp & Ryder – early 1990s

Depp 2004

Depp 1990s

Depp 1990s

Depp, 20, wife Lori Allison, 25

Johnny & Kate

JOHNNY DEPP DIAGNOSED: UNAUTHORIZED PSYCHOLOGICAL DIAGNOSIS OF HIS SECRET LIFE

Depp: arrest for trashing a NYC hotel room.

Depp promoting *Fear and Loathing*

Depp, 1993

Depp 1990

Depp & Ryder 1990s

Johnny & Winona 1990s

Depp in *Cry-Baby*

Moss & Depp

Depp 1990s

Depp 1990s

Depp 1990s

SELECTED REFERENCES

Agence France Presse. (2012, October 29). Medical professor sues Johnny Depp over alleged bodyguard assault.

"Alice in Wonderland". Box Office Mojo.

Arnold, Gary (October 2, 1994). "Depp sees promise in cult filmmaker Ed Wood's story". *The Washington Times*.

"Baby boy for Depp and Paradis". BBC News. September 18, 2002.

Barnes, Henry (29 July 2013). "Johnny Depp says he may retire from acting soon". *The Guardian*.

Beck, A.T., Freeman, A. (1990). *Cognitive Therapy of Personality Disorders*. New York: Guilford publications.

Bingham, J. (2006). *Johnny Depp*. Chicago: Raintree.

Bradshaw, Peter (November 10 2011). "The Rum Diary – review". *Guardian*.

Breznican, Anthony (May 8, 2011). "Johnny Depp on 'The Lone Ranger'". *Entertainment Weekly*.

Breznican, Anthony (July 10, 2006). "Crazy for Johnny, or Captain Jack?". *USA Today*.

Brown, August (April 20, 2012). "Johnny Depp jams with Marilyn Manson at Golden Gods Awards". *Los Angeles Times*.

Bryan, D. (2013). *Johnny Depp*. Mankato, MN: The Child's World.

"Celebrity Central: Johnny Depp". *People*.

"Charlie and the Chocolate Factory." Box Office Mojo.

"Charlie and the Chocolate Factory." *Hollywood Foreign Press Association*.

"'Charlie and the Chocolate Factory'". Rotten Tomatoes.

"Charlie's Chocolate Wars: Sweet tooth for cash?" *Entertainment Weekly*.

Child, Ben (May 10, 2011). "Johnny Depp solves Thin Man remake". *The Guardian* (London).

Daly, Steve (October 31, 2007). "Johnny Depp: Cutting Loose in *Sweeney Todd*". *Entertainment Weekly*.

Dawson, P. (2013). *Angelina Jolie Psychoanalyzed*. Los Angeles: Vistar Pictures Ltd.

Dawson, P. (2013). *Borderline Personality Disorder*. Los Angeles: Vistar Pictures Ltd.

Dawson, P. (2013). *BPD Recovery: Borderline Personality Disorder Recovery*. Los Angeles: Vistar Pictures Ltd.

Dawson, P. (2013). *Marilyn Monroe Diagnosed*. Los Angeles: Vistar Pictures Ltd.

Dawson, P. (2013). *Princess Diana Diagnosed*. Los Angeles: Vistar Pictures Ltd.

Dawson, P. (2013). *Rock Stars Diagnosed*. Los Angeles: Vistar Pictures Ltd.

Dean, M. (2006). *Borderline Personality Disorder*. Kansas City, MO: Compact Clinicals.

"Depp arrested after scuffle". BBC News. January 31, 1999.

"Depp's Pirates Plunders Record $132M". ABC News.

"Depp shows hospital gratitude with £1M". *Windsor Star*. January 16, 2008.

"Depp talks of daughter's illness". BBC News. May 10, 2007.

"Depp to play Tonto, Mad Hatter in upcoming films". Reuters. September 25, 2008.

Derschowitz, Jessica (November 30, 2010). "Johnny Depp: Disney Hated My Jack Sparrow". CBS News.

"Disney Exploiting Confusion About Whether Depp Has Indian Blood". June 17, 2013.

"FEATURE-It's a pirate's life for actor Johnny Depp". Reuters. Archived from the original on December 17, 2007.

Gleiberman, Owen (July 19, 2013). "The Lone Ranger (2013)". *Entertainment Weekly*.

Gornstein, Leslie. "Why Can Johnny Depp Play Tonto, but Ashton Kutcher and Sacha Baron Cohen Get Slammed?" *E!* May 23, 2012.

Grasser, Marc. "Johnny Depp in Talks to Join Disney's 'Into the Woods'". *Variety*.

Graziano, J. (2008). *Johnny Depp*. Broomall, PA: Mason Crest Publishers.

Harrington, Maureen; Rodriguez, Brenda (January 14, 2008). "Johnny Depp 'Overjoyed' by Golden Globes Win". *People*.

Higgins, K. (2004). *Johnny Depp*. Farmington Hills, MI: Lucent Books.

Hiscock, John (June 25, 2009). "Johnny Depp interview for Public Enemies". *The Daily Telegraph* (UK).

"Inside The Actors Studio – Johnny Depp". YouTube.

"Interview: Johnny Depp". *MoviesOnline*.

"Is 'Tonto's Giant Nuts' a Good Name for Johnny Depp's Band?"". Indian Country Today Media Network. May 22, 2013.

"Johnny Depp & Vanessa Paradis Officially Split". *People*. June 19, 2012.

"Johnny Depp at People". *People*. May 19, 2011.

"Johnny Depp — Box Office Data Movie Star". The-numbers.com.

"Johnny Depp Buying Country Mansion?" Showbizspy.com. January 26, 2012.

"Johnny Depp Co-Editing Lost Woody Guthrie Novel". *Rolling Stone*.

Johnny Depp moves back to America to avoid paying taxes in France, Houston Chronicle, November 11, 2011

"Johnny Depp Moving Away From Pirate Role". MetroMatrix.com. Archived from the original on January 7, 2008.

"Johnny Depp Not the Marrying Kind". SoFeminine.co.uk.

"Johnny Depp on playing Ichabod Crane in *Sleepy Hollow*". *Entertainment Weekly*. May 2007.

"Johnny Depp Stars in Tim Burton's 'Dark Shadows'". *The New York Times*. May 10, 2012.

Kreger, Randi (2008). *The Essential Family Guide to Borderline Personality Disorder*. Center City, MN: Hazelden.

Kreger, R., Shirley, J. *The Stop Walking on Eggshells Workbook*. Oakland, CA: New Harbinger Publications.

Lowe, Ben (March 20, 2012). "Johnny Depp to Feature on Marilyn Manson's New LP!" *MTV*.

Makarechi, Kia (April 14, 2012). "'My Valentine': Johnny Depp & Natalie Portman Star in Paul McCartney-Directed Video (EXCLUSIVE)". *Huffington Post*.

Makarechi, Kia (March 19, 2012). "Johnny Depp, Marilyn Manson Team Up For 'You're So Vain' Cover". *Huffington Post*.

Mandell, Zack (July 9, 2013). "Johnny Depp's Career Continues to Soar". *Yahoo*.

Mason, P.T., Kreger, R. *Stop Walking on Eggshells*. Oakland, CA: New Harbinger Publications.

McNary, Dave (July 12, 2013). "Johnny Depp Moves Production Company to Disney (EXCLUSIVE)". *Variety.com*.

"Monitor". *Entertainment Weekly* (1263): 40. Jun 14, 2013.

Nashawaty, Chris (April 4, 2008). "Johnny Depp and Tim Burton: A DVD Report Card". *Entertainment Weekly*.

Pomerance, M. (2005). *Johnny Depp Starts Here*. New Brunswick, N.J.: Rutgers University Press.

Reardanz, Karen (November 26, 2007). "Depp Gifts Paradis with Vineyard". *San Francisco Examiner*.

Rosen, Christopher (March 19, 2012). "Johnny Depp '21 Jump Street' Cameo: Inside the Star's Appearance in Big Screen Reboot". *moviefone.com*.

"Self Injury: A Struggle". *Famous Self-Injurers*.

Shaw, Lucy; Styles, Oliver (November 27, 2007). "Johnny Depp buys girlfriend vineyard estate in France". Decanter.com.

Silverman, Stephen M. (September 3, 2003). "Johnny Depp Calls U.S. a 'Dumb Puppy'". *People*.

"The Tourist". Box Office Mojo.

Thomas, W.D. (2007). *Johnny Depp*. Milwaukee, WI: Gareth Stevens Publishing.

Tracy, K. (2008). *Johnny Depp*. Hockessin, DE: Mitchell Lane Publishers.

"UPDATE: THAT'S NOT JOHNNY DEPP ON THE SET OF 'HUGO CABRET'" *hollywood.com*. March 28 2011.

Williams, L. (November 2, 2012). "UC Irvine prof can seek damages from Johnny Depp in concert scuffle". *Los Angeles Times*.

Wyllie, Sophie (January 9, 2012). "Rumors rife that megastar Johnny Depp has bought a Burnham Market house". *Fakenham and Wells Times*.

Zakarin, Jordan (July 12, 2011). "Johnny Depp: Paul Revere, Night Stalker Films Get Disney Deal". *Huffington Post*.

www.ingramcontent.com/pod-product-compliance
Ingram Content Group UK Ltd.
Pitfield, Milton Keynes, MK11 3LW, UK
UKHW051336280925
8114UKWH00029B/619